For My Friend
truth searcher ~~Michael~~ Michael of the
family Stott on this day
26th June 2021 for his
bright nature his resolve and
good heart as we journied to
london for the freedom march
together in the hope of a future
to come against the future that
authority would place upon us if
it could

all that was concealed
will be revealed

Stephen ~~foster~~

Gabriel Bebington Dave ~~Parry~~

~~Mumten Han~~

EUSTACE MULLINS

THE CURSE OF CANAAN

A demonology of history

OMNIA VERITAS

EUSTACE CLARENCE MULLINS

(1923-2010)

THE CURSE OF CANAAN

1987

Published by

OMNIA VERITAS LTD

OMNIA VERITAS

www.omnia-veritas.com

ABOUT THE AUTHOR

In forty years of dedicated investigative research, Eustace Mullins has drawn considerable return fire. He was kept under daily surveillance by agents of the FBI for thirty-two years; no charges were ever placed against him. He is the only person ever fired from the staff of the Library of Congress for political reasons. He is the only writer who has had a book burned in Europe since 1945.

After serving thirty-eight months in the U. S. Army Air Force during World War II, Eustace Mullins was educated at Washington and Lee University, Ohio State University, University of North Dakota, and New York University. He later studied art at the Escuela des Bellas Artes, San Miguel de Allende, Mexico, and the Institute of Contemporary Arts, Washington, D.C.

While studying in Washington, he was asked to go to St. Elizabeth's Hospital to talk to the nation's most famous political prisoner, Ezra Pound. The outstanding literary figure of the twentieth century, Pound had seen three of his pupils awarded the Nobel Prize, while it was denied to him because of his pronouncements as a native American patriot. Not only did Eustace Mullins become his most active protege, he is the only person who keeps Ezra Pound's name alive today, through the work of the Ezra Pound Institute of Civilization, which was founded shortly after the poet's death in Venice.

With the present work, Eustace Mullins hopes to end a three-thousand-year blackout behind which the enemies of humanity have operated with impunity in carrying out their Satanic program. It is very late in the history of our civilization. This book is written solely with the goal of renewing our ancient culture, and of bringing it to new heights.

PREFACE

After forty years of patient study of the crises which faces humanity, I arrived at a very simple conclusion-all conspiracies are Satanic! In retrospect, this conclusion should surprise no one. I admit that it came as something of a surprise to me. I had never anticipated that my decades of work would lead to such an all-encompassing and unchallengeable solution. This answer had eluded me through the years, not because I was on the wrong track, but because I had not yet consulted the ultimate source of knowledge - the Bible. To trace the machinations of the materialist conspiracy, I had deliberately limited myself to materialist sources-reference material on banking, politics, economics, and the biographies of those who were most deeply involved in these affairs.

When at last I did decide to look up some references in the Bible, a task which was greatly simplified by a number of excellent Concordances, such as Nelson's and Strong's, I was overwhelmed by its immediacy, by its directness, and by the applicability of its words to present-day happenings. As the months went by and I continued this research, I was not overwhelmed by a sense of deja vu, but by an overpowering conviction that very little had changed in the last three thousand years. My first revelation was that "God has no secrets from man." It is Satan who must confine his work to stealthy conspiracies to deception, and to promises which will never be kept. "And the great dragon was thrown down, that ancient serpent, who is called the Devil and Satan, the deceiver of the whole world" (Rev. 12:9).

It is for this reason that politicians, of necessity, must become followers of Satan in the rebellion against God.

Politicians must deceive the people in order to gain power over them, just as Satan must deceive the whole world if he is to continue his rebellion against God. Satan takes you to the top of the mountain and offers you all the kingdoms of the earth (Martin Luther King proclaimed, "I have been to the top of the mountain," but he never revealed what had taken place there); the politician offers you free food, free lodging, free medical care - everything will become "free at last!" The politician offers to defend you against your enemies, so that he can deliver you to the ultimate enemy-- Satan.

God does not make offers to you in competition with Satan and his politicians. What could God offer you when he has already given you the whole world? What more could He do than to send His Only Begotton Son to preserve this world for you when it was threatened by Satan? And why would God wish to veil His love for you behind arcane mysteries, occult conspiracies, and obscene practices?

Once my return to the Bible had given me the answers for which I had been seeking so many years, I realized that I had arrived at the culmination of this life's work. I had eagerly sought out the facts about each of the many conspiracies, and I now was able to define their interlocking into the one world "Conspiracy of Conspiracies." I had traced the names and activities of the principal actors in the Satanic drama which this world has become, a world which I described in 1968 in "My Life in Christ" as "Satan's Empire." This was an over-simplification, although I was not aware of it at that time. I had written this book under great stress; my father had died as the result of harassment by federal agents. Their goal was to force me to give up this work.

Other members of my family continued to undergo daily harassment because of the federal campaign against me. I had not been overcome by despair, but it did seem to me, in that period of my life, that Satan had indeed achieved a temporal victory over this world - not a permanent victory, but a gain which he could defend and which he might consolidate for years to come.

The next forty years brought me many startling revelations of the behind-the-scenes forces which had planned and perpetrated the mass murders of humanity. I had finally, as one writer put it, "uncovered the forces of war."

I was also able to find the sources of the Satanic ideology which has been consistently employed to deceive humanity, and to trick them into becoming unwitting tools of the Satanic programs, an ideology which we encounter today in various forms, such as Communism, Fabianism, secular humanism, and other disguises.

February 22, 1987

CHAPTER 1

THE WAR AGAINST SHEM

They sacrificed unto demons, which were no gods.
Deut. 32:17

In the churches of America, Christians worship a somewhat paternal God; the bearded patriarch whom Michelangelo depicted on the ceiling of the Sistine Chapel, an authoritarian figure who is also the Father of our Teacher, and our Saviour, Jesus Christ. God is revered as the original Creator of our universe, and as the ultimate moral guide. In this scenario, humanity is a somewhat innocuous group, placed in a pastoral setting, generally obedient to the laws of God, and subject to punishment when disobedience occurs. Religious observance based on this concept is adequate until this Arcadian scene is disturbed by misadventures or calamities. It also begs the question of innate or inescapable evil. Satan, the fallen angel, and rebel against God (Satan, a Hebrew word meaning "adversary") appears in the Bible. There are frequent references to God's admonishment, and often, chastisement, of wrongdoers, both individually and in large groups. Here again, the persistent appearance of evil throughout the history of mankind is dealt with as it occurs, but it is difficult to fix either its sources or its causes. Therefore, humanity has existed under a considerable disadvantage, unable to recognize or understand evil before being injured by it.

Indeed, the great movement of modern history has been to disguise the presence of evil on the earth, to make light of it, to convince humanity that evil is to be "tolerated," "treated with greater understanding," or negotiated with, but under no circumstances should it ever be forcibly opposed. This is the principal point of what has come to be known as today's liberalism, more popularly known as secular humanism. The popular, and apparently sensible, appeal of humanism is that humanity should always place human interests first. The problem is that this very humanism can be traced in an unbroken line all the way back to the Biblical "Curse of Canaan." Humanism is the logical result of the demonology of history.

Modern day events can be understood only if we can trace their implications in a direct line from the earliest records of antiquity. These records concern pre-Adamic man, a hybrid creature whose origins are described in ancient books. The Book of Enoch (which itself is part of an earlier Book of Noah, written about 161 B.C.), says that Samjaza (Satan), the leader of a band of two hundred angels, descended on Mt. Carmel. They had lusted after the daughters of men from afar, and now they took them for wives. These fallen angels, known as the Order of the Watchers, taught their wives magic. The issue of these unions was a race of giants, known as Nephilim.

The Bible does not mention the Nephilim specifically by name, and Strong's Concordance does not list them. However, Nelson's Concordance has several listings under Nephilim. The verses of the Bible to which it refers are Genesis 6:4, "There were giants in the earth in those days." The Revised Standard Version does give the name of the Nephilim, the same verse reading, "The Nephilim were on the earth in those days." These giants later became known as "the sons of Anak." In Numbers 13:33, we read, "And there we saw the giants, the sons of Anak, which come of the giants." These giants constituted a powerful menace to other peoples. In Deuteronomy 9:2 is the complaint, "Who can stand before the children of Anak?" Nevertheless, they were finally killed or driven out. "There were none of the Anakims left in the land of the children of Israel." (Joshua 11:22)

These early giants would be considered as mutations by modern scientists. Because of their peculiar parentage, they had habits and lusts which horrified their neighbors. Their leader, Satan (the adversary of God), also known as Satona, was the serpent who entered into and seduce Eve, producing the first murderer, Cain.[1] Not only were the Nephilim a menace to others, their uncontrollable hatred and violence sometimes led them to attack and kill each other. They then ate their victims, introducing cannibalism to the world. According to some accounts, God slaughtered them, while the Archangel Michael imprisoned the fallen angels, the Order of the Watchers, in deep chasms in the earth.

Unfortunately for humanity, this was not the end of the matter. Satan, through his children, the Nephilim, and also through Cain, had now established a demonic presence on the earth. His rebellion against God world result in continuous suffering and travail on earth for centuries to come. The history of mankind since his rebellion is the history of the struggle between the people of God and the Cult of Satan. With this understanding, it is now possible to trace the historical events which reveal the actual archives of the two adversaries.

---

[1] According to mythology.

The Book of Zohar stresses the talmudic legend that demons originated in sexual congress between humans and demonic powers. This offers a reasonable explanation as to why all occult ceremonies stress three things: drugs, incantations (which express hatred of God), and bizarre sexual practices.

The study of demonology in history discloses answers to otherwise inexplicable aspects of man's history. The torture and murder of children, obscene rites and mass killings of innocents in worldwide wars, as well as other catastrophes, are phenomena which bear little or no relation to mankind's day by day routine of tilling the soil, raising families, and maintaining the standards of civilization. On the contrary, these types of calamities are direct assaults on the normal existence of humanity. Furthermore, they are expressions of the rebellion against God, as attacks on His People.

Because of their extraordinary powers, demons have always attracted a certain number of followers on earth. "Secret" organizations, which insist on concealing their rites and their programs from all "outsiders" must do so in order to prevent exposure and the inevitable punishment. While they were wandering in the desert, the Jewish tribes worshipped demons and monsters. They revered their mythical monsters, Leviathan, Behemoth, aid Raheb, who well may have been survivors of the tribe of giants, the Nephilim. They also made sacrifices to the demon of the desert, Azazel.

Their mythology developed a certain hierarchy of demons. A Demonarch, who presumably was Satan, ruled over all demons on earth. He was also known as the Prince of Evil, Belial (the Hebrew Be'aliah, meaning Yahweh is Baal). Next in the hierarchy of demons was Asmodeus, King of the Demons, and his wife, Lilith, chief demoness of the Jews. Lilith is well known today as the patron goddess of the lesbians. Her name survives in many current organizations, such as the Daughters of Lilith. This choice of a patroness suggests that there may always have been a certain amount of demoniac impulses in homosexual practices. This motivation would fit in with the basic rites of occultism, such as defiance of God, and the development of "unusual lifestyles." The inevitable retribution for these practices has now appeared among us in the form of the widespread plague of AIDS.

Lilith is typical of the demons who were created by sexual intercourse between the daughters of man and the Watchers. They first appeared during the six days of creation as disembodied spirits, and later took physical form. The Book of Zohar says, "Every pollution of semen gives birth to demons." The Encyclopaedia Judaica refers to "the impurity of the serpent who had sexual relations with Eve." The Kabbalah claims that Lilith had intercourse with Adam and produced demons as part of the cosmic design, in which the right and the left are the opposing currents of pure and impure powers, filling the world, and dividing it between the Holy One and the serpent Samael . (Zohar Bereshit 73b., 53 et seq.)

Webster's Dictionary says of Lilith: "Heb. meaning of the night. 1. Jewish folklore, a female demon vampire. 2. Jewish folklore, first wife of Adam before the creation of Eve." Many legends identify Lilith as the first wife of Adam. These myths claim that God formed Lilith out of mud and filth. She soon quarrelled with Adam. Because of her overweening pride, she refused to let him lie on top of her. It is for this reason that she was adopted as the patroness of the lesbians. She left Adam and fled to the shores of the Red Sea, where she was said to indulge in her sexual fantasies with demons, living among the wild beasts and hyenas. Her presence gave rise to many terrifying legends; she became the chief of Jewish demonesses and was said to prey on newly born children, sucking the life out of them. She also was known to suck the blood from men who were sleeping alone and is referred to as "the night hag" (Isaiah 34:14 - And wild beasts shall meet with hyenas, the satyr shall cry to his fellow; yea, there shall the night hag alight, and find for herself a resting place.) Except for this one verse, her name was excised from all Scripture because of her unsavory reputation.

Other legends claimed that Lilith and her accompanying demonesses ruled over the four seasons, as Lilith-Naameh, Mentral, Agrath, and Nahaloth. They were said to gather on a mountaintop near the mountains of darkness, and there celebrate the Witches Sabbath, when they would have intercourse with Samael, the Prince of Demons.

It was because God had had such an unfortunate result with Lilith, after creating her out of mud and filth, that he decided to go to Adam's rib for his next creation, Eve. She was subsequently known as "haw wah," "Mother of All the Living," and also as "the Serpent Mother" because of her later association with Satan. The Prince of Darkness had a number of disguises, but when he incarnated sexual desire, as he did for Eve, he always appeared as a serpent.

Because evil was now established on earth, through the presence of the demons and their followers, it was necessary for God to punish mankind. In inflicting this punishment, He resolved to be just. For this, it was necessary for Him to select those who were without stain, and who would be allowed to survive the punishment. His method of selection was a simple one. He chose those who had not been contaminated. His choice was Noah and his family. Noah is described in Genesis 6:9, "Noah was perfect in his generations." The word generations here is an imperfect translation of the Hebrew word "to-Ied-aw," which means ancestry. An earlier and more appropriate translation is "Noah was a just man, and perfect, without blemish in his generations." He was God's choice because he and his family were the last remaining pure blooded Adamites in the world. (The Revised Standard Version has an even greater error in its wording, "Noah was blameless in his generations," since it does not state what he would have been blamed for.)

The site of the Flood, which was God's prescribed punishment for mankind, was not in the Near Eastern area, as is commonly supposed. Archaeologists have been puzzled for years that they could find no evidence of such a flood in this area. In fact, because Cain had been banished "east of Eden," Noah and his family lived in the Tarim Basin, located in the Upper Sinkiang Province. This basin was fed by the River Tarim, and here the Deluge took place.

Having been warned by God of the impending catastrophe, Noah succeeded in building the Ark, one of the greatest engineering feats of all time. Weighing 36,750 tons, it was built entirely of wood. It was 450 feet long, 75 feet wide, and 45 feet in depth. On this Ark, God commanded Noah to "take of every living thing of all flesh." Because of the limited space on the Ark, there could be no possibility of further reproduction of these species during their time aboard, and God commanded that no intercourse should take place. This commandment was violated by an inhabitant of the Ark, Ham, the second son of Noah. Ham had intercourse with a preAdamite woman on the Ark, a dark skinned person. Their offspring was a black son named Cush, who became the symbol of Ethiopia.

Noah was dismayed when he learned that his son had violated God's commandment, because he knew that retribution would come. After the Flood had subsided, and life on earth went back to its usual routine, Noah continued to be haunted by his fears. The subsequent occurrences have since had dire consequences for all of mankind. In the Bible, it appears as somewhat of a riddle, since the characters are identified and misidentified in sequential verses. Neither the exact sequence of events, their explanation, or the identification of the principals can be followed as it appears in Genesis, possibly due to mistranslations or editing over the centuries.

Although life on earth had resumed its pre-Deluge felicity, Noah continued to be distressed by Ham's transgression. So vexed was he that he drank too much wine, and he lay exposed in his drunkenness. As it is recounted in Genesis 9:24-27, Ham's son Canaan saw his grandfather exposed, although at one point he is referred to as "Noah's youngest son," instead of the correct designation as his grandson. Noah's other sons, Shem and Japheth, seeing their father exposed, hastened to cover him with a cloak. However, when he awakened, Noah was greatly infuriated by what had taken place, and he pronounced a curse on Canaan, "Cursed be Canaan; a slave of slaves shall he be to his brothers (Shem and Japheth)." Here again is something of a riddle, as Shem and Japheth were the uncles of Canaan, not his brothers. The "riddle" is probably an intentional one, because it is intended to evoke a special study of these verses to come to an understanding of these very important messages, warnings to all future generations.

Various explanations have been offered for Noah's tremendous anger at Canaan, and his Curse of Canaan. One, which has now largely been discounted, is that Ham may have slept with Noah's wife, or that he had made an attempt to do so. No basis for this conjecture has ever been established. Another explanation is that Noah cursed Canaan because he was still vexed at Ham's violation of God's commandment to the inhabitants of the Ark, that they should refrain from intercourse while on board. Because Ham had slept with the pre-Adamite woman on the ark, Noah finally vented his wrath in the Curse of Canaan.

This also fails to ring true; the men of the Old Testament were very direct in their dealings; if Noah was vexed with Ham, he would have cursed Ham, not Canaan. None of these explanations offers a valid reason for the vehemence of Noah's curse, a curse which has blighted humanity for three thousand years. The only rational explanation for the curse is Noah's anger that Canaan had done something which thoroughly outraged his grandfather. Looking on him while he was exposed would hardly have caused such a reaction. Scholars finally concluded that Canaan had done something so degrading that Noah had to pronounce a curse upon him. What would this have been? The Bible as presently translated does not really give us a clue. These scholars decided that Canaan, being of mixed race, and therefore not bound by the rigid moral code of the Adamites, had probably committed a homosexual act on his grandfather. Being of pure stock, Noah would have been exceedingly wroth at such an act, and would have reacted as he did.

The Curse of Canaan was extended to the land which was named after him, the Land of Canaan. The Canaanites themselves, the people of this land, became the greatest curse upon humanity, and so they remain today. Not only did they originate the practices of demon-worship, occult rites, child sacrifice, and cannibalism, but as they went abroad, they brought these obscene practices into every land which they entered. Not only did they bring their demonic cult to Egypt, but, known by their later name, the Phoenicians, as they were called after 1200 B.C., they became the demonizers of civilization through successive epochs, being known in medieval history as the Venetians, who destroyed the great Byzantine Christian civilization, and later as "the black nobility," which infiltrated the nations of Europe and gradually assumed power through trickery, revolution, and financial legerdemain.

The reputation of Canaan is to be found in many ancient records, although its foul history has been carefully expunged from even more of the historic archives and libraries. In 1225 B.C., the Pharaoh Merneptah, who, because of his victories in the Canaanite region, was known as "Binder of Gezer," set up a stele to commemorate his successes. Among the inscriptions placed thereon was this: "Plundered is the Canaan, with every evil; All lands are united and pacified."

This inscription did not mean that Merneptah had used every evil to plunder the Canaan; it meant that he had in his sojourn there encountered every evil practiced by this notorious tribe.

Ham had four sons; Cush, who founded the land of Ethiopia; Mizraim, who founded Egypt; Put, who founded Libya; and Canaan, who founded the land of the Canaanites, the area now in contention as the State of Israel. In the Aggidah. Cush is said to be black-skinned as punishment for Ham's having had intercourse on the Ark. "Three copulated in the Ark, and they were all punished - the dog, the raven, and Ham. The dog was doomed to be tied, the raven expect rates his seed into the mouth of his mate, and Ham was smitten in his skin. Note 9, San. 108b. i.e., from him descended Cush, the negro, who is black-skinned."

In talmudic literature, Cushi always means a black person or the negro race. Cushite is synonymous with black. (Yar Mo'ed Katan 16b).

The Bible as presently translated makes no reference to "ush's color. Reference to his descendants, the Cushites, appears only in Numbers and in Samuel Book Two. Numbers 12:1 reveals that "Miriam and Aaron spoke against Moses because of the Cushite woman he had married, for he had married a Cushite woman." Here again, no explanation is given as to why Miriam and Aaron turned against Moses, yet the matter is obviously of some importance, because the same verse emphasized by repetition that he had married a Cushite woman. We find the explanation by turning to the Talmud, which tells us that "Cushite" always means black. The verse in Numbers should read, and originally may have read, "Miriam and Aaron spoke against Moses because of the black or Cushite woman he had married." Second Samuel contains seven references to Cushites, but again no descriptions are given.

Prof. Sayee, the noted Egyptian scholar, and authority on the ancient Near and Middle East, explains that Canaan means "low," and Elam means "high." The Canaanites were those who inhabited the low places; the Elamites occupied the high ground. Col. Garnier, in his great work, "The Worship of the Dead," quotes Strabo's observation that "the Cushites inhabit the coastal regions of all Asia and Africa." They were never aggressive enough to fight for or remain on higher ground, and were forced to remain in the low, swampy areas, exposed to the elements, areas which other peoples would not contest them for.

Garnier continues, p. 78 of "The Worship of the Dead": "We have also seen that Osiris was black, or of the Cushite race, and this was characteristic of the Egyptians. Herodotus speaks of the Egyptians generally as black and wooly haired. There were two races in Egypt, the Mizraimites, who first colonized the country, and the black Egyptians, the latter receiving their name from Aegyptus, the son of Belus, i.e. Cush. There can be little doubt, therefore, that Aegyptus, the father of the black Egyptians, and son of Belus, is the same as the black Osiris." On p. 92 Garnier informs us: "The Aryan immigration and Brahmanism were subsequent to that of a Cushite race more or less hostile to them and their religion. We find Aryan traditions speaking of themselves as white and the Dasyns as black, i.e. Cushite." Garnier quotes a description of the Cushites as follows: "They call them demons and devil-worshippers, and lascivious wretches who make a god of the Sisna, the Lingam, and the Phallus."

Garnier goes on (p. 131) to observe that "Buddha must be identified with those gods whose human origin was Cushite, from Cush, the great prophet and teacher of the ancient Paganism, the father of the black or Ethiopian race. Buddha, although the chief god of the yellow race, is constantly represented, as black with wooly hair and negro features, the flat noses and thick lips of many of the ancient statues which occur in Hindustan, for these are clearly the well-known features of the genuine African negro; the human origin of Buddha was Cush."

Ham's subsequent acts did nothing to clear his reputation. He stole the garments which God had made for Adam and Eve before He expelled them from the Garden of Eden. Cush inherited these garments from Ham and passed them on to his son, Nimrod. Because of these garments, Nimrod became known as "the mighty hunter." He was considered to be invincible as long as he wore these garments, which are recorded in Genesis 3:21. Animals and men cowered before the onslaught of Nimrod because of these garments, which conferred great powers upon him (Encyclopaedia Judaica). Nimrod, who was born on December 25th, the High Sabbath of Babylon, was the founder of Babylon and the city of Nineveh.

In the history of mankind, Nimrod stands unequaled for his symbolism of evil and Satanic practices. He is credited for having founded Freemasonry and for building the legendary Tower of Babel, in defiance of God's will. In talmudic literature, he is noted as "he who made all the people rebel against God." Pes. 94b. The legend of the Midrash recounts that when Nimrod was informed of Abraham's birth, he ordered all the male children killed, to be certain of eliminating him. Abraham was hidden in a cave, but in later life he was discovered by Nimrod, who then ordered him to worship fire. Abraham refused and was thrown into the fire.

The legendary symbol for Nimrod is "X." The use of this symbol always denotes witchcraft. When "X" is used as a shortened form meaning Christmas, it actually means "to celebrate the feast of Nimrod." A double X, which has always meant to double-cross or betray, in its fundamental meaning indicates one's betrayal into the hands of Satan. When American corporations use the "X" in their logo, such as "Exxon," the historic Rockefeller firm of Standard Oil of New Jersey, there can be little doubt of this hidden meaning.

The importance of Nimrod in any study of the occult cannot be over-emphasized. Because of the powers given him by the clothing of Adam and Eve, Nimrod became the first man to rule the whole world. He indulged that power by launching excesses and horrors which have never been equalled. Ever since the time of Nimrod, Babylon has been the symbol of depravity and lust.

Nimrod also introduced the practice of genocide to the world. His grandfather, Ham, having consorted with other races, and brought children of mixed race into the world, was persuaded by his consort, the evil Naamah, to practice ritual murder and cannibalism. She informed Ham that by killing and eating fair-skinned people, his descendants could regain their superior qualities.

Throughout the ensuing centuries, the fair-skinned descendants of Shem, Noah's oldest son, have ritually been slaughtered by the darker descendants of Ham and Nimrod, in the world's most persistent campaign of racial and religious persecution.

Not only did Nimrod kill and eat the fair-skinned descendants of Shem, in his fury and hatred he often burned them alive. The type of human sacrifice involving the eating of the slaughtered human victims derived its name from the combined names of his uncle, Canaan, and the demon god Baal, the two names being combined to form the word "cannibal." Nimrod was also known in ancient history by the names of Marduk, Bel, and Merodach. Because of his importance in its history, Babylon was known as the Land of Nimrod. Nimrod is also cited in the most ancient Masonic constitutions as the founder of Freemasonry.

Nimrod's downfall reputedly came about when he began to build the Tower of Babel, a ziggurat, or temple tower, which was planned to rise up into the heavens. Because of this offense against God, Shem, the eldest son of Noah, pronounced judgment against Nimrod, and executed him.

Josephus says that "Ham's black grandson, Nimrod, was beheaded by Shem." Other accounts add that Shem then cut Nimrod's body into pieces and sent the pieces to the pagan temples of Babylon, as a warning to the priests that their sex orgies and child sacrifices would result in a similar judgment of execution. Instead of abandoning their hideous ceremonies because of this warning, the priests literally went underground. No longer did "their altars smoke with human blood," as Kitto, the great Palestinian authority, described them. The priests took the pieces of Nimrod as relics to their secret meeting places, which were hidden in "groves" and "shrines." This was the origin of the secret Mystery cults, whose orgies could no longer be performed in public temples. Because of the power of Shem, the priests from that time on conducted their forbidden orgies out of the light of day, in their secret hiding places. Their meetings were bounded with secret rites, which no one outside of their order was permitted to know, on pain of death. This was the origin of the Gnostics, the Knowing Ones, who knew the secrets. It may be for this reason that Nimrod became known as the founder of Freemasonry, because its fundamental rites were established and invoked after he was killed, in order to carry on his work of evil.

The history of mankind for the past three thousand years has been the history of struggle between the fair-skinned descendants of Shem and the darker-skinned descendants of his brother, Ham, yet you will not find this struggle defined in any historical work. The records of the genocide against the people of Shem are apparent throughout the archives of history, but there is not a school or university whose faculty will apprise its students of this simple fact. This in itself explains much which is usually dismissed as being "beyond explanation." The reason for this odd development is that the descendants of Ham traditionally have usurped the educational process, through their earlier usurpation of the priesthood to carry on their Satanic work. They have controlled the educational system ever since, converting it to their own evil purposes. It is of even greater interest that not a single school of theology anywhere in the world takes note of this central fact of history, a red thread which runs continuously through the record of events.

In the Greek language, Shem appears as Ehu; in Egyptian mythology, he is Shu, the son of Ra, the Sun God. It was through claimed descent from Shem that Louis, King of France, called himself the "Sun King." However, a much more important point, and one that has again been obscured or hidden by the priests who controlled the educational system throughout the last three thousand years, is the fact that it was Shem who founded and built the great civilization of Egypt.

The rulers of Egypt were called Pharaohs, from the Hebrew word pira, meaning "long hair." The native Egyptians were short-haired. Not only was Shem long-haired, he was also fair-haired. In their records, the priests call Shem "Shufu," or "Khufu," which means long hair. Being a great warrior, Shem easily led his people in the conquest of the native Egyptians. He immediately set about to commemorate his reign by building the Great Pyramid at Gizeh. Babylon was then overcome by the son of Shem, Elam; a later descendant, Cyrus of Persia, an Elamite, completed the final conquest of Babylon and built the great Persian Empire. It was to signify his great military successes that Shem adopted as his symbol the lion, which is still the symbol of rulers today. The Great Pyramid was later called Khiut, the Horizon, in which Khufu had been swallowed up, as the western horizon swallowed up the sun each evening.

After extensive archaeological investigations, the Royal Astronomer of Scotland concluded that the evidence was irrefutable that the Great Pyramid at Gizeh had been built by Shem. He found the name Shufu inside the pyramid, painted in red, which signified Shem's fair hair. Also inside the pyramid is an inscription placed there after the death of his descendant, Amenhotep IV, "He stopped the barbaric practices of the priests which had been introduced by Naamah and her followers from Babylon, including Nimrod." The priests murdered Amenhotep IV, so that they could resume their orgies of lust and child sacrifices. They had admitted to Herodotus that the Great Pyramid had been built by "a wandering shepherd," an odd observation, as shepherds do not usually create such grandiose monuments to themselves. However, this was one of the terms of derision by which they always referred to Shem after his death. Other inscriptions by the priests throughout centuries of Egyptian history revile Shem as "pig," "dwarf," and other terms signifying their hatred of him, possibly because he slew their mentor, Nimrod. In the same areas, other inscriptions extol the degenerate Ham, who had been corrupted by his consort, the evil Naamah, and introduced to the practices of human sacrifice and cannibalism.

Egyptian civilization reached its peak during the reign of Shem. The Sphinx is now admitted to be a portrait of him. After his death, the priests not only resumed their evil practices, but they embarked on a successful campaign to black out his name from recorded history, a campaign which has largely succeeded during the ensuing three thousand years. They also launched terrible punitive actions against Shem's fair-haired descendants, often murdering them, or burning them alive. Not only did the priests falsify the records of Shem, but they also succeeded in eliminating most of the subsequent history of his fair-skinned descendants, the Shemites, or, as they are sometimes called, the Semites.

The Arab scholar Murtadi noted that Num and Khufu (Shufu), the builders 'of the Pyramids, lived with Noah. (British Museum Catalog, 1909). Shem was also referred to by the name of Menes, from the Hebrew Meni, or man, which appears in the Egyptian Book of the Dead, referring to Uranus and his three sons, an obvious reference to Noah. Ham later became known as the Egyptian God Amon.

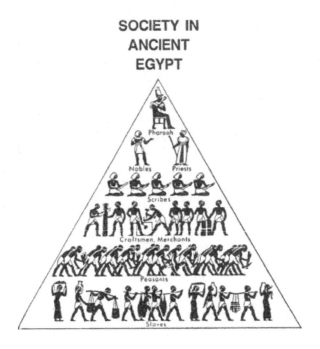

SOCIETY IN ANCIENT EGYPT

Herodotus writes that the first king of Egypt, who reigned until 2320 B.C. Eusebious says that three hundred successive sovereigns descended from him, the Thinite Kings, who had succeeded the demigods. The historian Murtado referred to Shem as Menes. As the most able son of Noah, Shem exemplifies the qualities upon which all subsequent civilizations have been built; courage, the desire to build, and the willingness to subdue those who have adopted a lower form of life.

He is the Adamite who created civilizations as we have known it. On the other hand, the descendants of Ham, the Canaanites, exemplify the Satanic urge to destroy civilization and the rebellion against God. J. Hewlitt points out that Adamite meant a "thinker," and mena or man produced Menes, the thinking man. This survives today in the intellectual society, Mensa. The distinction was made to distinguish the lineage of Adam from the pre-Adamites, or non-thinking men. (Ruling Races of Prehistoric Man, v. 2 p. 364). The Jewish Encyclopaedia says that Shem became king of Jerusalem as the representative of YHWH, so that he could carry on the battle against the slave people, the Canaanites.

In Genesis, we find this verse: "Bless be the Lord, the God of Shem!" Genesis 9:26. Shem had five sons: Elam, from whom came the Persian Empire; Asshur, from whom came the Assyrian Empire; Arpachshad, Lud, and Aram. So great was the reverence for the name of Shem in the ancient world that his name in many records became synonyous with YHWH. Yahweh, or, in a later version, Jehovah, derives directly from the Hebrew verb Hava (h), meaning, "I am." Historically, this was read as the older Khufu, or HWFW, instead of YHWH, and thus it refers to Kufu, or Shem, the builder of the Great Pyramid. It was because of the persecutions of the fair-skinned peoples by the priests that Khufu, which phonetically is almost identical with the Hebrew Hava (h), became YHWH, the God of the Exodus from Egypt. The Encyclopaedia Britannica notes of "Jehovah," "The pronunciation 'J' is an error resulting among Christians combining the consonants YHWH with the vowels of 'adhonay' Lord, (Adonis) which was substituted by the Jews for the sacred name YHWH, commonly called the tetragrammaton, or four consonants. The name 'Jehovah' first appears in the manuscript of Martin's Pogio in the fourteenth century." Thus the name of Jehovah, which is commonly used in our churches, is only five hundred years old!

In order to understand why the name of Shem was systematically reviled and concealed throughout the records of history, we must return to the record of his thoroughly degenerate and evil nephew, Canaan. Canaan was so wicked that his last will and testament to his children was a formula for vice. It read, "Love one another (that is, of this tribe only), love robbery, love lewdness, hate your masters, and do not speak the truth." This remarkable document, the Will of Canaan, is to be found in only one place in all the world's theological literature, the Babylonian Talmud, where it is presented thusly, "Five things did Canaan charge his sons: love one another, love robbery, love lewdness, hate your masters, and do not speak the truth." Pes. 113b.

The Will of Canaan has been the Canaanites prescription for all of their operations during the ensuing three thousand years. Meanwhile, the people of Shem, knowing nothing of this document, vainly tried to "convert" the Canaanites, and turn them from their evil ways. If the descendants of Shem had been warned of the precepts imparted by this document, the history of the last three thousand years could have been very different. The Will of Canaan today remains the operating instructions of the Canaanite heirs, who presently control the World Order. At the same time, it remains unknown to the peoples whom the Canaanites continue to rob, enslave, and massacre. The Will of Canaan contains the instructions necessary to resist the results of the Curse of Canaan, which condemn them to slavery. The instructions to "hate your masters," that is, Shem and Japheth and their descendants, is a command to commit genocide against the people of Shem. For this reason, all subsequent Canaanite rites are based upon these exhortations to struggle and commit acts of violence against the people of Shem. It is not only the basis for all of the revolutions and "liberation movements" since that time, it is also a basic incitement to commit genocide and to carry on racial wars. Because of the three-thousand-year historical blackout, the people of Shem have never understood their peril, and they have frequently been subject to massacre because their essential goodness made it impossible for them to believe the vileness of the Canaanites. The Will of Canaan has always been concealed from them because it is the basic program of conspiracy and secret rites which enable the Canaanites to wreak their hatred upon the descendants of Shem.

Much of the continuous hostility between these two forces is mentioned in the Bible, but never in the basic form which has been stated here for the first time. In his book, "The Mystery of the Ages," Herbert Armstrong comments, "Canaanites, who were racially dark, had settled the land; God commands the Israelites to drive them out" (p. 172). Armstrong cites Numbers 33 as the basis for his reference.

During the centuries of oppression and mass murder, God has not stood aside from His people. On the contrary, He has frequently exhorted them to attack and to rid themselves of the peril of the Canaanites. In the early years of this struggle, it was still possible for His children to hear and to obey. The vision of Obadiah is recounted in Obadiah 20, "And the capacity of this - host of the children of Israel, shall possess that of the Canaanites, even unto Zarephath; and this capacity of Israel which is in Sepharad, shall possess the cities of the south." Significantly, the Revised Standard Version omits the mention of the Canaanites entirely.

The battle continued over a period of centuries. In Joshua 17:13, we read "Yet it came to pass, when the children of Israel were waxen strong, that they put the Canaanites to tribute but did not utterly drive them out."

God expressed His will in the strongest terms to His children in Number 33:52-56: "Ye shall drive out all inhabitants of the land [Canaan] before you ... And ye shall dispossess the inhabitants of the land, and dwell therein: for I have given you the land to possess it ... But if ye will not drive out the inhabitants of the land before you; then it shall come to pass, that those who ye let remain, of them shall be pricks in your eyes, and thorns in your sides, and shall vex you in the land wherein ye dwell ... It shall come to pass, that I shall do unto you, as I thought to do unto them."

The children of Israel, that is, the descendants of Shem, obeyed God, and did war against the Canaanites, but in later generations, they lost sign of this goal, permitting the Canaanites to live with them. During this period of history, there were great victories against their historic enemy, as recounted in Judges 1:17: "And Judah went with Simeon, his brother, and they slew the Canaanites that inhabited Zephath, and utterly destroyed it."

This victory came about because the children of Israel were distraught, and they sought guidance from the Lord. Judges 1:1-5: "Now after the death of Joshua it came to pass that the children of Israel asked the Lord, saying, 'Who shall go up for us against the Canaanites first to fight against them?' And the Lord said, 'Judah shall go up: behold, I have delivered the land into his hands.' And Judah said unto Simeon his brother, 'Come up with me into my lot, that we may fight against the Canaanites' ... And Judah went up; and the Lord delivered the Canaanites and the Perizzites into their hand... and they slew the Canaanites and the Perizzites."

Later, the victors again fell into the evil practices of those whom they had conquered, and again they were punished by the Lord. Judges 4: 1-2: "The children of Israel dwelt among the Canaanites. And the children of Israel again did evil in the sight of the Lord, and the Lord sold them into the hands of Jabin, king of the Canaanites." A later verse in Judges notes that the Israelites prevailed against Jabin and destroyed him and the Canaanites.

Exodus 15:15 says, "Then shall the dukes of Edom be amazed; the mighty sons of Moab, trembling shall take hold of them: all the inhabitants of Canaan shall melt away."

Nelson's Concordance lists more than eighty-five Biblical verses referring to the Canaanites. Most of the references are unfavorable, and invariably they reveal God's determination to punish his people for their misdeeds. Ezekiel 16: 1-3: "Again the words of the Lord came to me: 'Son of man, make known to Jerusalem her abominations ... Your origin and your birth are of the land of Canaan.'" Considering the frequency of references to Canaanites in the Bible, it is surprising that religious leaders rarely make any mention of them. In fact, many of the wealthier religious leaders today are actively in league with the Canaanites, enabling them to garner millions of dollars in contributions from gullible Christians.

Certainly the barbaric practices of the Canaanites were never secret, nor were they unknown in ancient times, as evidenced by the number of references available. Psalms 106:37-38: "They sacrificed their sons and daughters to the demon; they poured out innocent blood, the blood of their sons and daughters, whom they sacrificed to the idols of Canaan." Because of this well-documented record of their fiendish practices, God issued numerous orders that other tribes should not intermarry with this people. Isaac passed on one of these orders to Jacob. Genesis 28:1: "Isaac called Jacob and blessed him, and charged him, 'You shall not marry one of the Canaanite women.'" We have previously noted that Miriam and Jacob turned against Moses for marrying a Cushite, or black. The men of old were aware of the necessity to protect their genetic heritage, and they were equally aware that it could vanish in a single generation, if the wrong marriages took place.

The prohibition against mingling with the demon-worshipping Canaanites remained one of God's strongest commands. God said, "So shall we be separated, I and all of Thy people, from all the people that are upon the face of the earth" (Exodus 3:16).

God characterized the Canaanites thusly: "And I will make them a terror and an evil for all the kingdoms of the earth [referring to the Diaspora-Ed.], as a reproach and a proverb, a taunt and a curse on all places where I shall scatter them" (Jeremiah 24:9).

Thus we see the Canaanites, newly named the Phoenicians, dispersing along all of the trade routes and avenues of commerce throughout the earth. As God prophesied, they spread corruption, terror, and devastation wherever He scattered them. Later known as the Venetians, they dominated the avenues of commerce; when they settled inland, they specialized as merchants, and later, as bankers, at last comprising a group now loosely known as "the black nobility," which holds seemingly irresistible power today.

God further warned His people against the dispersed Canaanites. Deuteronomy 7:2-5: " ... thou shalt smite them, and utterly destroy them; thou shalt make no covenant with them [such as the League of Nations or the United Nations-Ed.] nor shew mercy unto them. Neither shalt thou make marriage with them: thy daughter thou shalt not give unto his son, nor his daughter shalt thou take unto thy son. For they will turn away thy son from following me, that they may serve other gods; so will the anger of the Lord be kindled against you, and destroy thee suddenly. But thus shall ye deal with them; ye shall destroy their altars, and break down their images, and cut down their groves, and burn their graven images with fire."

This was a direct command to destroy the groves and shrines of the demon-worshipping Mystery cults, now known as Freemasonry. The prohibition against "graven images" has been misunderstood by many well-meaning Christians. God did not prohibit graven images - He prohibited the obscene images of the Baal and Ashtoreth cults, which were made to create sexual excitement as part of their obscene rites. The battle against obscenity goes on today, although it often seems that American Christians are losing it.

In making these demands (they were not requests), God was not offering a program for a school picnic; He was laying out the only program which would allow His people to survive on this earth. Otherwise, He warned, "And a mongrel race will dwell in Ashdod" (Zechariah 9:6).

Should His people fail to carry out His instructions, God specifically described what would happen, and in so doing, He accurately described the world of today.

"But it shall come to pass, if thou wilt not hearken unto the voice of the Lord thy God, to observe and to do all His commandments and His statutes which I command thee this day, that all these curses shall come upon thee and overtake thee: ... The stranger that is within thy gates [the Canaanites or their descendants-Ed.] shall get up above thee very high, and thou shalt come down very low. He shall lend to thee, and thou shall not lend to him; he shall be the head and thou shalt be the tail" (Deuteronomy 28: 15, 43-44).

Certainly this is the situation which exists in the United States today. The Venetians control the Federal Reserve System; they lend to us, but we do not lend to them; they are the head, and we are the tail.

Having become Satan's curse on humanity, the Canaanites now spread across the earth like some evil plague. Genesis 10:18: "The families of the Canaanites were spread abroad." This diaspora brought troubles to every nation in which this people landed. Ezekiel 16:3, 45, and 46 lists the racial tribes of the Canaanites, denouncing them individually, "thy father an Amorite, their mother a Hittite, their older sister Samaria, their younger sister Sodom." Jesus, the minister of compassion, when he was asked to cure a Canaanite, denounced them as dogs. Matthew 15:22: "And, behold, a Canaanite woman from that region came out and cried, 'Have mercy on me, o Lord, son of David; my daughter is severely possessed by a demon.' But He did not answer her a word." At last He did answer her, verse 26, "And He answered, 'It is not fair to take the children's bread and throw it to the dogs." By children, He meant the children of Israel, and that the Canaanites were dogs. She persisted and he finally did heal her daughter.

The Canaanite political parties were the Pharisees, Sadducees, Zealots, Essains, Assissins, Herodians, and Scribes. A later group, the Edomites, descended from Esau and later intermarried with the Turks, producing a Turco-Edomite mixture which later became known as the Khazars, the present occupants of Israel, according to the great Jewish scholar, Arthur Koestler.

The Canaanites were divided into the Amorites, Hittites, Moabites, Midianites, Philistines, Ammonites, Edomites, Zidonians, Sepharvaims, Perizzites, and affiliated tribes, all of which are routinely denounced in the Bible. Genesis 3:17: "The Perizzites are the enemies of God; the Ammonites worshipped Moloch Chemos and were demon-possessed." The Ashodites worshipped the fish and god, Dagon-they were robbers and hated God (as recorded in the British Museum --Ed.). The Egyptians were known as worshippers of black magic, which resulted in God's rebuff to Hagar. The Amorites were cursed by God (Ezra 9:1). Hittite was defined as meaning to destroy or to terrify; Perizzite came to stand for strife and disorder; the Sepharvaim (later Sephardim) were revolutionaries; Jebusite stands for trampling underfoot.

In his monumental work, "The History of the Jews," Joseph Kastein writes, p. 19, "The Canaanitish cults were closely connected with the soil and expressive of the forces of nature, particularly the force of fertilization ... This force or divinity, was called Baal ... Whenever any question arose Involving their existence as a nation, they knew only one God, and recognized but one idea-the theocracy."

Thus Kastein admits that the Canaanites were fertility cults, but he does not explain that the worship of Baal as a god of fertility, with the obscene rites of his queen, Ashtoreth, was so abominated in the ancient world that whenever Baal was used in this context, in referring to proper names, the suffix for Baal was "bosheth," or shameful; thus we get the names Ishbosheth, Mephibosheth, etc.

The destructive nature of the Canaanites upon other nations in which they settled is nowhere more strongly demonstrated than in Egypt, the first land to be corrupted by their barbaric practices. Originally, "Baal" simply meant Lord in the Canaanite language. The obscenity of the rites soon developed a popular image of Baal which had three heads, the head of a cat, the head of a man, and the head of a toad. His wife, Ashtoreth, also known as Astarte and Ishtar, was the principal goddess of the Canaanites. She also represented the reproductive principle in nature, and in case anyone might overlook it, all of her rites were sexual observances. In Babylon, the temples of Baal and Ashtoreth were usually together. Mainly, they served as houses of prostitution, in which the priestesses were prostitutes, and the male priests were Sodomites who were available for the worshippers who were of that persuasion. The worship of the Canaanite gods consisted of orgies, and all their temples were known as centers of vice. They also originated voodoo ceremonies, which became the rites of observance in Ethiopia through the Ethiopian Jethro, the tutor of Moses. These same rites now enthrall tourists in the Caribbean.

It was not long before the simple ceremonies of vice began to pall on the worshippers of Baal. They sought greater excitement in rites of human sacrifice and cannibalism, in which the torture and murder of small children were featured. To consolidate their power over the people, the priests of the Canaanites claimed that all firstborn children were owed to their demon gods, and they were given over for sacrifice. This lewd and barbaric practice was noted in Isaiah 57:3-5: "But you, draw near hither, sons of the sorceress, offspring of the adulterer and the harlot. Of whom 'are you making sport? Against whom make ye a wide mouth, and draw out the tongue? Are ye not children of transgression, a seed of falsehood? Inflaming yourself with idols under every green tree, slaying the children in the valleys under the cleft of the rocks?"

Thus Isaiah inveighed not only against the obscene expressions of the blood-maddened orgiasts, their salacious grimaces, but also their now well-established custom of practicing their horrible rites in "groves" and "shrines," where they could murder children without being seen and punished by the descendants of Shem.

King Solomon came under the influence of the child-murderers, and he rebuilt an altar to Milcom (Molech, from the Hebrew melekh, meaning king). I Kings 11:5-8. Molech, or Moloch, was honored by his worshippers by the building of a great fire on his altar. The parents were then forced by the priests to throw their children into the fire. In excavations at Gezer (the Pharaoh Merneptah had called himself the Binder of Gezer after he put a stop to the obscene rites of the Canaanites at Gezer) Macalister, under the auspices of the Palestine Exploration Fund, from 1904 to 1909, found in the Canaanite stratum of about 1500 B.C., the ruins of a "High Place," a temple to Ashtoreth, containing ten crude stone pillars, five to eleven feet high, before which human sacrifices were offered. Under the debris in this "High Place," Macalister found great numbers of jars containing the remains of children who had been sacrificed to Baal. "Another horrible practice was what they called 'foundation sacrifice.' When a house was to be build, a child would be sacrificed and its body built into the wall, to bring good luck to the rest of the family. Many of these were found in Gezer. They have been found also at Megiddo, Jericho, and other places." (Halley's Bible Handbook)

Halley's also notes that in this "High Place," Macalister found large piles of images and plaques of Ashtoreth with rudely exaggerated sex organs, designed to stimulate sexual acts. Ashtoreth images found in many areas of the Canaanite influence emphasize over-sized breasts, sensuous smiles, heavily accented eyes, and nudity. The demonic nature of this sex worship is traced directly to Ham's intercourse with the witch Naamah on the Ark. Col. Garnier, in his "Worship of the Dead," writes, "Naamah was celebrated for her beauty, talent, energy, lustfulness, and cruelty, and she was of Nephilim (fallen angel) parentage."

The Encyclopaedia Judaica describes the Canaanite demonology as featuring Lilith, the vampire; Reseph, the god of the plague; Dever, god of pestilence; and the god of the underworld, Mot, from mavet, the Hebrew word for death.

Despite their prominence as destructive influences in the ancient world, the Canaanites and their demon-god Baal seldom appear in the authoritative works on the ancient Near East. Gaston Maspero's great history of Egypt, "The Dawn of Civilization," published in 1894, and republished in 1968, does not mention either Baal or Canaan. H. R. Hall's "Ancient History of the Near East" does not mention Shem or Canaan in the index. Baal has a single mention. How much of this is due to the deliberate falsification and destruction of historical records by the Egyptian priesthood cannot be ascertained, but the results are obvious. Another contributing factor is the sudden disappearance of the names' 'Canaan" and "Canaanites" from all historical records after 1200 B.C. How did this come about? It was very simple. They merely changed their name.

Chambers Encyclopaedia notes that "After 1200 B.C. the name of Canaanites vanished from history. They changed their name to Phoenician." Thus the most notorious and most hated people on earth received a new lease on life. The barbaric Canaanites had disappeared. The more civilized Phoenicians, seemingly harmless merchant folk, took their place. Having obtained a monopoly on purple dye, which was highly prized throughout the ancient world, the Canaanites advertised their control over this product by calling themselves Phoenicians, from phoenicia (phoenikiea), the Greek word for purple. From the outset of their history, the Phoenician Canaanites always managed to get a monopoly on some essential product. They later had a monopoly on tin for some centuries, until the Greeks discovered tin in Cornwall in 233 B.C. Joseph of Arimathea, the uncle of Jesus, was said to have owned large tin mines in Cornwall.

The change of name did not mean that the Canaanites had abandoned their worship of Baal and Ashtoreth. They became more prudent in their worship of Baal, and in the colonies which they established along the length of the Mediterranean, they built their temples to the female of the species, Ashtoreth. In the Egyptian city of Memphis, the Phoenician Temple of Ashotoreth was the largest religious edifice. She was known there as the wife of the supreme god, El, and his seventy deities. In their rituals, Ashtoreth was sometimes worshipped as the male demon, Astaroth, who survived in European rites as Astara or Ostara. In this form, he became the patron god of the Nazi movement in Germany.

The westernmost outpost of the Phoenicians was Cadiz, a Phoenician colony which derived its name from the Semitic gadir, or fortress. Their most important colony, which soon became a rival to Rome itself, was Carthage, which they established about 900 B.C. The name derived from Hebrew, Kart-hadshat, or new city. The Phoenicians often named their cities with the prefix of "new." During the fifth century, the Carthaginians had fought the Greeks and survived, but in 264 B.C. Rome attacked in full force. A series of wars ensued, called the Punic Wars, because the Carthaginians called themselves the Punics. St. Augustine noted that the Punics among themselves referred to their people as the "Chanani," or Canaanites, but this name was like a secret code; they never used it in dealing with other people.

Whether for purely commercial reasons, or because they feared a military power astride their avenues of commerce in the Mediterranean, the Romans determined to utterly destroy Carthage. They succeeded in this resolve so absolutely that present-day archaeologists are not sure just where Carthage was located. From 264 to 201 B.C., Rome waged three Punic Wars against Carthage, culminating in the defeat of their leader, Hannibal, by the Roman armies under the command of Scipio Africanus. The Romans killed or took into slavery every Carthaginian and razed the city. They completed their task by sowing the land with salt, so that nothing would ever flourish there again. Nothing ever did.

This defeat, although a major setback, did not destroy the world operations of the Canaanites, but it did inculcate in them a fierce hatred of all things Roman, which ever since has been characterized by the Canaanite school of propaganda as "fascism," from the Roman rods, or fasces, which were carried by the magistrate to symbolize his determination to maintain order. The later Masonic assault upon the Catholic Church was largely dictated by the fact that it was headquartered in the city of their most ancient enemy, Rome, and therefore the papacy became to the Phoenicians the modern embodiment of the force which had destroyed their most important headquarters. Few Americans realize that when the New School of Research in New York denounces "fascism," joined by the columnists of the New York Times and the New York Post, they are merely echoing their ancient anger over the destruction of Carthage. Here again, our historians have only one goal, to obscure the past and to prevent us from realizing the nature of the forces at work.

It was not only the Canaanites who spread across the earth. The descendants of Shem also multiplied and journeyed to find greater opportunities for their families. They moved from country to country, founding great kingdoms and dynasties, which have survived to the present day. There are many people who can agree that the kings and leaders of the Western nations are descended from the tribe of Judah, but they fail to recognize an important fact, which is entirely omitted in the King James version of the Bible, that there were three branches of the tribe of Judah. Those who lump all the descendants of the tribe of Judah together do not realize that there was a tainted branch. There were the families of Pharez and Zarah, Judah's pure bred sons out of Tamar, and there was a third branch, Judah's descendants from a Canaanite mother, Shuah, who were known ever afterwards as "the cursed Shelanites." Tamar was the daughter of Aram, the youngest son of Shem. Shuah called Tamar's sons bastards because they had been born out of wedlock, while the twins claimed to be the rightful heirs of Judah because they were of pure-blooded stock, the Adamite strain. From the Shelanites descended thirty-one cursed tribes of Canaanites of Judea and Samaria, including the Sepharvaims, a name which the Canaanites had adopted for deceptive purposes.

At the birth of Pharez and Zarah, the midwife, seeing that there were twins in the womb, realized that it would be necessary to mark the firstborn, who would have primogeniture. She quickly wrapped a red thread around the wrist of Zarah, but it was Pharez who came out first from "the breach." The Messiah was descended from Pharez, and he was said to have been sent by God to heal "the breach" which had existed since the birth of Pharez and Zarah.

Tamar, mother of Pharez and Zarah, had a descendant named Tamar Tephi, known in Irish legend as "the daughter of Pharaoh." She married Eochaidh, king of Ireland, who was known as the Prince of the Scarlet Thread. Thus the two lines of Pharez and Zarah were again reunited.

The Scarlet Thread subsequently became an integral part of British history. A red thread is symbolically woven into every rope which is used by the Royal Navy; and every British monarch has delivered to him official documents which are wrapped with a red cord. The term also survives in "red tape," that is, the official red cord which must be unwound before any state business is transacted. There is also the red carpet which tradition required to be unrolled before royalty walks in.

Before he would give Tamar in marriage, Heremon, the father of Tamar, demanded that serpent worship and the rites of Bel, which were then practiced in Ireland, be renounced. The serpents then disappeared from Ireland, and there are no poisonous serpents there today. A later legend is that St. Patrick expelled the serpents from Ireland. Both legends call attention to the demonic practices of the Canaanites, as well as their descent from the serpent; its banishment established Ireland as a land of the true religion of YHWH, or the descendants of Shem. The disappearance of the serpents also signified that the evil powers of the Canaanites had vanished from Ireland.

Both Spain and Ireland show their direct connection to the descendants of Shem in their names. Spain occupies the Iberian Peninsula, from Iber, or Hebrew; Ireland is known as Hibernia, the land of the Hebrews, as are the Hebrides Islands. In his History of Ireland, Roger Chauvire says that Ireland is the last remaining part of Atlantis which is still above the surface of the sea. In his History of Ireland, A. M. Sullivan writes of the legendary origin of the present Irish race.

"The Milesian colony reached Ireland from Spain, but they were not Spanish. They were an eastern people who had tarried in that country on their way westward, seeking, they aid, an island promised to the posterity of their ancestor Gadelius. Gadelius was the son of Niul, who was the youngest son of the King of Scythia. As a child, Gadelius had been bitten by a poisonous serpent. He was near death when his father persuaded Moses to use his rod to cure him. From that day, the Milesians carried westward their banner, which was emblazoned with a dead serpent and the rod of Moses, until they found an island which had no poisonous snakes."

The sons of Milesius, Gadelius' descendants, who sailed from Spain to Ireland were Heber the Fair, Amergin, Colpa, Heber the Brown, Ir, and Heremon. Their descendants ruled Ireland for one thousand years, the dynasty being established by Niall (Niul), who ruled at Tara from 310 to 405. He is described by Sullivan as "a splendid hero of the Gaelic blood, tall, fair-haired and blue-eyed, a great and noble-minded warrior, 'kind in hall and fierce in fray'; from him descended the kings of Ireland, the Neills."

These conquerors of Ireland, the Milesians, derived their name from Milesius, the soldier (from the Latin miles, from which we get the word militia). Gadelius, the founder of the line, derived his name from the Hebrew "gadil," meaning to become great, or in plural the exalted, the fortune-seekers, or the fortunate ones. Because of their great pride and their natural abilities, the Irish were later referred to as being from "the Land of Kings." Of almost any Irishman, it could be boastfully said, "Sure, and he's the descendant of kings."

From earliest records, the Irish and the Britons are shown to be historic enemies. Apuleius wrote in 296 A.D. of the "two races, the Britons and Ibernia." Eumenius always wrote of Hibernia as the enemy of Briton. Caesar's Notes on the Gallic Wars, 58-50 B.C., wrote of "Hibernia, west of Britain."

The world was now swept by two diametrically opposed tides of history. On the one hand were the highly creative and productive descendants of Shem, who have since become known as Semites, and on the opposing side were the "cursed Canaanites," who historically were the anti-Semites, the foes of the tall, fair-haired, and blue eyed descendants of Shem. Because the Semites were always known as great warriors, they handily defeated the Canaanites in every military encounter, and in many cases obeyed God's command to drive them out and to destroy them utterly. But the anti-Semites seemed to have great staying power; when driven out of one country, they appeared in another to continue their same type of corruption and betrayal. While the Semites were busily establishing one great empire after another, Asshur's building the Assyrian Empire, Cyrus the Great building the Persian Empire, and Shem himself creating the great Egyptian civilization, the anti-Semites were developing their own talents. These included a talent for trade and commerce, for travel, for making themselves at home in any country, and among any race of people. Generally they established their trading colonies along the seacoasts, for they lacked the courage to venture into the great wildernesses of Europe, where the Semites always made themselves at home. The Canaanites always remained true to the precepts of the Will of Canaan; they were true to each other, regardless of the circumstances; they were constant in their love of robbery, their love of lewdness, and their hatred of the masters, that is, anyone who tried to interfere with their corrupt way of life. And they always refused to tell the truth. By remaining loyal to these unchanged precepts, the anti-Semites had at their disposal vital weapons for their war against the people of Shem. The Shemites, on the other hand, being fiercely individualistic, never hesitated to pit their empires against each other, or even family against family, their overweening pride always taking precedence before any racial or historical imperative.

During the Middle Ages, the people of Shem found their typical characteristics best expressed in such organizations as the Teutonic Knights, a group of warriors which was invincible for hundreds of years. At the same time, the anti-Semites were busily expanding trade routes, and amassing their profits from trade (to this day, the British aristocracy professes disdain for anyone who sullies his hands with trade, an ancient prejudice against the Canaanites); with these profits, they eventually became bankers to the world. In pursuing this objective, they found a great opportunity during the Crusades. Not only did the Crusades open up trade routes throughout the known world, but they also opened up new avenues of graft and corruption, which allowed the Canaanites to amass even greater profits. When the Christian knights departed for the Crusades, dedicating themselves to the service of Christ, the Canaanites, who prudently remained at home, now perfected various schemes to rob the knights of their money and property while they were away. In "Ancient Knighthood and the Crusades," we find that some of the crusaders "found shelter and protection at the hands of the Teutonic Knights, who were engaged in looking up the frauds perpetrated by the rapacious monks and clergy, who had forged title deeds and mortgages upon lands and property of absent Crusaders or those who had fallen in defense of the Cross in the Holy Land ... time for reflection and study of the causes of the Crusades at home and abroad, when, other than the scum of Europe which settled upon its dregs, the best people had been almost entirely obliterated from the face of the continent. The rapacity of the popes and clergy down to the lowest monks was appalling to those self- sacrificing, stalwart warriors of the Cross, who had returned and found utter strangers in the places and homes of their kindred, tad upon investigation it was discovered that frauds, forgeries of title deeds, and confiscations under pretexts of heresy had despoiled their kindred, and the meagre few who had survived were beggars upon the highway and lanes, perishing as tramps by the wayside."

The Knights of the Teutonic Order built the city of Riga In Latvia in 1201; they conquered Estonia in 1220; they conquered Prussia in 1293, establishing a military tradition there which ended only after World War II. Although they were disbanded in 1809, the Teutonic Knights remained the inspiration of the German military establishment, which guided Germany through two World Wars. It was Hitler himself who wrote "finis" to their proud traditions, when he concluded the Molotov-Ribbentrop Pact in 1939. Not only did this pact cede the nations of Estonia, Latvia, and Lithuania, the ancient strongholds of the Teutonic Order, to the Communists or Canaanites, but subsequently, all of the great estates of the last heirs of the Prussian tradition, the last survivors of the Teutonic Order, fell into the hands of the onrushing Soviet hordes.

By this time, the reader must be thoroughly confused. The "Semites" are really the "anti-Semites" or Canaanites, the heirs of the Curse of Canaan, whose corrupt acts are dictated by the Will of Canaan; the true Semites are the fair-haired warriors who built one great civilization after another-then how do we recognize these various forces in today's world? "By their deeds ye shall know them." Those who are engaged in murderous conspiracies, those whose only loyalty is to secret international organizations, those who promote the use of drugs, bizarre sexual practices, and criminal undertakings, in short, those who continue the rebellion against God, these are the Canaanites, the anti-Semites. Those who remain true to Christ are the Semites. Despite great calamities and the sweep of powerful historical forces, the genetic pools of the original people of Shem, as well as those of the Canaanites, remain fairly consistent. How do we recognize the one group from the other? You should have no problem in looking about you and deciding who are the true descendants of Shem, often fair-haired, fair-skinned, predominantly blue-eyed, healthy, creative, productive, proud, disdaining to engage in any dishonest activity, and always fiercely individualistic, these are the people who remain true to the tradition of the people of Shem. The Canaanites, on the other hand, are generally shorter, darker, more furtive, and almost always engaged in some type of criminal activity, usually with special government approval or license. Roget equates license with "anarchy, interregnum, mob rule, mob law, lynch law, nihilism, reign of violence," in other words, the acts of the Canaanites; yet in the United States today, we have imposed on the citizens requirements for license to do any of the things free men would not be licensed to do; to drive or own a car, to engage in a profession, and many other intrusions into the individuality of the people of Shem. "License," which does not appear in the Constitution written by and for the people of Shem, means setting up requirements that only the Canaanites can meet, or license which only the secret clubs of the Canaanites will grant to their own; no others need apply. This is the cohesiveness required by the Will of Canaan in everything they do, socialistic and communistic, the individual submerged in the mass, and committed to conspiratorial social and business practices. They are also frequently involved in some sort of extracurricular sexual activity which can be traced directly back to the orgies of Baal, human sacrifice, and obscene sexual rites. At the same time, these "anti-Semites" will go to great lengths to conceal their true identity and their real loyalties. In their communities, they are often found to be leaders in activities advertised as "compassionate" and "caring"; they are often to be found in government offices, in the media, and in the educational institutions. In these areas, they ruthlessly promote the interests of their own kind, while presenting a solid phalanx of opposition to any one of the individualistic descendants of Shem who enter these professions. The great asset of the Canaanites is that the people of Shem have no idea what is going on; they rarely find success in a profession despite their great natural talents and appetite for hard work. Throughout their careers, they are oppressed by the realization that "luck" never seems to favor them while others find promotion almost automatic, if they are members of their rivals, the Canaanites. Now time grows short. History will not allow the people of Shem additional centuries, or even decades, to come to their senses and realize what is going on. Just as they have been victims of massacre and genocide for centuries, the people of Shem now face the determination of the Canaanites to exterminate them utterly and finally, a goal which they hope to achieve by the end of this millennium.

CHAPTER 2

THE TRANSGRESSION OF CAIN

"Not as Cain, who was of the evil one, and killed his brother. And wherefore did he kill him? Because his own works were wicked, and his brother's just" (I John 3:12).

The transgression of Cain, the first murderer, is of remarkable significance in tracing the development of occult organizations in history. The Hebrew word for Cain is Kajin, from Koon, to chant, and from which we derive the slang terms for persons of mixed race, Kajuns and coons. From Cain descended Tubal Cain, whose name is used as the secret password of Freemasonry. Tubal Cain was the son of Lamech, and brother to Noah, but he was born of a bigamous marriage. Tubal Cain became a blacksmith, and he later became renowned as the father of witchcraft and sorcery. His father, Lamech, was the son of Methuselah, of the line of Cain.

We might suppose that the two sons of Adam, Cain and Abel, having the whole world before them, would have little cause for discord, but Cain, being of the Evil One, sought a quarrel with his brother. The Bible recounts that they made offerings to God, and that God accepted the offering from Abel, but rejected the offering of Cain because he was unworthy, that is, he was of the serpent. Cain, overcome by wrath and jealousy, then slew Abel. The midrash gives a somewhat more extended version, that Cain persuaded Abel that they should divide the world between them. Cain would get all the land, and Abel would have all the chattels thereon.

Cain then informed Abel that he was standing on his land, and that he should remove himself. Abel retorted that Cain was wearing clothes of animal skins, which belonged to Abel. They fought, and Cain slew Abel.

God then banished Cain "eastward of Eden," in "the land of Nod." He wedded a woman of pre-Adamite stock, and thus compounded his fault. Genesis 4:17 says, "Cain knew [that is, had relations with] his wife." That Cain's wife was of forbidden or strange flesh is borne out later, in Jude 11, in referring to the men of Sodom and Gomorrah, "Woe unto them! for they have gone the way of Cain," that is, seeking after strange flesh. The pre-Adamites were referred to by the Hebrew word Nachash, to hiss, as a serpent-meaning Negro. The Arab word Chanas comes from this Hebrew word, as well as Khanoos, or Ape, and the Arab word for devil, Khanas. Thus the mixing of the races and the appearance of the devil in history are conjoined in the misdeeds of Cain. Cain is also reputed to have celebrated the first Black Mass, or Satanic Mass, on earth.

The name of Cain survives today in Freemasonry in two forms, which are integral to the most crucial tenets of this association. First of all, murder, the threat of murder, and the constant reenactment of murder are basic to the most important Masonic rituals, as Stephen King pointed out in his book, "The Brotherhood," shortly before his untimely death. Thus a direct link to the first murderer, Cain, is established by these rituals. The importance of the Cain legend to Freemasonry is also revealed by the fact that Cain slew his brother. In Freemasonry, if you are asked to act against your own brother in behalf of a fellow-Mason, you must do so, under pain of death. There have been many instances where a man who was pursuing a lawsuit against a Mason was astounded to have his own brother, who would be a Mason, come into court and commit perjury against him to help his brother Mason. This custom also survives in other organizations (which may be related to Freemasonry). In La Cosa Nostra, leaders often request a member to murder a close relative upon whom the death sentence has been passed, as the ultimate test of his loyalty.

The name of Cain also survives in a second important element of Freemasonry. The secret password of Freemasonry is "Tubal Cain" (Heckethorn, "Secret Societies," p. 26). Tubal Cain, a descendant of Cain, was the son of Lamech, the father of Noah, who had two wives, Adah and Zillah. 'Zillah bore Tubal Cain; he was the forger of all instruments of bronze and iron. The sister of Tubal Cain was Naamah" (Genesis 4:22). Naamah's revelries with her blood relative, Ham, resulted in the Curse of Canaan; she is also recorded as the person who brought human sacrifice and cannibalism into the world. Tubal Cain, grandson of Methuselah by Lamech, was of the line of Cain, hence his name. He is known as the father of witchcraft and sorcery, hence his importance to Freemasonry and their use of his name as their password.

Ham's descendant by the Negro Cush, Nimrod, son of Cush, became the world's most demonic ruler, and the first ruler of the world. He used his power to indulge in sex orgies and child sacrifices, until Shem beheaded him for his offenses against God. Shem cut his body into pieces and sent these gory relics to the priests as a warning to cease and desist their vile practices of demonic worship. Instead, the priests hid the pieces, revering them as objects of worship, concealing them in their "groves" and "Shrines" as the first "Mysteries." The secret of the relics, or Mystery, was made known to initiates only after a long period of indoctrination, when they could be trusted not to betray the worshippers of Baal. This was the true origin of the "Mysteries," from which, as Albert Pike notes in "Morals and Dogma," all Masonic rites originate.

Satanic practices throughout the world can be traced in an unbroken line directly back to Gnosticism, from gnosis, or knowing. Gnosis refers to knowing the secrets of the Mysteries, that is, the place where the relics are hidden, the pieces of Nimrod's body. The "G" which is prominently featured in Masonic symbols indicates not only its origins in Gnosticism, but also "Generation," that is, the fertility rites of the sex cult of Baal and Ashtoreth. This "G" is also featured in the logo of the Gannett chain, a group which is rapidly swallowing up newspapers and television stations all over America, as well as publishing the newspaper "USA Today," which loses over $100 million a year. This is considered a small price to pay for controlling the minds of American people.

The fate of Nimrod also survives in the myth as Osiris and his sister Isis. Osiris, another name for the Canaanite god Baal and his consort Ashtoreth or Isis, whose rites the Canaanites brought into Egypt, were worshipped as fertility gods. The Egyptian legend is that Osiris' brother Set (or Shem) dissected him into fourteen pieces. Isis gathered up the pieces, but the most important part, the phallus, was missing; the legend says that a crab had eaten it. Isis made a substitute phallus out of wood, and thus restored her brother.

Because of its origin in the temples of Baal, which were dedicated to both male and female prostitution, Freemasonry has been the unseen force behind the drive to make the United States into a bisexual nation. Its philosophical director, Albert Pike, makes this plain in his authoritative book, "Morals and Dogma," p. 849: "Reversing the letters of the ineffable name, and dividing it, it becomes bisexual" This is pure Kabbalism, and it refers us directly to the cult of Baal and Ashtoreth. Pike makes the point clearer on page 741, "Masonry is a search after Light. That search leads us directly back, as you see, to the Kabbala. All truly dogmatic religions have issued from the Kabbala and return to it; everything grand in the religious dreams of the Illuminati, Jacob Boehm, Swedenborg, Saint-Martin, and others, is borrowed from the Kabbala; all the Masonic associations owe to it their secrets and symbols."

This is the most definitive revelation of the true origins and purposes of Freemasonry. Originating in the Kabbala, it accomplishes its devious purposes through the even more secret organization of the Illuminati, the inner circle which controls the six million Freemasons of the world.

From their inception, the "Mysteries" were always bisexual; rather, they sought to indulge any passion in their dedication to pleasure, which meant constantly seeking after new and perhaps more exciting sensations. Our modern psychologists explain these diversions as "the alternative lifestyle." The symbol of the obscene rites is the Delta, or triangle (the large pornography collection at the Library of Congress is called the Delta collection; each card in the catalogue listing a book in this collection has the symbolic triangle in the upper lefthand corner). The Delta represents the triune circles of eternity, the Hebrew Yod. The double Delta, or six pointed symbol of Judaism, represents the male triangle supreme over the female triangle below, and penetrating her. The inverted triangle in the Rite of Kadosch Freemasonry represents Lucifer as the Grand Patriarch and Grand Emperor. This triangle comprises the Indivisible Trinity to which the Kadosch takes his oath of blind obedience. The Delta is also the symbol of the Chapter in Royal ArchMasonry. This triangle represents the Indivisible Masonry.

The Delta, or Triad, now is featured as the new symbol of Hundreds of American business organizations, perhaps as a notice to the elect that this business is now part of the Masonic Empire. The present writer has many pages which researchers have gathered showing the predominance of this symbol in American business. The Triads are also the name of the ancient Chinese underworld gangs, for whom murder is a customary method of doing business.

Throughout the world, the Triad has become the symbol of international business conspiracies. When Kashoggi, the munitions dealer whose arms dealings resulted in the 1980's Iran scandals, formed an American branch of his operations, he called it Triad America. Also symbolically, it has now gone into bankruptcy, after inveigling many Americans into multi-million dollar deals in many areas.

Captain William Morgan, who was murdered for having written of the Masonic rituals, and thereby gave rise to the Anti-Masonic Party in America during the nineteenth-century, noted in his historic book, "Freemasonry Exposed," that when a Fellow Craft Mason was asked in interrogatory (interrogatory has since become a prime technique of lawyers In their manipulation of a bill of attainder proceeding known us "Discovery") what was his work, he answered that he worked at building King Solomon's Temple. "What does a Master's Lodge represent? The Sanctum Sanctorum, or holy of holies, King Solomon's Temple."

Albert Mackey's "Encyclopaedia of Freemasonry" lists under Orient, "The place where a Lodge is situated is sometimes called its 'Orient,' but more properly, its 'East.' The seat of a Grand Lodge has also sometimes been called its 'Grand Orient,' but here 'Grand East' would, perhaps, be better. The term 'Grand Orient' has been used to designate certain of the Supreme Bodies on the Continent of Europe, and also in South America, as the Grand Orient of France, the Grand Orient of Brazil, the Grand Orient of Portugal, and the Grand Orient of New Grenada, etc. The title always has reference to the East as the place of honor in Masonry."

The reverence for the East throughout Grand Orient Freemasonry is revealed by their activities in Western civilization. They have consistently worked to impose Oriental despotism on the citizens of Western Republics through totalitarian government apparatus. Oriental despotism has become especially predominant in all of our legal proceedings, the "court" where the despot rules, the symbolic bow, or standing, when the despot comes into the room, and the refusal of the despot to brook any questioning of his decision by a citizen, who can approach the judge only through an anointed priesthood, the legal profession. Some Americans optimistically decide to come into court representing themselves, which the people of Shem provided for specifically in their Constitution of the United States, but judges usually give such "attorneys pro se" short shrift. In states such as Virginia, where Masonic power rules the courts, judges have been known to boast that no attorney pro se will ever get a favorable decision in their court. A non-Mason who enters an American court today is placing himself at the mercy of an Oriental despot, hence the tyrannical actions of judges in sentencing to indeterminate prison sentences anyone who happens to displease them, or whose property is coveted by a Mason.

This Oriental type of despotism can be traced back to Zoroaster in Persia, to Ishtar and Tammuz in Babylon, to the graeco-Thracian Mysteries at Eleusis, the Mysteries of Demeter, Persephone, and Dionysus; to Cybele and Altis in Phrygia; to Aphrodite and Adonis in Syria; to Isis and Osiris in Egypt; and to Mithra in Persia.

These Mystery cults were formally combined into much of the text of the Babylonian Talmud, a book of religious precepts which had been formulated after the fall of Jerusalem in 586 B.C. Nebuchadnezzar took this people to Babylon as captives from 586 to 537 B.C., after which Cyrus of Persia captured Babylon and authorized the return to

Jerusalem. During the Babylonian captivity, there was a free admixture of the various Canaanite tribes; the Edomites intermarried with the Canaanite branch of the Judahites and Chers. Edom means red; ever since the Captivity, red has meant revolution and Canaanite massacre of the innocents. The Rothschilds, when they backed the formation of the Illuminati, changed their name from Bauer to Roth (red) child (shield). This intermixture of various strains caused a great deal of confusion among the offspring as to what heir customs should be. To resolve this difficulty, the captives began to compile a great book of religious teachings. Talmud means "teaching" in Hebrew. By the second century A.D., the Talmud had been completed as oral law, the Mishnah, or older part, and the Gemara, or commentary on the law.

It first appeared in print in 1520, when Daniel Bomberg published it in Venice.

Because of its origins in the demon-worshipping capital of the world, Babylon, demonology plays an important part throughout the text of the Talmud. It refers to the Demiurge, or Chief Demon, as the Creator of the Universe, and it defames the various appearances of demons as (1) mazzikim; (2) shedim; (3) ruhot (Avot. 5-6). Asmodeus is listed as the King of the Demons (Pes. 110a-112b).

The Mishnah taught in the second century B.C. that two things should never be revealed to the public, or the uninitiated: (1) the work of creation, and (2) the work of the chariot (meaning esoteric operations, the "Divine Throne"). These precepts later became further formalized in the secret rites of Freemasonry.

In 1280 A.D., a further development of Talmudic thought, The Zohar, or Book of Splendour, appeared. This was known as the Cabal, or tradition. It was based on two things: (1) generation, or the fertility rites, as the most sacred word in the new instructions (which, of course, also became the "G" featured in Masonic symbols), and (2) the precept that Israel alone is to possess the future world (Vayschleh folio 177b). The Zohar derived from the Sefer Yetsirah, or Book of Creation, which had appeared in the Babylon of the third century; the ten Sephiroth or numbers, based on the belief that the universe derives from the ten numbers and two letters of the Hebrew alphabet; this later was developed into the twenty-two trumps of Tarot, or the twenty-two Paths which lead to Sephotorth.

In Cabala,[2] evil takes on a mysterious existence of its own, which its precepts trace back to the physical appearance of life on earth, or Adam. Cabala claims that Adam throws the entire stream of life out of balance, and that the Church, or Christianity, by formalizing the physical existence of the Adamite people on earth, have become a problem which must be resolved. This is the essence of the basic anti-life principle underlying all Cabala and its heir, Freemasonry. These precepts declare that Satanism will achieve its final triumph over the Church and Christianity, thus ending the "dualism" of this world, the struggle between good and evil. In short, the problem of good and evil will be ended when evil triumphs and good is eliminated from the earth. This program may sound somewhat simplistic, but it is the basic premise of the Cabala and Freemasonry.

These anti-life precepts are now to be encountered, and dealt with, in many of the developments of our civilization. The descendants of the Canaanites instinctively hate and

---

[2] Cabala appears in various spellings through history, principally "Cabala." Also Kabbalah, Kabala, etc.

actively oppose such progress as technology, urban life, industrialism, and the cultural achievements of humanity. Their basic goal is to return the earth to the primitivism of its pre-Adamic state, when a Neanderthal type of human roamed at will over an earth which had no "civilized" aspects to remind him of his primitivism. The end purpose is to "restore" pre-Adamic man, so that Adamite man, as a creation of God, no longer presents an obstacle to Satan and his rule over this world.

Thus cabbalistic Freemasonry aims for the extermination of life as we know it, culminating in the final triumph of the Canaanite Curse on this earth. In retrospect, this amazing observation offers an irrefutable reason for the otherwise inexplicable massacres, wars, and human devastation which have been regularly visited upon a long-suffering humanity by the Canaanite conspirators.

The Encyclopaedia Judaica has an entry of some sixty-one pages on the Kabbala alone, by far the largest single entry in this encyclopaedia. This entry notes that "Christian Kabbalah," that is, the central development of secular humanism, first appeared in the theosophical systems of the Freemasons in the second half of the eighteenth century, that is, during the period of "the Enlightenment." It was this predominant element in secular humanism which led to the revolutions of the eighteenth and nineteenth centuries, and which had previously led to the Reformation. These political results were the logical outcome of the teachings of Zohar, which declares that En Soph (the Ultimate Deity) brought the world into being in an indirect manner, in order to avoid being contaminated by physical being, or life; this again expresses the basic anti-life direction of this philosophical system. This deity's only manifestation on earth is through the Ten Sephiroth, or Divine Emanations. The teachings of Zohar deny any presence on earth of God or His Son Jesus

Christ; it places all of its emphasis on 'non-God or humanistic doctrines.

Orthodox Jews base their religious practices entirely on the Cabala. They celebrate their coming triumph, the Feast of Tabernacles, which is defined in the Zohar as the period when they triumph over all the peoples of the world. "That is why during this feast we seize the loulab and carry it as a trophy to show that we have conquered all the other people (the populace)" (Toldoth Noah 63b).

In his definitive work, "The Magical Mason," W. Wynn Westcott, the founder of the Hermetic Order of the Golden Dawn in England, traces the origins of the Freemasons back to the Essenes in Jerusalem; Pharisaic Jews, the practitioners of the most strict Judaism; the ancient Mysteries of Egypt and Greece; the Vehm-Gerichte of Westphalia in Germany; the trade guilds of the Middle Ages; the Roman Collegia; the French Compagnons; and the Rosicrucians. Westcott points out that the cornerstone of the Capitol of Rome has the keystone mark of "the Overseers," a sacred group. The Royal Arch has an altar of white stone in the form of a double cube; it is engraved with "the Sacred Name." He says that the Mysteries, from which all Masonic ritual is derived, were intended to end the fear of death in the initiate, by re-enacting the descent into Hades, and thus finding the great first cause of all things revealed to the initiate. Westcott claims that the famous Black Stone in the Sacred Mosque at Mecca is also part of this ritual. There is also the Sacred Stone placed beneath the Throne of England, which is said to have been the Stone of Jacob in Biblical times.

From such ancient symbols of power came the Masonic motto, "Per me reges regnant," "through me kings reign." By controlling kings, the Masons exercised their power from behind the scenes. If the kings were overthrown by revolutions (which were often of organized by the

Freemasons themselves), the kings might be beheaded, but the instigators behind the throne would be forewarned and escape unscathed. They would then continue to reign through the next chosen leader, usually designated by their inner councils.

Although it is dedicated to the usurpation and maintenance of absolute power through an Oriental despotism, Freemasonry has attained much of its worldwide influence through its emphasis on and sponsorship of the power of revolutions against the established order. Their slogan became the motto of the French Revolution, "Liberté, egalité, fraternité." Liberty, equality, that is, equality for Masons only, with slavery as the fate of everyone else, and fraternity, that is the brotherhood of the Masonic Order of the Canaanites. This slogan appears throughout documents of Freemasonry, which also advertises itself as "The New Age" movement. Many of its publications, such as the magazine of the Washington Freemasons in our nation's capital, feature the name, The New Age, and the symbolic triangle on the cover of its magazine, the triangle being emblazoned in its borders with the motto, "Liberty, Equality, and Fraternity." The New Age, or New Order, refers to the era which will be inaugurated after the final Armageddon, when the Canaanites exterminate the last survivors of the people of Shem.

In the Masonic world, Jerusalem has always been heralded as the birthplace of Freemasonry. Another tradition has it that the earliest Masonic lodges built the Temple of Solomon. King Solomon completed the Temple in 1005 B.C. Solomon died at the age of sixty, after a reign of some forty years, and was succeeded by his son Rehoboam. Mackey's "Encyclopaedia of Masonry" says under the entry, "Oriental Chair of Solomon," "The seat of the Master in a Symbolic Lodge, and so called because the Master is supposed symbolically to fill the place over the Craft once occupied by King Salomon. For the same reason, the seat of the Grand Master ill the Grand Lodge receives the same appellation. In England it is called the Throne."

In Masonic symbolism, the Rainbow appears as the sacred depiction of Lucifer, the Light Bearer, and it indicates his Brightness. On Masonic diplomas is inscribed the verse, "And God said, Let there be Light, and there was Light." In fact, the use of God's name here is a typical subterfuge whose true meaning is known only to the higher degrees of Freemasonry, the occult degrees, and is an example of the internal deception by which the occult degrees rule the fellow crafts. Lucifer in the true name of the being whom they worship as a god, as their mentor, Albert Pike, made plain in his communications to Mazzini and other Masonic leaders.

The symbols of Freemasonry, to those unaware of their Cabbalistic meaning, may seem innocuous enough, particularly to the great majority of Masons, the members of the three degrees of the Blue Lodges. They are never informed that the "All-Seeing Eye" of their symbolism refers not to light, but to the genitals, the Eye of Hoor, which is the anus, and which signifies the homosexual or bisexual commitment of our present ruling class, the World Order of the Canaanites. "G" stands for both Generation, or the act of coitus, and for Gnosticism. It also glorifies the Great God Baal, and the missing part of his anatomy, the phallus, which according to the legend of Set and Nimrod, had been removed.

The worship of the phallus appears in Masonic ceremonies in the Master degrees Ma-ha-bone, signifying the hermaphroditic son of Loth. The Master's Lodge represents the Uterus, the Middle Chamber. The acacia signifies that all the Mysteries originated in India, or rather, that their initial inspiration came from that area. In the Acacia Rite, the fellow crafts are dressed in white, from the Greek signifying innocence, although it also signifies the corruption of innocence in many religious rites.

The Acacia Mutual Life Insurance Company headquarters occupies a prominent place in Washington near the halls of Congress. During his lifetime, J. Edgar Hoover, longtime head of the Federal Bureau of Investigation, accepted only one business association. He was named a director of Acacia Mutual, which was almost directly across the street from his headquarters at the FBI. Because of this association, it proved impossible to remove him from the FBI during his lifetime.

EMBLEMS OF MASONRY

The Masonic points also derived from the ancient Mysteries; the triple degrees of the system correspond to the mysteries of Serapis, Isis, and Osiris. The entered apprentice is referred to the three lights, Osiris in the East, Isis in the

West, and Horus, who was master, or living lord in place of Osiris, in the South.

The Hexapla, or Seal of Solomon, is a six-pointed star. In the Cabala, six is esteemed as a male number, which has been assigned by the Kabbalists to Microprospus, the Vau of the Hebrew alphabet, and the six middle signs. The Cabala itself is the basis of Theosophy; in the Encyclopaedia Judaica, under the entry "Theosophy," it merely says, see Kabbala. The Kabbala took shape as a definite system, a secret Sophia or body of knowledge, after the fall of Jerusalem. It relied heavily on numerology and incantations. The Hebrew gematria is a code which is based upon numerology. Devious explanations and prophecies are worked out by laboriously tracing various numerological values. For instance, through gematria it is shown that Moses wrote the Farewell Song; the first six letters of the first six sentences are the same as Moses name in Hebrew-345. The Cabala claims that the sacred number offers the prospect of knowledge. This number, 142857, is divided from the Eternal Number, One, or one million, or God plus six symbols of endlessness; divided by 7, it always comes out 142857. The primary numbers, 1 through 9, make up the triangle of the ternary, the completed Image of the three worlds. 9 is also the number for Mars; the secret name of god is number 9, and the period of gestation is 9 months; all of this information is to be found in the Cabala.

The chants and incantations from the Cabala include such esoterica as the Key of Solomon, which gives the formula for summing up Lucifer: "So come forth! Enter! or I shall torture you endlessly by the force of the powerful names of the Key: Alglon, Tetragram, Vaycheons, Stimulametion, Ezphraes, Petregrammaton, Olzaran, Irion, Erython, Existron, Erzona, Onera, Orosyn, Mozan, Messias, Soter, Emanu, Saboot."

A symbol which is to be found in every Masonic Lodge is the representation of a blazing star. Masons, apparently not knowing its true origin, claim it is the symbol of prudence. In fact, it represents the dog star, Sirius. The inundation of the Nile occurred in Egypt when the sun was under the stars of the Lion. To the Egyptians, it was known as the god Anubis; we know it by the name from the Hebrew, Sihor, which in Greek became Serios, and in Latin, Sirius. Its appearance was the sign to the ancient Egyptians to retire to higher ground, before the rising of the Nile, a tradition of prudence unknown to the present-day Masons, who nevertheless ascribe to it the correct interpretation of prudence. The character emblazoned on the Masonic apron is the triple Tau, a compound of three T's, or, in Greek, Tau. It stands for the old Egyptian Nilometer, which was used to ascertain the height of the Nile's inundation, on which the life of the inhabitants depended. It thus became the symbol of health and prosperity, having the power as an amulet to avoid evil.

A key Masonic ceremony is based on the tradition that the three great secrets of the mystery school of Moses were known to no one man; the three secrets, also called "the three words," were known by King Solomon, King Hiram of Tyre, and Hiram Abiff of Tyre, who is called "the widow's son" by Masons. Tyre, of course, was one of the key Canaanite cities. Three Masons of lower degree sought to force Hiram Abiff to tell them the word which was in his keeping; he was murdered by them because he refused. The murder ritual of Hiram Abiff is one of the key Masonic ceremonies, and it is intended to impress upon them the importance of submitting to murder rather than to give away any secret of the Masons. It also, as Stephen King points out, emphasizes the importance of the element of murder in all of Freemasonry, perhaps the single most constant factor which links all of their ceremonies. The murder of Hiram Abiff is solemnly re-enacted at the reception of a Master

Mason. The chamber is draped in black, with death's head painted on the walls. A body is displayed in a coffin, and the entire story is then re-enacted, culminating with the murder of Hiram Abiff by two apprentices. This impresses upon the members of the fellow craft that the blood-curdling oaths which they are required to take are no idle ceremonies, and that they must be faithful to the Masonic Canaanite rite, or their lives will be forfeit.

In the Masonic ceremonies, a new name for God (whom they always hated) was coined by the ritualists, because they dared not use the name of their real God, Lucifer. They now called on the mystical Jah-Bul-On, a name which they originated by combining the various deities of the Canaanite devil-worshippers: Jah, from the original Jahweh; Bul, the Hebrew name for the Canaanite god Baal; and On, representing the Egyptian God, Osiris.

Because of their Kabbalistic origins, the number 13 is of great significance in Masonic rites. A Council of Five, which is composed of the family leaders of the Rothschilds and their closest associates, governs the World Order of Canaanitic Freemasonry. Below it is the Council of 13, which also has great authority; after them comes the Council of 500. The council of 500 is made up of the leading politicians and business leaders of the world; if also includes the most prominent men from education and religion. The members of this Council are often present at the policy meetings of the Bilderberger Organization, with which it basically corresponds.

Key elements in the world program of Freemasonry are frequently enacted on their special date, the thirteenth. Thus, the Federal Reserve Act, a key point in the control of the world's economic systems by the Canaanites, was enacted onto law on the 23rd of December, 1913. The 16th Amendment to the Constitution of the United States, the income tax amendment, which was also a key element in the program, was adopted on May 31, 1913. This amendment gave the Canaanites control over every economic aspect of the captive population of the United States.

From that day on, they had to report every penny of both income and assets, as had been laid down by Lenin in his program, "The Threatening Catastrophe," which he had published in 1917. This program called for the confiscation of assets as punishment for "concealing income"; it was adopted by the Internal Revenue Service. The Lenin program now is the official operating doctrine of the IRS. The 17th amendment to the Constitution of the people of Shem, the amendment changing the requirements for electing Senators to the Congress, was adopted on May 21, 1913. These three amendments effectively sabotaged the Constitution, removing its historic protections of the people against a tyrannical government. Because income is actually property, the 16th amendment stripped citizens of the United States of all property rights, as did the later provisions for confiscation of all money and property. The Senate election amendment stripped the state legislatures of their historic right to elect Senators; it had been required to maintain the balance between the less populous and the more populous states; it now costs ten million dollars to elect a Senator. This amendment left the inhabitants of the several states bare to the most vicious intrigues of the barbaric and devil-worshipping Canaanites. In effect, the people of Shem lost a racial and religious war, because of these three acts of 1913. The emphasis on the number 13 also restates the resolve of the Freemasons to destroy their historic enemy, Christ, and His Twelve Disciples.

When the Rockefellers set up their criminal control of the state legislatures, the Council of State Governments, they symbolically installed it at a building numbered 1313. In 1813, the Duke of Sussex, the second son of King George

III, became the Grand Master of English Freemasonry. Thirteen small stars, the Seals of Solomon, were placed on United States currency, to form a six-point Mogen David (Shield of David).

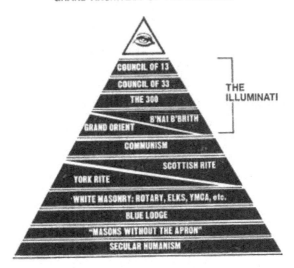

GRAND ARCHITECT OF THE UNIVERSE

COUNCIL OF 13
COUNCIL OF 33
THE 300
B'NAI B'BRITH
GRAND ORIENT
COMMUNISM
SCOTTISH RITE
YORK RITE
WHITE MASONRY: ROTARY, ELKS, YMCA, etc.
BLUE LODGE
"MASONS WITHOUT THE APRON"
SECULAR HUMANISM

THE ILLUMINATI

The various degrees of the Masonic ritual are of great hidden significance. The first three degrees, known as the Blue Lodge, are (1) entered apprentice; (2) fellow craft; (3) Master Mason. The initiates of the Blue Lodge are purposefully deceived throughout their membership as to the true purposes of Freemasonry. Any Mason of high degree who informs them of the behind-the-scenes occult program of the Order is subject to the death penalty. Consequently, the Blue Lodges, found in most American towns and cities, seem little different from the organizations of other fraternal orders, such as the Puritans and the Lions. Superficially, all three groups seem to be drawn from the same strata of society, earnest, family men, often church-goers, representing the essential qualities of small town life, but the resemblance is only superficial. The Masonic Order usually draws its members from the leading merchants, and from the professions, bankers, doctors, and lawyers. They come to their meetings, they dabble in some charity work, and in general, they mark time until that day when they are asked to perform some unusual task for a fellow Mason, or for the national or world order. At that time, they finally realize that the blood oath does have significance, but by that time it is usually too late. They may be asked to support a Masonic candidate for political office, to swing a business deal to a fellow Mason, or even to commit perjury or some other illegal act for a brother Mason. Even then, they are never offered any confidences; they are merely told what they must do, and they must obey. The Lions and the Ruritans, on the other hand, have no such demands on their members.

The first seven degrees of Freemasonry are the same novice crafts as the first seven degrees of the Great Mysteries of Osiris. They are also the same seven degrees as the requirements for advancement in the Jesuit Order. Heckethorn's "Secret Societies" notes that the apprentice ceremonies are thought to be of Jesuitical origin; Weishaupt had had a Jesuit chair at the University of Ingolstadt when he organized the Illuminati. Heckethorn says, "He [the apprentice] is then deprived of all metal he has about him; his right knee, and sometimes his left side, are uncovered, and the heel of his left shoe is trodden down. These ceremonies are supposed by some writers to be of Jesuitical origin. The deprivation of metals is to typify the vow of poverty, the baring of the breast and knee is intended to prevent the admission of women, and the treading down the heel of the shoe to remind the candidate that Ignatius de Loyola, who had a bad foot, thus began his pilgrimage."

The Scottish Rite has twenty-nine higher degrees, such as the 16th degree, Prince of Jerusalem; Grand Pontiff; the

20th degree, Knight; the 26th degree, a Rite which calls for Luciferian worship, demanding in the sacred name to cast out "obscurantism," a Masonic code term for the teachings of Christ; the 30th degree, Kadosch, a Yiddish term meaning "Noble," whose initiation rite contains the significant phrase, "I, I alone, All mine, All for me, by any and every means." The important 32nd degree, Sublime Prince of the Royal secret, means that he has now advanced sufficiently to be given information of a high degree, that is, Gnosticism, the "knowing" of the secret, which goes back to the dismemberment of Nimrod, when the sect went underground. The Rite of the 32nd degree ritually denounces property, law, and religion as "assassins of the Grand Master de Molay. Once Religion is dead, Law and Property will fall to our mercy, and we shall be able to regenerate society by cofounding on the corpses of the Assassins of man, Masonic Religion, Masonic Law, and Masonic Property."

This Rite reveals the basic purpose of Freemasonry, to overthrow the established institutions of society and to replace them with Masonic institutions of society controlled by the Canaanites. The Scottish Rite also has the Rite of Herod, the French Rite, the Grand Orient Rite, Mizraim Rite, which is a Rite of Ancient Egypt named after the son of Ham. Of these degrees, the Rite of Herod memorializes the most brutal king in history. Many Jews denounced Herod because of his bloodlust. He ordered all newborn babies to be killed, so as to ensure killing the newborn Christ.

It is the 33rd degree which is of the most importance in learning about the real aims of Freemasonry. Known as "the revolutionary degree," it confers the title of the Supreme Pontiff of Universal Masonry. Only those who reach the 33rd degree are allowed to wield world power, hence the title "Universal." Consequently, most heads of government, or persons of like importance, are 33rd degree Masons. Of course they cannot be loyal to any nation they head, because their loyalty has already been pledged, on penalty of death, to Universal Masonry.

A typical 33rd degree Mason was the late President of the United States, Harry S. Truman. Lacking any known talents, he had a disastrous career as a haberdasher; he was then deemed unemployable for any known profession. His problem was solved when he became the chief organizer for the Masonic Lodges throughout the State of Missouri. This miserable creature later allowed his mother's farm to be sold to pay his debts, while he continued on the nonpaying course. After he had served the Masonic Order well for a number of years, the Order then nominated him for a judgeship, as is often done by the Order in maintaining its iron control over the courts of the United States. His subsequent political career was then assured. To draw attention away from the Masonic sponsorship of his career, a great deal was made of a passing association with the boss of the Kansas City underworld, Boss Pendergast, as the man behind his meteoric rise. In fact, Pendergast was also a Mason. After attaining the 33rd degree, Truman secretly changed his name by adding the initial S., which stood for Solomon. He frequently told journalists that "The S doesn't stand for anything." As President, he was consistently loyal to the revolutionary tradition of the 33rd degree. Hailing the bloodsoaked dictator, Joseph Stalin as "Good Old Joe," he initiated the Marshall Plan to continue the secret shipment of supplies to the Soviet Union. He publicly labelled the Alger Hiss treason case "a Red Herring," and he authorized the State Department's George Kennan to draw up the "containment policy," which guaranteed that Russia would continue to occupy the Central European nations without any interference, after they had conquered them by armed aggression. In all of his revolutionary work, he was ably assisted by his closest personal confidant, David Niles, or

Neyhus, a Communist homosexual who had one sister holding an important position in the Government of Israel, and another sister who had a policymaking position in Moscow. To protect him while he was on his nightly drunken cruising sprees in the back alleys of Washington, Niles had J. Edgar Hoover assign two FBI agents to follow him. They had to crouch behind garbage cans while he engaged himself in his customary pursuits, and then saw to it that he returned safely to the White House. This FBI tradition was continued for Walter Jenkins during the Lyndon Johnson occupancy of the White House.

One of the most revolting personalities in the history of the United States was the chief organizer of Freemasonry, Albert Pike. Born in Boston, he went to Harvard University and later moved to Arkansas. He served as a general in the Confederate Army during the Civil War, after which he devoted the rest of his life to promoting Freemasonry. He is credited with having brought the Scottish Rite into prominence in the United States. Significantly, the Scottish Rite dates all of its official communications with the year of the Hebrew calendar. Pike maintained worldwide ties with such noted Masonic revolutionaries as Garibaldi and Mazzini. They cooperated in establishing four Grand Central Directories for Freemasonry; the North American branch was headquartered at Washington, D.C.; the South American branch was headquartered at Montevideo; the European branch at Naples; and the Asia and Oceania branch at Calcutta. He and Mazzini were succeeded as heads of world Freemasonry by Adriano Lemmi. Pike and Lemmi had an extended disagreement over the name of the God of Masons which they were to use in their rites; Pike was determined to call him Lucifer, while Lemmi held out for Satan; they finally settled on Lucifer. Pike subsequently used the term, Sublime Pontiff of Lucifer, to describe himself.

Although he came from modest origins, Pike, during his years in Arkansas, seemed to possess unlimited funds, for which no source has ever been established. A gross, obese creature of the most perverted tastes, he frequently organized expeditions of as many as three wagonloads of friends and prostitutes. They rolled out into the countryside, laden with casks of brandy, every available delicacy, and other refreshments. They then would gorge themselves for days on end, indulging in wild orgies, and blind to the world.

After rising to control of American Freemasonry, Pike forbade the mention of the name of Jesus Christ in a prayer in a Masonic Lodge. He organized the Adonaicide Mass for the top officials of the New Palladian Rite. It was based on the initiation rite of the 25th degree, in which the serpent is portrayed as the true friend of man, and Christ, or Adonais as the real enemy of mankind. Actually, it was a somewhat conventional Black Mass, to which Pike added some original touches of his own; the highlight of the initiation of a nude prostitute, called Eve, into the rites of intercourse. A fowl or animal was then immolated as a bloody sacrifice to Lucifer, to celebrate the victory of the Synagogue of Satan over Christ; followed by the ritual defiling of the Host. The blood was passed around to the celebrants to be drunk, after which the flesh was ritually eaten. All those present then abandoned themselves to a drunken orgy.

Despite his frequent dissipations, Pike was a tireless organizer. He managed to produce the massive textbook, "Morals and Dogma," which is the Bible of American Freemasonry to this day. First published in Charleston (the Mother Lodge) in 1871, the book indicates from its very first page the tyrannical intent of Freemasonry. "The blind Force of the People is Force that must be economized, and also managed-- It must be regulated by Intellect. ... The Force of the People ... cannot maintain and continue in action and existence a Free Government once created."

This is the bald resolve that Freemasonry cannot tolerate the existence of a free government. Therefore, the American Republic and the Constitution of the United States, written by and for the people of Shem, must be eliminated. Pike's book, by and large, is simply a formulation of the program which the Canaanites had already been pursuing for three thousand years. It gave a precise set of instructions by which the American people could be brought under control and bent to the ends of Freemasonry.

Pike positively identifies the demonic origins of Freemasonry on page 22: "Masonry, successor of the Mysteries, still follows the ancient manner of teaching. Masonry is identical with the ancient Mysteries." This also explains Freemasonry's close cooperation with the leaders of secular humanism, which also stems directly from the Mystery cults.

Another meaningful statement is found on page 152: "Masonry is activism." These three words explain the furious involvement of Freemasons in every type of activist movement in the United States, whether it is feminism, humanism, racial integrations, or Communism. Pike had laid down the law --Masons must be activists, and they have obeyed his dictum. As a result, much of the drive, as well as the financing, for all types of activist agitation in the United States comes directly from the Hidden Hand of the Masonic Order. Wherever you see a group marching in this country, you will probably find that Masons are the instigators.

Pike explains Freemasonry's commitment to One World Government, on page 220. He writes, "The whole world is but one republic, of which each nation is a family and every individual a child." This explains the Socialistic paternalism of the present American Government, which seeks a Fabian, cradle to grave control over the daily life of every citizen. The well-oiled machinery of the national Masonic movement is able to implement such a humanistic program, which is devoid of religious inspiration or values. "Children" cannot be trusted to handle their own money; only a wise central government in Washington can decide to send our earnings to other nations, who deserve our help, but as individuals, we might not be generous enough to rob our children for the sake of tyrants in other lands. Consequently, the agents of the IRS take our earnings from us, and the federal government in Washington then puts it to "better" use.

Pike, the final arbiter of all of American Freemasonry, defines the occult origins of Freemasonry, as well as its determination to set up a one-world tyranny. Such an anti-Christian doctrine could only come from the smoking altars of Baal and his demon-worshipping disciples.

To stress the importance of his dogma, Pike writes that "Every Masonic Lodge is a temple of religion, and its teachers are instructors in religion." Because of his previous statements, he is actually saying that every Masonic teacher is an instructor in the Kabbalah. This is reflected in the Master Mason's oath: "I will acknowledge and obey all due signs and summons sent to me from a master mason's lodge or given to me by a brother of that degree ... I will fly to his relief. ... Failure to do so meant "no lesser penalty than having my body severed in two, my bowels taken from hence and burned to ashes." This oath, for greater impact, is taken while kneeling blindfolded. This is the true revelation of a "fraternal lodge" which is supposedly dedicated to charity and good works. Has anyone ever been solicited for charity work with the admonition that if they refuse, they will be severed in two and their bowels taken out and burned?

Albert Pike, who was born in 1809, died in 1891 in Washington, D.C. His funeral was held in the Masonic

Temple at midnight, with the Rite of the Kadosch funeral. The room was draped entirely in black, lit only by a few candles burning eerily, a true Witches Ceremony for a man who had devoted his life to the cause of Lucifer.

From 1859 to 1871, Pike had worked on his master plan for the World Order of Freemasonry. He formulated the program which included three world wars; the first to overthrow the Czar and set up a Communist state; the second world war which would build up the Communist empire; and the third world war which would destroy Christian civilization for all time throughout the world. On August 15, 1871, he wrote a letter to Mazzini, which is now on exhibit at the British Museum, of his program for the Luciferian world conquest, planned to unleash "the Nihilists and the Atheists ... everywhere the citizens will receive the one pure Light through the universal manifestation of the pure doctrine of Lucifer ... which will follow the destruction of Christianity and atheism, both conquered and exterminated at the same time." It was Pike who formulated the secret technique whereby initiates of the Blue Lodge would only pass through "the outward doors of their philosophy"; the initiates must be deceived by false interpretations; true interpretations were reserved for those of high degree, the Princes of Masonry, who were forbidden to reveal the true interpretations to the lower initiates.

Because of the numerous Papal Bulls which had been issued against Freemasonry, Pike and Lemmi resolved that the papacy must be destroyed. The Bulletin of the Grand Orient of France, September 18, 1885, called for the destruction of the Catholic Church.

Monsignor Dillon was perhaps the first person to perceive that the real power behind the Communist movement was that of Freemasonry. He wrote in 1884 that the New Age actually is built on the desire for the coming of a New Messiah, a false one; that the Temple of Solomon was destroyed in fulfillment of the prophecy of Christ, and the Grand Orient and the Scottish Rite Lodges were the source of modern revolutionary activity. Pope Leo XIII denounced Masonry as Naturalism: "The ultimate aim of Freemasonry is to uproot completely the whole religious and political order of the world which has been brought into existence by Christianity, and to replace it with another in harmony with their way of thinking. This will mean that the foundation and laws of the new structure will be drawn from pure Naturalism."

Abbe Lerudan had written in 1747 in Amsterdam: "The real secret of Freemasonry is disbelief in the Divinity of Christ and replaced with Naturalism or the doctrine of Rationalism which was preached by Socinus in Poland." Oliver Cromwell, the regicide of England, was a Socinian by belief; the made it possible for Freemasonry to formally organize in England. Napoleon, whose brother Joseph Bonaparte was Grand Master, was believed by the Masons to be too powerful; Bernadotte, a Mason, persuaded him to launch his disastrous campaign against Russia, which led to the destruction of his army.

In Italy, Lord Sackville of England had founded the Grand Orient of Italy, which was directed by the highly secret Carbonari through the Alta Vendita, its operating arm. The instructions to the members contained this admonition, "Let each act of your life tend to discover the Philosopher's Stone. The alchemists of the Middle Ages lost their time and the one of their dupes in the quest of this dream. That of the secret societies will be accomplished for the most simple of reasons, because it is based on the passions of man. Let us not be discouraged then by a check, a reserve, or a defeat. Let us prepare our arms in the silence of the lodges, dress our batteries ... flatter all passions the most evil and the most generous, and all lead us to think our plans will succeed one day above even our most improvident calculations."

Another instruction of the Alta Vendita read: "We do not cease to recommend to you, to affiliate persons of every class and every manner of association, no matter what kind, only provided that mystery and secrecy shall be the dominant characteristic. Under a pretext most futile, but never political or religious, created by yourselves, or better yet, cause to be created by others, associations having in common music, the fine arts for object. Then infiltrate the poison into those chosen arts; infiltrate it in little doses. A prince who has not a kingdom to expect, is a good fortune for us. There are many of them in that plight. These poor princes will serve our ends, while thinking to labour only for their own. They form a magnificent signboard, and there are always fools enough to be found who are ready to compromise themselves in the service of a conspiracy, of which some prince or other seems to be the ringleader. There is little morality even among the most moral of the world, and one goes fast in the way of that progress. A good hatred, thoroughly cold, thoroughly calculated, is of more worth than all these artificial fires and all these declarations on the platform. Presently, we shall have a printing establishment at Malta placed at our disposal. We shall then be able to act with impunity, with a sure stroke and under the British flag, to scatter from one end of Italy to the other, books, pamphlets, etc. which the Alta Vendita shall judge proper to put into circulation."

Nesta Webster, in "World Revolution," page 14, discloses further threats' to potential betrayers: "If you are only a traitor and perjurer, learn that all our brothers are called upon to arm themselves against you. Do not hope to escape or find a place of safety. Wherever you are, shame, remorse, and the rage of your brothers will pursue you and torment you to the innermost recesses of your entrails." This was no idle threat; the Masons were known to poison whose whom they suspected of having betrayed them, so that they died slow and agonizing deaths, with terrible pains "in the innermost recesses of their entrails."

The manner of execution is often symbolic, intended to convey a warning to other Masons or to outsiders who might know more than is good for them. Such was the execution of Robert Calvi, a principal in the Banco Ambrosiano scandal. Calvi was found hanging from Blackfriars Bridge in London, the place having been chosen to signify that he had fallen from grace. A warrant was recently issued by a judge in Milan for another principal in this case, Archbishop Paul C. Marcinkus, a native of Chicago, who had been in charge of the Vatican's finances. The bank failure cost the Vatican $250 million, although its liability at one time was estimated to be some $3 billion. Archbishop Marcinkus was in charge of the Instituto per Ie Opere di Religione, the Vatican's Institute for Religious Works, which controlled its finances. The scandal was not really about banking, but about Freemasonry.

Lord Sackville had established the first Masonic Lodge in Italy in 1733; by 1861, Italy was beginning to organize as a world power. There were then three Masonic groups in Italy, at Turin, Naples, and Palermo. Garibaldi succeeded in uniting them in 1864 and thus became the most powerful political leader in Italy; so great was his reputation that President Lincoln asked him to become Commander-in-Chief of the United States Army during the Civil War. When Mussolini came to power after the First World War, he declared Freemasonry "a danger to the peace and quietude of the State." The Lodges were proscribed by the Anti-Masonic Law of 1925, which unleashed a furious worldwide propaganda campaign against Mussolini as a "dictator." After World War II, some five hundred Lodges promptly resurfaced in Italy. The Lodges were lavishly financed with as funds thoughtfully provided by the taxpayers of the United States. Money was coming in such amounts that a super-secret group was required to handle it. One Lucio Gelli had joined the Grand Oriente d'Italia in 1963; he now organized a new lodge, which he called Propaganda Due, or P-2. It was named after Mazzini's Lodge, Propaganda Uno, which he had founded to lead the Revolution of 1848. Gelli assumed the Masonic title of "supremo regulatore dell universo," Supreme Regulator of the Universe. Within a short time, almost every prominent official, banker, and editor of Italy was a member of P-2.

P-2 became deeply involved in many underhanded banking transactions, including control of Banco Ambrosiano. Another bank was set up, Banco Privata, which seemed to be a vehicle for funds which had been hidden since World War II, OSS millions which had been stashed in secret hiding places. The principals of Banco Privata would indicate this; they included John "McCaffery, the Italian representative of Hambros Bank (Charles Hambro has been head of SOE, British Intelligence in London); he purchased 24.5% of Banco Privata for Hambros; Michael Sindona bought 51 %. Sindona later sold Banco Privata to the IOR through Archbishop Marcinkus; the control was shifted to a Sindona firm in Lichtenstein, Fasco A. G. Another holding company, La Centrale Finanzaria, was set up by Sindona, which had Robert Calvi, Evelyn de Rothschild, and Jocelyn Hambro on its board. Sindona was soon moving $49 billion in Eurodollars through this and other bank holding companies which he operated. He netted some $10 million in profits. Banco Ambrosiano was at the vortex of all this activity; it went bankrupt. Gelli withdrew $50 million and fled to Switzerland, where he was arrested. Calvi was found hanging from the Blackfriars Bridge in London. Sindona, who also was involved in the collapse of the Franklin National Bank in New York, was arrested and sentenced to prison. He died in an American prison. Before his death, he explained to an interviewer the complexities of the great grain swindle, when the Soviet Union bought wheat from the United States in July, 1972. The Soviet Union was allowed to pay for its purchases in the following manner: the central bank of Hungary, acting for the Soviet Union, placed an order to sell the dollar short for $20 billion; Secretary of the Treasury John Connally then devalued the dollar by 10%; the Soviet Union made $4 billion on its short selling operation, and paid for the grain; they had $2 billion profit from the short selling operation and $2 billion from the 10% devaluation of the dollar. Sindona observed, "In its fathomless naivete, the United States has provided the Soviets with $4 billion, money that has since doubtless been invested in the destruction of its benefactors; I began to see then that America was the consort of her own ruin. I tell you, in all of history, no power has so blindly armed and succored its enemies as she."

In fact, "America" is not encompassing its own destruction; it is being destroyed by the Masonic Canaanites who have infiltrated its highest offices, and who now employ their power to destroy the people of Shem and the Republic which they established.

The Calvi murder brought some interesting names to the surface, including one Francesco Pazienza, a Washington figure who was close to former Secretary of State, General Haig; Flavio Carboni, a consultant to Banco Ambrosiano who was also close to Armando Corona, head of the Grand Orient of Italy; Ernesto Diotallevi and Danil Abbrudati, the heads of the Roman underworld. Abbrudati was killed by bodyguards of Roberto Rosone, deputy chairman of Banco Ambrosiano, when he tried to assassinate Rosone. Carboni was in London with Calvi when Calvi was disposed of. Carboni was registered at the Sheraton Hotel in London while Calvi was nearby at Chelsea. Sindona later said that

South American Freemasons had carried out the murder of Calvi.

Carboni had previously received from Calvi $100,000 which Was paid to the Swiss bank account of his mistress, Laura Concas; Calvi had also paid $530,000 to Ernesto Diotallevi. A London judge reversed the ruling that Calvi had committed suicide and declared it to be death at the hands of persons unknown. The investigation was halted.

The Masonic Order of Canaanites operates in the United States in open defiance of the statutes against criminal syndicalism. 46 CJS 1 states: "Syndicalism is the doctrine which advocates abolishment of the existing political and social system by means of a general strike, peaceful demonstration, or revolutionary violence ... it is within the powers of the legislature to punish the advocacy of propaganda which has for its purpose the destruction of government, or the rights of property which that government was founded to preserve, then before there is a present and imminent danger of the success of the plan advocated. The initial and every other let knowingly committed for the accomplishment of that purpose may be forbidden and declared to be a crime. They may also prohibit and penalize the association with or membership in organizations advocating such doctrines or inviting others to join such organizations ... advocacy within one state, or advocacy of acts of violence against another state, or against the United States, may constitute criminal syndicalism."

Thus there are adequate statutes on the books to protect the people of Shem from their planned extermination by the Masonic Canaanites. Freemasonry also violates statutes prohibiting restraint of trade, combinations entered into to injure other persons, and many other illegal activities. Continuous damage is done to the entire economy by the existence of a small, supersecret group which controls all advancement in business and the professions, which controls the issuance of bank loans, entering into a publishing business such as books, magazines, or newspapers, operating a radio and television station, chartering a bank, and many other avenues of trade. Parents always want the best possible future for their children, making great sacrifices to put them through school and to send them to college. They never realize that without the "Open Sesame" of the Masonic Order, their children are condemned to be hewers of wood and drawers of water, that they can never hope to earn any large sums or to make advancements in their field. Everything is already pre-empted by the Canaanites for their own kind. Only the children of the conspiratorial elite will be admitted to the best schools, be offered the best jobs, and live the good life. For the rest of America, the party is over.

CHAPTER 3

SECULAR HUMANISM

The Masonic Order of Canaanites has flourished because it has chosen its propaganda vehicles with great care. Perhaps the most efficient of these, one which has converted a large and vocal segment of the Christian church to its work, is secular humanism. The basic premise of secular humanism is that human interests should take precedence over all things. Because of its insistence that "government interests" are the primary instrument for implementing the good of human interests, secular humanism has become the primary advocate or statism, or big government, which means, of course, totalitarian government. This implementation by government bureaucrats always pits "human interests" against "spiritual interests." The spiritual interests are soon shunted aside. Secular humanism, more properly, is the humanism of temporal affairs, the affairs of this world. For those who believe there is no afterlife, it is of supreme importance to maintain total control throughout this life, believing that there is no other. Those who believe in the afterlife, on the other hand, are tempted to be too tolerant of outrages on the earth, supposing that things will be better in the next world.

Many people confuse in their own minds the term "humanitarianism" with that of humanism. Humanism is never humanitarian; its most widely perceived example in the twentieth century is the death camps of Soviet Russia, where some sixty-six million souls have perished.

Humanitarianism results from compassion--and the desire to alleviate someone else's suffering. Humanism, on the other hand, stemming it does directly from the demon worship and the child murders of ancient Babylon, has as its ultimate goal the inflicting of suffering on its enemies, or anyone whom it perceives as an enemy. Humanistic social agencies in the United States continually degrade and humiliate the persons whom they claim to be "helping." The Internal Revenue Service is the outstanding humanistic agency in the United States; its goal is to redistribute the wealth of the citizens to "more deserving" recipients; quite often, these recipients are resident in foreign lands, and they would like nothing better than to see the United States destroyed.

Humanism always has a specific political direction. Its aim is to usurp and replace man's political institutions, and to set up in their place a permanent type of socialism, in which "the good of humanity" will be administered by the bureaucracy of a totalitarian state. The "welfare state" which has been established in so many Western nations is a giant step on the path leading to this goal.

Despite the many references to secular humanism by both its advocates and its opponents, one seldom hears any concrete discussion about what secular humanism is, or about its sources. This is particularly surprising, because both its origins and its history are easily available from standard reference sources. Also, the more vocal advocates of secular humanism are often found in academia, where scholarship is a way of life, and where this subject offers many tempting avenues of research.

In the present work, this writer had not expected to take up the subject of humanism. Indeed, when beginning the researching of the demonology of history, it seemed unlikely that humanism would appear in any role. Like most other scholars, the present writer had failed to consider one essential aspect of humanism. For the revelation of this particular aspect, we are indebted to a Russian emigre, Vladimir Voinovich. He quotes A. Surkov, a speaker at the First Congress of Soviet Writers, "Poets somehow or other overlook a fourth aspect of humanism, one expressed in the severe and beautiful concept of hatred." Indeed, most writers would fail to perceive that hatred is a vital aspect of humanism. Perhaps it is more obvious in Soviet Russia than in other countries. Voinovich goes on to characterize hatred as perhaps the most important single component of humanism. But how is this possible? How could humanism, the placing of humanity's interests above those of spiritual concern, the improvement of mankind by denying any spiritual role in man's development, and concentrating strictly on "his own" humanistic interests, contain the fundamental ingredient of hatred? Only someone experienced in the horrors of the modern Soviet State could be qualified to identify hatred as the prime ingredient of humanism. The Soviet Government, administrator of the world's most humanist state, has murdered some sixty-six million of its own citizens since the Bolshevik Revolution, according to its leading writer, Aleksander Solzhenitsyn. All this has been done in the name of "socialist realism," or humanism.

The essential ingredient of humanism, hatred, can be traced directly back to its source, the demon worshippers of Baal in ancient history, the Canaanites who indulged their appetite for human sacrifice in the name of "religion," cannibalism in the rite of honoring their gods, and child murder in the name of Moloch. These are the same Canaanites who operate the great nations of the world today, and who eagerly look forward to more of the massacres which they have perpetrated in the twentieth century, and which has made our time the scene of the greatest mass murders in the history of mankind.

The demonic sources of humanism are reflected not only in their denial of God and the Kabbalistic claim that God took no part in the actual creation of the world, but also in its philosophical inspiration, which stems solely from Satan and his evil activities. As I. M. Haldeman writes, "All of the spirit world is moved with the wisdom of the fallen angel. The spirits of the dark zone are coming forth in a spiritistic period ... Spiritism is but the agency in the hands of that great fallen angel who still retains the title as the prince and god of this world and of long date is determined to fulfill and function it." Thus we see that a great many people, spiritists, spiritualists, and their like, believe that Satan is in control of this world. From their actions, the humanists also seem to believe this. Certainly they would not have taken hatred of life as a principal ingredient of their philosophy if they had not adopted the practice of Satanism.

As we examine the long history of humanism, and trace its manifestations from the ancient world to the present time, we find singular coefficients which appear in all of its various historical periods. The first, of course, was the Canaanite world of Baal and Ashtoreth, with its focus on demonic methods of worship. In its subsequent manifestations, probably due to increasing public resistance, it took on a protective coloration of "intellectual" costume. Baal became Dr. Faustus. The smoking altars of the Canaanites were obscured by a growing emphasis on philosophical discourse. The first of these "schools of humanism" was that of Pythagorus (582-507 B.C.). The Pythagorean school, which was set up at Crotona, functioned as a "mystery school," that is, a school in which the "mystery" aspects of philosophy were emphasized to a limited group of carefully chosen "initiates." The Pythagorean equation was based on the dualism of first principles - the limited, or source of definitiveness, and the unlimited, or source of divisiveness. In effect, this was the first school of dialectic, a form of teaching which was to reach its apogee in the nineteenth century work of Hegel, and his most famous disciple, Karl Marx.

The Pythagorean School also featured many precepts which in later centuries would appear in the Book of Zohar, the Kabbalah. One of these precepts was numerology, an attempt to concentrate upon the universe as a mathematical equation, and thus to work out, or to discover, a magical formula which would give control over it. The pythagoreans featured tetraktys, the sacred number ten, which was arrived at by adding the first four numbers.

The Pythagorean School at Croton has an interesting correlation in our own time. During the 1930s, the American headquarters of the Theosophical Society was at Krotona, California.

Whether this town was deliberately named after the Pythagorean town is not known.

The Pythagorean Theorem or metaphysic of numbers greatly influenced Plato. Although he is known to us primarily as a philosopher, he exercised considerable political influence throughout his adult life. He was the acknowledged leader of a Mediterranean political faction which was opposed to the expansion of the Persian Empire. Plato led in the development of an elite which could bring the Greeks back to political dominance in the Mediterranean. The influence of the Pythagoreans caused him to develop a program much like that of the Freemasons today, a secret elite which could exercise its influence from behind the scenes, but always dedicated to its own hidden program, whose principles were known only to an elite.

Plato supported Dionysus I, ruler of Syracuse, as leader of the Greek coalition forces. Dionysus became Plato's model for his future philosopher-king. In return, Dionysus' brother-in-law, Dion, gave money to Plato to establish his school of philosophy, advancing funds to build a group of buildings which are now known to history as the Grove of Academe. It was in these buildings, on the outskirts of Athens, that Plato wrote "The Republic" as a guide for humanists of the future, so that they could achieve total control over their society. Plato then advised Dionysus II in his sacred war against Delphi. During this war, the Temple of Apollo was captured, including the vast amounts of gold which had been stored there. Plato later wrote the dialogue "Timaeus" as an elegy for his mentor, Dion.

Both Plato and Pythagorus believed in the doctrine of transmigration of souls, a favored theory in mysticism. Plato remains the single most important figure in the development of humanism, because, almost single-handedly, he transformed it from a creed based on the demon-worship of Baal to a more respectable "school of philosophy," a process which had been initiated by Pythagorus. Nevertheless, humanism remained a creed which was devoted to the conspiratorial enslavement of mankind by a secret elite, which considered itself specially "chosen," and Gnostic, that is, knowing, as contrasted to the not-knowing. While become more and more engaged in the secular aspects of society, humanism has remained true to its basic precepts, which are comprised of a mixture of the doctrines of the principal "mystery" cults; pantheism, worship of nature, Gnosticism (which is always a manifestation of Satanism, irrefutably based in Gnosticism, or knowing the secrets), and hermeticism. It was the threat of these doctrines which caused Christ to issue his famous warning, "Beware of false prophets, who come to you in sheep's clothing, but inwardly they are ravening wolves. Ye shall know them by their fruit. Do men gather grapes from thorns, or figs of thistles?" (Matthew 7: 15-16). Humanism is the wolf in sheep's clothing. It comes advertising its compassion for humanity, its concern for the homeless and poor, but as Christ says, know them by their fruits. Do not ask what they intend to do. Find out what they are doing. In this way, you will not try to gather grapes from thorns, or figs of thistles.

Hermetic philosophy is traced back to Hermes Trismegistus, the Greek name for the Egyptian god Thoth, the god of wisdom and letters. The name itself means "thricearmed," the precept being that he who has more information than others has greater protection. Francis Yates points out in "Giordano Bruno and the Hermetic Tradition," "The theory of universal animation is the basis of magic. The Hermetic sequence par excellence is alchemy-the famous Emerald Tablet, the bible of the alchemists, is attributed to Hermes."

Despite the efforts of Christian leaders to stamp out heresy, the Middle Ages were rife with many forms of superstition and black magic. While the alchemists sought to transform base metals into gold, a new dialectic of mysticism, the Kabbalah, became a potent force throughout Europe. "Cabala" simply means traditions. It was formulated as the Book of Zohar, written by the Jewish mystic Moses ben Shemtob de Leon in 1280 A.D. as a midrash on the basic law.

Legend had it that when God gave the Law to Moses, he also gave a second revelation as to the secret meaning of the Law. It was forbidden to write down this secret meaning for centuries; it was passed along orally to a select group of initiates. "Secret meanings" are basic to the "mystery" cults. Theosophy is based on secret meanings; its doctrines were taken directly from the Kabbalah, yet the most widely circulated book on American cults, "The Kingdom of the Cults" by Walter Martin, Bethany Press, 1965, in the chapter on Theosophy, does not once mention the Kabbalah.

The Book of Zohar is described as a theosophical system based on the ten Sephiroth, or divine emanations, and twenty-two letters of the Hebrew alphabet comprising the names of God. In 1492, the expulsion of the Jews from Spain sent teachers of the Kabbalah throughout Europe. Their doctrines produced the most dominant school of philosophy of the Renaissance, the Neoplatonic School. Neoplatonism, in turn, became the fount of other philosophical developments, which led directly to the Reformation, the Enlightenment, and the Age of Revolution.

Zohar stresses the talmudic legend that demons on earth originated in sexual congress between humans and demonic powers, creating such well known demons as Lilith. For this reason, demonic rites always emphasize sexual acts. The Neolatonists were widely criticized because many of its teachers and students were well known for their involvement in homosexuality.

Neoplatonism combined hermetic writings with Gnosticism, organized against the background of the Kabbalah. It emphasized internal illumination (a precept which led directly to the development of the Illuminati cult in Germany), ecstasy, and the correlation of mysticism and nationalism. Neoplatonism's attraction to its adherents was the offer of "liberation of the self" through mystical experience. This system of philosophy soon made the Renaissance the dominant cultural force in Europe. Influenced by the Byzantine Plethon, it found its apogee in the career of Pico della Mirandola. In Neoplatonic philosophy, the soul has definite affinities within the sphere. The soul substance is laid around the concentric sphere of the four elements above the fiery heaven.

As in the case of Plato, this school of philosophy was seen to have powers of attraction to the ruling order, and it was soon placed in service. The most powerful banker of the Renaissance, Cosimo de Medici, leader of the "black nobility" in Italy, the Guelphs, gave the money to found the Accademia Platonica in Florence during the fifteenth century. With this financial and political support, Neoplatonism won rapid acceptance. In 1486, Pico della Mirandola presented 900 theses on this new philosophy at the Accademia; 72 of these theses were obvious Kabbalist concepts. A noted Hebrew scholar, della Mirandola based much of the philosophy of Neoplatonism on his studies in this field. By his emphasis on a universe, which is centered on man, he is credited with having anticipated the twentieth century philosophy of existentialism. Della Mirandola was succeeded at the Accademia by Johann Reuchlin, who became famous for his development of "Christian cabbalism," that is, a Christian version of the Kabbalah. He also became a principal figure in the spread of the Neoplatonic doctrine. Later known more simply as "Renaissance humanism," Neoplatonism, or Christian Kabbalah, often excluded belief in God from its philosophy. Its principal thesis was the cabbalistic theory that matter (or life) is essentially imperfect, and thus causes disorder in an otherwise perfect world. Plato's Republic also sought to "correct" the imperfections of society by setting up a "perfect" nation, whose perfection would have to be protected and sustained by a dictatorship; this became the foundation of all future schemes for "utopia," the most well known of these being Communism. Marx proclaimed that when this state of perfection had been reached, the state would wither away and would no longer be required to exercise dictatorial powers. However, no Communist state has yet reached this state of perfection. This was the goal of perfection which originated in a revulsion against the life process; because of this revulsion, "humanists" had no qualms about murdering sixty-six million humans in Soviet Russia. This was the result of Neoplatonism's "perfect marriage" between the Kabbalah and the Oriental precepts of Gnosticism, a union based on the denial of God's role in the Universe.

The combination of high finance, in the person of the Medici, and Neoplatonism, which offered the possibility of unlimited behavior control, created a situation which was made to order for the Canaanites in their continuing battle against the people of Shem. Plotinus and his pupil, Porphyry, had developed the basic aspect of Neoplatonism, that the First Principle and source of reality, the One, or Good, transcends being and thought, and is naturally unknowable.

Gnosticism always begins with the precept that certain things are "unknowable," but that their hidden meanings can be revealed to a select group who have gone through the proper rites of initiation. Thus the doctrine of Neoplatonism became the ideal vehicle for the new worldwide secular priesthood, the heirs of the rites of Baal, but clothed now in the cultural garments of the Renaissance, and later, the Enlightenment. Its final phase was the Illuminati, the secret sect which directs Freemasonry.

The Oxford English Dictionary defines humanism as concern with merely human interests, as distinct from divine. In the Notes, we find, "1716; M. Devion Athen. Brit. 170, 'Their Jesuit boasting Monopoly and bragging tyranny over Humanistical Schools.'"

Because humanism was based on the relativism of Protagorus, it developed successively into the Renaissance, the Reformation, the Enlightenment, Marxism, and Freudianism ... Freudianism then developing its own offshoots of feminism, bisexuality, and the drug culture. Humanism became the guiding force of the development of Socialism and Fabianism in England and the United States. Its principal propagandists were careful to establish that humanism was based on atheism, amorality, and a Socialist One World State. Corliss Lamont, the son of a partner in the firm of J. P. Morgan Co. became the principal spokesman for humanism in the United States.

He says, "A truly Humanist civilization must be a world civilization." He drafted a Humanist Wedding Ceremony which is now widely used to replace the traditional Christian rite.

In 1953, an official Humanist Manifesto appeared. It states (I) the universe is self-existing and not created; (2) man is pure of nature (the noble savage, as defined by Rousseau, the precursor of the French Revolution); (3) modern science provides the only acceptable definition of the universe or of human values; (4) exclude any supernatural explanation of the universe or of human values; (5) the end of life is the complete realization of human personality through liberalism and liberal education. The emphasis on "personality development" became effective only after traditional values had been destroyed. People no longer knew who they were or what the purpose of their life might be. They were then ripe for the school of "personality," that is, humanist propagandists who could recruit them for "alternative life styles," or homosexuality, and for the program of the Communist Revolution. Humanism also provides the absolute justification for the oppressive intervention of liberal officials in every aspect of citizens' lives. Our personal freedom and rights come directly from God; no government can either bestow them or take them away; it can only administer them. The doctrine of humanism, by denying God's role in mankind's affairs, opens the door for a cabbalistic state to take away all human rights, and thus set up a Soviet Gulag, or world concentration camp. This would ensure the final victory of the Canaanites over the people of Shem, enshrining the hatred which is the core of humanistic philosophy in their absolute power over their historic opponents.

The principal agencies of humanism in the United States are centralized in a small group of billion dollar foundations which were set up to subvert the American Republic. In *"The World Order,"*[3] I traced the history of these foundations back to the Peabody Fund, the chief carpetbagger power in the conquered Southern states after 1865. Peabody, an American who became secretly affiliated with the Rothschild banking house in London, founded his own banking house, Peabody and Co., which later became J. P. Morgan & Co. His carpetbagger Peabody Fund, working closely with the federal military forces, which maintained their occupation of the Southern states until 1877, later became the General Education Board. Still later, it was absorbed by the Rockefeller Foundation. Since World War II, at least four Secretaries of State have been presidents of the Rockefeller Foundation, including John Foster Dulles, Dean Rusk, Cyrus Vance, and Henry Kissinger (the latter was a director).

The humanist foundations use their tax-exempt billions to infiltrate and control American education, religion, and government. The humanist officials of the foundations, after undergoing extended brainwashing at subsidiaries of the Tavistock Institute (itself a branch of the British Army Dept. of Psychological Warfare) are thoroughly indoctrinated in the Canaanite program of world control. Thus Dean Rusk, who was of an old Georgia family, when he was informed by his World Order controllers that he must marry off his daughter to a black man, enthusiastically called a press conference to announce the happy event.

---

[3] Published by Omnia Veritas Ltd – www.omnia-veritas.com

Surprisingly enough, the major American foundations were the creation of one man, a member of the German Illuminati named Daniel Coit Gilman. In the "Brotherhood of Death" file is a card from the German group to Gilman. Gilman had been vice president of the Peabody Fund and another carpetbagger fund called the Slater Fund, which controlled Southern politics after the Civil War. Gilman met with Frederick T. Gates, the director of John D. Rockefeller's "charitable enterprises," and set up a new foundation for them in 1898, called the Southern Educational Board, which merged the Peabody and Slater Funds. This foundation was further centralized when Gilman advised Rockefeller to call it the General Education Board, a noteworthy move signifying that its purpose was not merely to control education in the South, but in the entire United States. It now operates under the name of The Rockefeller Foundation. In addition to being an incorporator of General Education Board, Gilman was also the incorporator of the Carnegie Institute, of which he became the first president, and the Russell Sage Foundation. In 1856, Gilman had set up the Russell Trust at Yale University with Andrew White and Timothy Dwight. This group became known as "Skull and Bones" because of its symbols featuring those parts. It is also known as the "Brotherhood of Death" because its members include many of the leading front men in the United States, the planners of war, peace, revolution, and financial calamities. They include the late W. Averell Harriman and many members of his banking firm, Brown Brothers Harriman, such as Prescott Bush and his son, George Bush, the vice president of the United States; the tireless propagandist William Buckley, and many others.

The three founders of the Russell Trust exercised a profound influence over our educational establishment; Dwight became president of Yale; White became the first president of Cornell; and Gilman became president of the

University of California, and later Johns Hopkins University, where Woodrow Wilson came under his influence.

The Russell Sage Foundation, also founded by Gilman, has played an important behind-the-scenes role in the United States for many years. Frederick A. Delano, one of the incorporators, and heir to his father's opium fortune, was a member of the original Federal Reserve Board of Governors in 1914; he was later named President of the Federal Reserve Bank of Richmond by his nephew, Franklin Delano Roosevelt. Another director of Russell Sage Foundation, Beardsley Ruml, served as president of the influential Federal Reserve Bank of New York, which is known as our money market bank. He also inflicted the withholding income tax on the American people during World War II as an "emergency" measure. The emergency seems to be still with us. We could go on for many pages, detailing the tremendous influence of the humanist foundations on every aspect of American life. They are solely responsible for implementing the increasing government control over every citizen, because each plan for more control and higher taxes is drafted by the foundations, whose staffs then present it to our willing Congressmen for almost automatic enactment into law. Because we do not understand the demonic influence and origin of these humanist revolutionaries in the smoking altars of human sacrifice in Babylon, we are not able to protect ourselves against their depredations. Yet the evidence exists, and it is available if we would but make use of it.

In 1876, an article about Skull and Bones appeared at Yale, which boasted of a clandestine entry into the sacrosanct premises of The Order. On one wall was an engraving depicting an open vault, four skulls, and other paraphernalia. Below it was a card with the following: "From the German Chapter. Presented by Patriarch D. C. Gilman of D. 50." Patriarch is a basic title for officials of both the Illuminati and Freemasonry. However, one would err in concluding from this discovery that Skull and Bones is merely another chapter of the Freemasons. It is one of the secret higher degrees through which the Illuminati exercises its world power, but it has no direct connection with any Freemason group.

CHAPTER 4

ENGLAND

The Canaanites, or Phoenicians, employed their command of various monopolies to gain control of the commerce of the entire Mediterranean area. Having established their bases along the shores of the Mediterranean, they found that the most centrally located headquarters for all of their operations was located on the Adriatic Sea. Here they founded the City of Venice (Phoenicia) in 466 A.D. Because of its unique location, and the dedication of the Canaanites to the pursuit of money and power, it soon became the command post of the commercial world.

The 1152 census shows some 1300 Jews in Venice; they paid a tax of five per cent on their money lending operations. They were also active as brokers in commodities. In 1366, they obtained the right to reside in Venice itself; prior to that date, they had been forbidden to reside in the city, and were confined to living on the mainland lit Mestre. They customarily charged from ten per cent to twenty per cent on loans. Because of Venice's great commercial possibilities, they flocked in from many parts of the world. In 1492, after their expulsion from Spain, many Jews and Marranos settled in Venice. The colony was then divided into three groups; the Germans, known as tudeschi; the levantini, from the Levant; and the ponantini, or westerners.

In 1797, the French occupation opened the gates of the Ghetto. Napoleon then gained power and established his

Italian kingdom, from 1805 to 1814, which gave them further rights. During the Revolution of 1848, Kastein reports in his "History of the Jews" that revolutionary Venice was ruled by Daniel Manini and two other Jews.

The Venetians were always known as masters of intrigue; they aided the Turks in the conquest of Constantinople in 1453, which ended the twelve hundred-year reign of the Emperors of Byzantium. The Turks were shocked at the rapacity of the Venetians, who carried off much of the city's legendary art treasures, gold, and jewelry. After they had returned home with their loot, the Venetians actively disputed control of the Mediterranean with the Turks, fighting them continually from 1453 to 1718. Venice had now become the headquarters of a ruthless, social-climbing band of entrepreneurs who purchased titles for themselves, or created them out of thin air, built splendid mansions, and collected the art treasures of Europe. They financed their new lifestyle with the enormous sums which they garnered from trade, piracy, and money lending.

From the year 1171, this group became known throughout Europe as "the black nobility," because they were of Canaanite origin, as contrasted to the fairskinned nobility of the people of Shem. The black nobility gradually infiltrated the noble families of Europe; today, they constitute most of the surviving European royalty.

Because of their ruthlessness, the Venetians attained a worldwide reputation as international arbiters of intrigue, revolution, poisoning, and other forms of assassination. They often conspired to bankrupt any opponent, and were known to cruelly rape the daughters of anyone in the oligarchy who dared to oppose them. From Venice, they rapidly spread northward like some new form of plague, setting up businesses and banking establishments in the northern cities of Italy. They bought more titles and intermarried with impoverished families of the old nobility. In Florence, the preeminent family was the de Medicis, who used their wealth to establish an Accademica which foisted humanism on the world. The de Medici established Florence as the European center of the black nobility, or Guelphs, as they were now called.

The black nobility also established close ties with the ruling families of England, through the Savoy and Este families. The Savoys ruled Italy from 1146 to 1945. The Este family ruled Ferrara from the twelfth century until Italy was united in 1860. Peter, the ninth Count of Savoy, married his niece, Eleanor, to King Henry III of England, and thereby became his privy councillor. King Henry granted him large estates, with the title of Earl of Richmond. Peter brought in other members of the black nobility to marry English noblemen, who included Richard de Burgh and the Earl of Lincoln. Peter's younger brother, Boniface, was appointed Archbishop of Canterbury. Peter died in 1268.

The founders of the European dynasties which lasted into the twentieth century were Rupert, Count of Nassau, who died in 1124, and Christian, Count of Oldenbourg, who died in 1167. From Rupert came the Hesse-Darmstadt line, the Hesse-Cassel line, the Dukes of Luxembourg, the Battenbergs, the Prince of Orange and Nassau, and the Kings of the Netherlands. From Christian came the Kings of Denmark and Norway, the Schleswig-Holstein line, and the Hanovers, who became Kings of Great Britain from 1717 to the present time. Also of the black nobility were the Dukes of Normandy, the Angevins and the Plantagenets, who became the Tudor and Stuart kings of England, the Saxe-Coburgs, and the Wittelsbachs.

The Hanover line was always deeply involved with Freemasonry. The Hanovers became Kings of England in 1717. hat same year, the first Grand Lodge was established in England. The Masons Company had been established in England in 1376 in London and had obtained a grant of arms from King Henry VIII in 1472; it was incorporated by King Charles II in 1677. But this was guild masonry, the builders, which was taken over in 1717 by "speculative Masonry," which opened the groups to members of other professions. A poem appeared in London in 1723, "The Freemasons; a Hudibrastic Poem," which rhymed: "If history be not ancient fable, Free Masons came from the Tower of Babel"

A tradition was established that a member of the royal family, or someone with close ties to Buckingham Palace, would be named Grand Master of the English Lodges. From 1782, the Duke of Cumberland, the Prince of Wales, and the Duke of Sussex were grand masters. The Duke of Sussex was King George II's second son; he married Louise, daughter of the King of Prussia. He later had two children by his mistress. They took the family name of Este. Queen Victoria was always proud of her connection with the House of Este, which had begun as the House of Azoll.

The House of Windsor is the world's preeminent family of reigning monarchs today. They represent the final triumph of the Guelph faction, or black nobility, the culmination of the Canaanite drive for power. Their rise had been continuous since the 13th century, when they defeated their most powerful opponents, the Teutonic Hohenstaufen dynasty, who were known as the Ghibelline faction. They had been named after one of the Hohenstaufen strongholds, Weiblingen. Frederick I, Barbarossa, as head of the Hohenstaufens, had extended his rule into northern Italy, where he was surprised by the unexpectedly strong challenge from the Guelph faction. The struggle, which lasted for more than a century, was won by the lower nobility faction of the Guelphs because of their strength among the rising merchant class; the Ghibellines, or high nobility, continued to be the knights on horseback, refusing to sully their hands with trade. The Ghibellines ruled the northern cities of Siena, Milano, and Pisa, while the strength of the Guelphs was centered in Florence and Farrara. Otto IV of Guelph carried on the fight against Philip of Swabia, a Hohenstaufen, but the Hohenstaufens found themselves outnumbered by the forces of the League of Rhenish Towns, a merchant alliance which was able to raise large sums to outfit the condottieri. By the end of the fifteenth century, the Guelphs had triumphed.

Alfonso I of Este married Lucrezia Borgia. His sister, Mary of Modena, married James II of England, bringing the Este line into the English ruling family.

The Ghibellines favored a strong central rule and imperial power, while the Guelphs agitated for decentralized power and the "Rights of Man," a motto which later became their rallying cry for their drive to power.

In the twentieth century, the surviving heirs of the Guelph and Ghibelline factions were arrayed against each other in two world wars. Germany had become a world power through the military instincts and drive of the Prussian Ghibellines. In 1866, Bismarck, to further his goal of unifying Germany, had dispossessed a number of German princes from their estates. The Duke of Nassau and the Elector of Hesse formally renounced their claims; only the princes of Hanover, who were the heirs to the throne of Brunswick, refused to relinquish their holdings. For decades afterwards, the Hanovers considered themselves to be at war with Prussia. Indeed, two world wars did take place, due in part to the continued resentment of the ruling family of England against the rules of Germany. It is an interesting point that the victorius Hanovers saw to it that a defeated Germany was split into two, small, militarily occupied countries after World War II, the final revenge of the victors.

Calvinism, a strong influence in England during the sixteenth century, capitalized on the growing power of the mercantile fleet and the black nobility, whose main interest was money. Unlike previous religious institutions, which had placed great emphasis on austerity and vows of poverty, this new religious doctrine stressed that the charging of interest in loans and the amassing of wealth was the new way of doing the work of the Lord. It was a welcome revelation to the growing merchant class that God really wanted us to become wealthy. "Enrichissez-vous!" became the new battle cry which swept across Europe as the Canaanites built great commercial empires. The prophet of this new divine revelation was one Jean Cauin of Noyons, France. He was educated at the College du Montagu, where Loyola, founder of the Jesuit sect, had studied. Cauin later moved to Paris, where he continued his studies with the Humanists from 1531-32.

During his stay in Paris, he was known as Cauin. He then moved to Geneva, where he formulated the philosophy now known as Calvinism. At first known in Geneva as Cohen (the usual pronunciation of Cauin), he Anglicized his name to John Calvin. This religious movement was based on a literal Jewish interpretation of the Ten Commandments, Old Testament philosophy, and the prohibition of graven images. The early disciples of Calvinism were known as "Christian Hebraists." The advent of Calvinism made possible the great expansion of Jews into further avenues of European commerce besides money-lending. For this achievement, the Encyclopaedia honors Calvin with the statement, "Calvin blessed the Jews."

In retrospect, Calvin can be seen as but one more of the Canaanite movements which have periodically swept across

Europe, creating revolutionary plots which were then exported to other countries. It is no accident that with the advent of Calvin, Switzerland became the private banking center of the world, or that the successive revolutionary plots have been both hatched and financed from Switzerland. Even Lenin found a haven in Switzerland during the years of toiling over the techniques which would allow him to seize Russia from the Romanov family, which had ruled that nation for one thousand years. Calvinism's welcome exhortation to amass more money was counter-balanced from the outset by the fact that it was inaugurated as a brutal, tyrannical system which functioned on a basis of Oriental despotism, again revealing its Canaanite origins. The people of Shem never believe in forcing anyone to do anything; this is a basis of their law; they believe that as a matter of natural instinct, people will always do the right thing. The Canaanites, on the other hand, always aware of the Curse on their people, and God's command to the children of Israel to exterminate them, realize that their survival depends on employing the most brutal measures. Calvinism ran true to form.

In November, 1541, Calvin issued his Ecclesiastical Ordinances, a body of instructions which imposed absolute discipline on all citizens. Calvin's ordinances imposed the death penalty against any opponent; his leading critic, Jacques Gruet, was beheaded for blasphemy; another religious opponent, Michael Servetus, was burned at the stake. Other critics were tortured and beheaded. Calvin encouraged the burning of witches and ruthlessly enforced his ordinances, creating the most tyrannical and autocratic theocracy in Europe.

The importation of Calvinism into England was calculated to drive a wedge between the Church and State. The traditional Church of England had as its titular head the King. Calvinism's divisive propaganda led to the triumph of

Cromwell and the replacement of the Kings of the Stuart line by the House of Orange-Nassau. The first victim of this purge was King Charles I, who was beheaded by the conspirators. Details of the plot were published centuries later in Lord Alfred Douglas' publication "Plain English," September 3, 1921: "L. D. Van Valckert came into possession of the missing volumes of the records of the Synagogue of Mulheim, lost since the Napoleonic Wars, which were written in German. These records have the entry, June 6, 1647, from O. C. to Ebenezer Pratt, 'In return for financial support will advocate admission of Jews to England; this, however, impossible while Charles living. Charles cannot be executed without trial, adequate grounds for which at present do not exist. Therefore, advise that Charles be assassinated, but will have nothing to do with procuring an assassin, though willing to help in his escape.' The reply came from Pratt July 12, 1647, 'Will grant financial aid as soon as Charles removed, and Jews admitted. Assassination too dangerous. Charles should be given an opportunity to escape. His recapture will then make trial and execution possible. The support will be liberal, but useless to discuss terms until trial commences.'"

Lord Alfred Douglas was subsequently imprisoned on a charge of having libeled Winston Churchill in his paper, a feat which most reasonable men would consider impossible.

The plot proceeded as outlined by Pratt. On November 12, 1647, King Charles "escaped." He was recaptured, and during his subsequent trial, the House sat all night, December 5, 1648, finally agreeing that Charles would negotiate a settlement on terms laid down by them. This resulted in the famous Pryde's Purge. Cromwell, infuriated that the House had not passed sentence of execution, dismissed all the members who had favored a settlement with Charles. The fifty members who remained were known as the "Rump Parliament." They had usurped absolute power. They then proclaimed a High Court of Justice on January 9, 1649. It was composed of Levellers from Cromwell's Army. Manasseh ben Israel's agent in England, Isaac Dorislaus, drew up the indictment against King Charles. Manasseh ben Isreal, who transmitted the funds from Amsterdam for Cromwell's revolution, is named "Cromwell's English Intelligencer" by the Encyclopaedia Judaica. On January 30, 1657, King Charles was beheaded at Whitehall.

Cromwell did not live long to enjoy his triumph. He died in 1661, making it possible for King Charles II to regain the throne. Many of Cromwell's most dedicated revolutionarie's emigrated to the American colonies, where they have exercised a pernicious influence ever since. The Cromwellians were the guiding inspiration of the abolitionist movement which precipitated the Civil War; they have been behind-the-scenes figures in many other disasters in the United States.

Because Charles II was now on the throne of England, the Amsterdam bankers instituted a great financial depression in England in 1674. The unrest caused by this development paved the way for the House of Nassau to seize the throne of England. England made peace with its nemesis, Holland, in 1677. As part of the deal, William of Orange married Mary, daughter of the Duke of York, who became King James II when Charles II died in 1685. James now became the only obstacle to William's taking over the throne of England. The Amsterdam bankers now launched a frenetic campaign of bribing King James II's leading aristocratic supporters. The first to succumb was the Duke of Marlborough, John Churchill, ancestor of Winston Churchill. As head of the army, Marlborough's support was crucial. He accepted bribes of some 350,000 pounds from de Medina and Machado. Next was Lord Shrewsbury (Charles Talbot) who had occupied high office during the reign of both Charles II and James II. Seeing that the tide was now turning, such luminaries as Sidney Godolphin, the Duke of Sunderland, and the Duchess of Portsmouth secretly went over to those who favored the accession of William of Orange.

Meanwhile, James II seemed unaware of the treachery which surrounded him. Marlborough even signed a renewed oath of fidelity to James on November 10, 1688. On November 24, he joined the forces of William of Orange.

Sailing with William's invasion force was Lord Polwarth, whose descendant, the present Lord Polwarth, is prominent in American and English banking and industry; Hans Bentinck, a Dutchman who had nursed William through a bout of smallpox; he named his son William after the King. The Earl of Devonshire was in secret correspondence with William at the Hague; Devonshire agreed to deliver the entire Midlands area to William, after signing a historic letter inviting him to take the throne of England. In the 1930's, his descendant, the Duke of Devonshire, briefly worked for J. P. Morgan in New York; Morgan often referred to him as "Lord Useless." The heir to the Devonshire estates married Kathleen Kennedy, daughter of Joseph P. Kennedy. He was killed in action during the war. The Devonshires now faced the bothersome prospect of a Kennedy claim to their estates. The problem was solved when Kathleen Kennedy was killed in an airplane accident while flying to France for a champagne tryst with her lover.

Now King of England, William III named Bentinck the first Earl of Portland. The second duke married into the Cavendish fortune; the third duke became Governor General of India and made the history books when he abolished the practice of suttee in 1829. Those who had aided William's invasion were well-rewarded; they have been the wealthiest families in England ever since. The first order of business was to charter the Bank of England in 1694, the mission for which William had been backed by the bankers of Amsterdam. This made the Canaanite cause a true world power. William's accession placed the throne of England firmly in the line of the black nobility, where it has remained ever since. Lord Shrewsbury became one of the first stockholders in the Bank of England, investing ten thousand pounds. He enthusiastically predicted that the Bank of England would not only finance trade, it would also carry the burden of her wars, a prediction which proved true. Because no revolutionary faction could obtain any financing after the Bank of England gained control of the money of England, there has never been another civil war or revolution in England. The Cavendish-Bentinck line, like others who supported William, has always prospered. The present Duke married a Mrs. Quigley of Kentucky and is a director of the Rothschild firm, Rio Tinto. During World War II, he was chairman of the Joint Chiefs of Staff (Intelligence).

The Scottish lords to a man had been loyal to James II; to the first to bend the knee to William was one Patrick Lyon. He became Earl of Strathmore. The daughter of the fourteenth Earl, Elizabeth Bowes-Lyon, is now the Queen Mother of England.

William III soon had a beautiful mistress, Elizabeth Villiers; he also conducted lengthy love affair with a handsome young nobleman, Arnold van Keppel, whom he named Earl of Albemarle. When William III died, two persons were specifically named in his will; the Earl of Portland, and the Earl of Albemarle. Both received bequests of land and jewels.

The Canaanites make sure to reward those who serve them well. Typical was the career of John Buchan, who married Susan Grosvenor. The Grosvenors (Duke of

Westminster) are the wealthiest family in England, owning some six hundred acres of prime London real estate. For three years, Buchan was private secretary to Lord Alfred Milner during Milner's promotion of the Boer War. Milner also founded the Round Tables (the present Council on Foreign Relations). Buchan became a widely published novelist and was named Governor General of Canada. He was given the title Lord Tweedsmuir. In his autobiography, "Pilgrim's Way," Buchan mentions en passant "the veiled prophets who are behind the scenes in a crisis." He offers no further identification. He also writes, "I dreamed of a worldwide brotherhood with the background of a common race and creed, consecrated to the cause of peace." In this seemingly innocuous fantasy, he was really citing his dedication to the worldwide Canaanite conspiracy, with its pseudo-program of "the Rights of Man," World Brotherhood, and world peace, all this, in reality, the screen for a universal tyranny imposed by the Canaanite despots.

The Bank of England was chartered as the result of regicide and an international conspiracy which successfully seized the throne of England. Yet John Buchan wrote in his autobiography, "I had long shared Lord Rosebery's view of him [Oliver Cromwell] as the greatest of Englishmen." Lord Rosebery had been the first of the English aristocrats to marry into the Rothschild family. It was to be expected that he would revere the memory of England's only regicide.

The Rothschilds had used the European network of the Illuminati as their transmission belt for their rapid takeover of the continent's financial structure. They used a number of stratagems, a few of which were revealed by Guy de Rothschild in his book, "Whims of Fortune": the Rothschilds correspondence was always written in Hebrew; it was never signed, so that any signature purporting to be from one of the five brothers would be seen to be a forgery. He reports, "Just after World War I, the French government needed to borrow dollars. They contacted the House of Morgan, who preferred, however, to deal with the Rothschilds rather than with a government."

This was a bit of gloating on the part of Rothschild; he knew that the vaunted House of Morgan had never been more than an appendage of the Rothschild network; it was instructed to deal with the House of Rothschild. He also notes, "My family had always been one of the major shareholders in the British Rio Tinto ... traditionally half the capital was French."

One of the marks which the Rothschilds left on the world was the traditional red shield of the Salvation Army. In the nineteenth century, Baron Rothschild began to give considerable sums to General Booth in London, always through an unidentified representative. One day, he came in and revealed that he was the mysterious benefactor. He stated that he would continue his donations, but he would like to make one suggestion. The Salvation Army could attract more attention if perhaps it could adopt some distinctive logo. "What would you suggest?" asked General Booth. "I suppose a red shield would be effective, don't you?" said Baron Rothschild.

The Salvation Army carried the red shield all over the world.

One of the principal agencies of the Canaanite network as been the Rhodes Trust, which has trained young men in the principles of the Canaanite program for world power for almost a century. Cecil Rhodes was the agent for the Rothschilds when he secured their control over the vast diamond and gold reserves of South Africa. They still exercise control through DeBeers (diamonds) and the Ango-American Corporation (gold). Rhodes had considerable holdings himself; when he died, Lord Nathan Rothschild emerged in 1891 as his sole trustee. This control was later expanded to include other members of the Society of the Elect, R. H. Brand of Lazard Freres, Sir Alfred Beit, another of the Rand millionaires, the Earl of Rosebery, and Sir Alfred Milner. This group not only set up the Rhodes Trust; it later financed the Royal Institute of International Affairs and its American subsidiary, the Council on Foreign Relations.

After gaining control in England, the Canaanites reverted to their traditional practices as demon-worshippers. England was soon rife with cults embodying witchcraft, Black Masses, and blood rituals. The Earl of Pembroke had been an early supporter of William of Orange, and a charter subscriber to the Bank of England. The Countess of Pembroke became a leader of the new "mystery cults," with her brother, Sir Philip Sidney, who brought mysticism into English literature with the publication of his "Faerie Queene" which he had dedicated to his sister.

Humphrey, Duke of Gloucester, also played an important role in the mystery cults. He was descended from black nobility, being descended from both of the bastard sons of the Duke of Normandy, Richard the Fearless. The Gloucesters followed William the Conqueror to England.

Mysticism became a dominant theme in English literature of this period. Sir Philip Sidney was greatly influenced by Hubert Languet, a French intellectual who openly espoused the "Rights of Man" and what is now known as the "liberation doctrine." He frequently spoke on the right of people to armed insurrection and the legitimacy of resistance. Sir Philip's father, Sir Henry, had been a protege of the powerful Cecil family; he later was named president of Ireland.

The work of Shakespeare contains many mystical influences, Prospero's revels, etc. One of England's greatest dramatists, whose work is largely ignored, is Christopher Marlowe. He wrote three great plays, all of them devoted to exposing the mystery cult: Tamburlaine, The Jew of Malta, and Dr. Faustus. After completing Dr. Faustus, he died somewhat mysteriously, being stabbed in what was called a quarrel. The Jew of Malta is said to be a dramatization of the career of Dr. Frederigo Lopez, former physician to the Earl of Leicester. In 1593, Lopez was accused of plotting to poison Queen Elizabeth; he was executed by hanging in 1594. Some scholars maintain that Queen Elizabeth had been secretly married to the Earl of Liecester, Robert Dudley, and that they had two sons, Sir Francis Bacon, who had been adopted by Sir Nicholas Bacon, and Robert, Earl of Essex. Lopez could have officiated at these births; his silence would protect the succession to the throne. Others claim that Bacon actually was the person who wrote the plays attributed to William Shakespeare.

Sir Francis Bacon introduced "the new philosophy" into England. It was based on the induction theory and "the pyramid of knowledge," both of which were mystical concepts. They were the principles of humanism, as stated in a more "scientific" or plausible form. From 1350 to 1425, the medieval guilds had died out by government decree, due to the aristocracy's fear of demands for higher wages. Bacon began the secret revival of these guilds, first through the Rosicrucian movement, which he is said to have founded, and later through the Free and Accepted (Speculative) Masons. The Rosicrucians, or Knights of the Rose Croix, flaunted the symbol of a rosy cross. The upright was the symbol of life; the cross bar the symbol of death. The rose symbol was said to mean, first of all, secrecy in all things; and second, the blooming of woman's genitals. The cult was known in Bohemia as early as 1615, where an alchemist, Dr. John Dee, organized its followers.

Francis Yates' important work, "The Occult Philosophy in the Elizabethan Age," traces some of Bacon's work to the Rosicrucian Manifesto. Yates notes that Marlowe's plays, with their merciless examination of the forces behind mysticism, may have been purposely overshadowed by the more mystical works of Shakespeare. The Jew of Malta touched upon some of the most sensitive court secrets of the Elizabethan Age; Tamburlaine is a play which exposes a Saturnian tyrant whose color was black (Canaanite), and a fulmination against dictatorial power. It may be his greatest work, but it has been shunted aside in favor of Dr. Faustus. This play openly portrays the process by which the demon-worshipping Canaanites, as agents of Satan, pledge themselves to the Devil in return for earthly riches and power. Marlowe's play takes up the power of incantations and chants, magical formulae, and shows Dr. Faustus' study, which is decked out with the planets and the signs of the zodiac. On the other hand, Shakespeare shows that he had been heavily influenced by cabbalistic works, such as Georgio's De Harmonica Mundi. His Merchant of Venice, although frequently denounced for its supposed anti-Semitism, actually is a powerful plea for racial tolerance.

In more recent works, English scholars go to great pains to deny that Sir Francis Bacon ever had any connection with either the Rosicrucian movement or the Freemasons. Because these were highly secret organizations, it seems odd that these scholars could be so positive in their denials. Bacon, who had been given the title, Viscount of St. Albans, became the Lord Chancellor of England. He was later removed from this office because of court intrigues led by Lord Buckingham. The Royal Society of London was founded thirty-four years after Bacon's death; in 1660, the Bishop of Rochester and the other founders paid official tribute to Bacon's works as the basis of their Society.

The Oxford English Dictionary offers some notes on the cabbalists during this period: "Scott Monast. ... I used to doubt the existence of cabalists and Rosicrusians' thought the SubPrior." "1891, Rosie Cross. 'It is commonly held ... that there is a close connection ... between the Alchemysts and the Rosicrucians." W. Taylor, Monthly Mag. VIII 797, "The disciples ... have formed in churches an esoteric gnostic or illuminated order, rather than congregations." This quote is important because it shows that the Illuminati were penetrating the established churches. The 9th edition of the Encyclopaedia Britannica identifies the missing link between these groups as Ignatius Loyola, who founded the Jesuit Order on the Feast of the Assumption on April 15, 1541 near Rome; this date is given by some authorities as 1534. He had formerly been a student at Salamanca; from 1520 on he was a member of an Illuminati sect in Salamanca called Alombrados; in 1527 he was tried by an ecclesiastical commission because of his membership in this sect; he was acquitted. In the Society of Jesus, he set up six degrees for advancement, which are the same as in Freemasonry; its doctrines are similar to those of the Jewish Mishnah.

EUSTACE MULLINS

Four Lodges met at the Goose and Gridiron alehouse in London on June 24, 1717, to form the first Grand Lodge of England. Jacob Katz, in his book, "Jews and Freemasonry in Europe," says that the initial members included Mendez, de Medina, Alvarez, and Baruch, most of whom were Marranos. During Elizabeth's reign, the Rosicrucians had organized themselves as Masons, perhaps under Bacon's guidance. The Encyclopaedia Judaica says that the coat of arms of English Freemasonry was designed by Jacob Judah Leon Templo. 1717 was the year that the Hanovers ascended the throne of England. Under the leadership of George III's son, the Duke of Sussex, the rival lodges of "Ancient" and "Modern" were now joined. The Royal Society's members, who had paid homage to Bacon, joined the Masons through Rev. John Desaguliers, England's second Grand Master. Elia Ashmole was an important figure in the growth of English Freemasonry. Not only was he an important intellectual figure; he also organized the various mystery cults into the functioning system of Freemasonry. Together, Lord Acton and Ashmole controlled William Pitt's foreign policy, as well as the Royal Society of London, the precursor of the Royal Institute of International Affairs. Ashmole's name survives today as the prestigious Ashmolean Museum at Oxford.

The growth of Freemasonry in Germany illustrates the power of the Canaanite force which brought the Hanoverian Kings to power in England. Its success focused on the career of Adam Weishaupt, born in 1748. At the age of twenty-two, he was elected to the chair of common law at Ingolstadt University; the post had been held by Jesuits continuously since 1750. He founded the Order of the Illuminati on May 1, 1776. The other founders were the Duke of Brunswick; Grand Duke Ernest of Gotha and the Elector of Hesse (whose transaction with King George III to provide Hessian mercenaries to defeat the American

122

revolutionaries was the foundation of the Rothschild fortune).

On July 16, 1782, Weishaupt formally combined the Order of the Illuminati with the Freemasons at the Congress of Wilhelmsbad. The combined groups now had over three million members, including some of the most powerful men in Europe. Weishaupt was the ideal front man for this organization, because of his ability to formulate ideas and his organizational ability. He wrote, "The Free Masons should control all men of every class, nation, and religion, dominating them without obvious compulsion; uniting them through a strong bond; inspiring them with enthusiasm to spread common ideas; and with utmost secrecy and energy, direct them towards this singular objective throughout the world. It is through the intimacy of secret societies that these opinions will be formed." (Munich, 1765, cited by Barruel.)

Far from being a starry eyed idealist or fantasizing intellectual, Weishaupt was backed in his plan for world power by many of the leading Canaanite bankers of Europe; Moses Mendelssohn of Germany, Daniel Itzig of Vienna; Friedlander, Mayer, Meyer Cerfbeer, Moses Mocatta, and the Goldsmid brothers of London, Benjamin and Abraham. Remaining behind the scenes of Weishaupt's operations, while liberally funding the growth of his movement, they secretly functioned as the Sovereign Patriarchal Council of Hamburg, the Supreme Jewish Lodge.

Jacob Katz, "Jews and Freemasonry in Europe," Harvard Press, 1970, states that the German Freemasons originated in the Order of the Asiatica, of which the wealthy banker Daniel Itzig was head. Itzig was also the backer of Weishaupt. In 1811, the Frankfurt lodge of free masons was formed by Sigismund Geisenheimer (Geisenheimer was the head clerk of the House of Rothschild) and Rabbi Zvi

Hirsch, chief Rabbi of Frankfurt. Hirsch later led in the Reform Judaism movement which formulated the political Zionist program. The Frankfurt lodge listed among its members all of the leading bankers of Frankfurt, the Rothschilds, the Adlers, the Speyers, the Hanuers, and the Goldschmidts; they later held joint meetings with the Sanhedrin of Paris. Duke Carl von Hessen of Schleswig then became the head of the German masons. As Landgrave, he administered the province of Schleswig for its absentee owners, the Danish monarchy. His principal emissary was a mysterious "Johnston," variously said to be a Jew named Leicht, Leucht, or Becker. He was arrested while on a mission for the masonic movement, and he died while held prisoner in the Castle of Wartburg.

Frederick the Great, while still crown prince, was initiated into Freemasonry in Brunswick in 1738. In 1761, he was named head of the Scottish Rite. As a young man, he had seen his father behead his lover in an attempt to force him to abandon his homosexual practices.

The leaders of Freemasonry-Illuminati were known as the Ordre of the Stricte Observance; they were Prince Charles of Hesse (Eques a Leoni Resurgente) and von Haugwitz, Frederick's cabinet minister, known as "Eques a Monte dancti." Behind him were still another group, known as "the Invisibles," or the Unknown Superiors, who have been previously identified as the Sovereign Patriarchal Council.

From its inception, the alliance of the Illuminati and the Freemasons had a clearly defined program: (1) abolition of all ordered government; (2) abolition of private property; (3) abolition of inheritance; (4) abolition of patriotism (5) abolition of all religions; (6) abolition of family, morality, and control of education of children; (7) creation of a world government.

This program may seem familiar to the reader; it has been encountered as the working instructions for every revolutionary movement in the world since 1782; Communism, liberation movements, resistance fighters, all obtain their program from this basic plan. It also states the goals of secular humanism in its attack on the family and the plan to control the education of children. Because messages were constantly being carried to and from the various chapters of the Illuminati, these instructions were seized from captured couriers and became known to European governments. Even then, no action was taken, possibly because of accomplices in high places. Also, there was an important stumbling block to convincing the threatened populations of the menace of the Illuminati revolutionists. This was the dominant presence of many of the world's most powerful bankers at the heart of the conspiracy. It was too much to ask the average official, or even a member of the public, to believe that the world's most prominent aristocrats, landholders, and bankers would be backing a program of this type. Surely bankers would not advocate the seizure of private property. Surely aristocrats would not abolish the right of inheritance. Surely landholders with vast acreage would not advocate the nationalization of all land. The problem was that no one understood that this was the program of the Canaanites, which was intended solely to rob and enslave the people of Shem. Of course, the Canaanite bankers did not intend to seize their own property. Of course the black nobility did not intend to nationalize their own inheritances. The Illuminati program nowhere states that this is the plan designed to overcome the Curse of Canaan; that the Illuminati plan merely formalizes the Will of Canaan as a working set of instructions. The admonition of Canaan to his heirs to "love robbery-hate your masters" was now the program of a worldwide group of conspirators. The people of Shem remain convinced that bankers do not finance Communism, and that wealthy people will not give up their holdings. The Illuminati-Communist plan continues the battle of the Canaanites against the people of Shem. Until they realize this, the people of Shem remain doomed to destruction.

From the Illuminati headquarters at Frankfurt came the twin Canaanite evils which have since plagued the world, Zionism and Communism. The first Communist International was composed of Lionel de Rothschilds, Heinrich Heine, and Karl Marx. Weishaupt had died in 1830, at the age of 82; he was succeeded as head of the Illuminati by Guiseppe Mazzini, the Italian revolutionary leader. Under Mazzini's leadership, the Illuminati moved rapidly toward a policy of more direct action, of revolutionary outbreaks and open attempts to seize and overthrow governments. The Communist International was the first step in this program of activism. At first it was simply known as The League of the Just, a branch of the Illuminati. This group commissioned Karl Marx to write the Communist Manifesto in 1847; it was published in 1848 and was immediately given worldwide circulation by the international offices of Freemasonry. Throughout his long political career, Marx was known to work actively with both the Jesuits and the Freemasons. In 1864, Marx organized the International Workingmen's Party in London; in 1872, he moved it to New York, where it was merged with the Socialist Party. Marx received a regular stipend from American newspapers as a columnist, employment which had been arranged for him by the Freemasons.

Mazzini appointed General Albert Pike head of American Freemasonry in 1860; Pike had only joined the Masons ten years earlier. On January 22, 1870, Mazzini wrote to Pike of his plan to establish a supreme governing council of secret Masons of high degree, who would govern all of Freemasonry; however, no federation of Masons would ever be allowed to know about the Supreme Council, a precept which remains in force today. Most Masons will emphatically deny that such a council exists anywhere in their organizational structure. Known as the New and Reformed Palladian Rite, it consisted of three Supreme Councils, with headquarters in Charleston, Rome, and Berlin. The chiefs of these three councils communicated daily by their Arcula Mystica Magic Box, which was actually an early development of radio. At that time, there were only seven such boxes in existence throughout the world.

The other arm of the worldwide revolutionary movement was Zionism, which aimed to enlist the international force of the Jews in a campaign to establish a State of Israel as the world's supreme ruling power. Since this was also the, vowed purpose of Freemasonry, to rebuild the Temple of Solomon, and to fill it with all of the wealth of the world, Zionism's initial appearance came through Freemasonry. It was first known as "Reform Judaism." Graetz' History of the Jews, v. 5, p. 674, States that: "the first Jewish Freemason Lodge, at Frankfurt-on-main, was the heart of the Jewish Reform Movement." In 1842, the Society of Friends of Reform (Judaism) at Frankfurt issued its principles: (1) the denial of the legal authority of the Babylonian Talmud, substituting for it instead the Old Testament; (2) the denial that the Messiah would lead them back to Jerusalem; (3) temple service was to be conducted in the vernacular; (4) women could now be allowed to sit beside men in the synagogue, instead of being segregated, as had always been required by Orthodox Judaism. Reform Judaism launched a number of programs besides Zionism; ecumenism, that is, active cooperation with leaders and congregations of other faiths; feminism, equality of the sexes; but their most important concept, that the Messiah would never appear on earth to lead them back to Jerusalem, opened the door for the seeking of this goal by political activism, that is, Zionism. The initial program of Political Zionism was first broached by Rabbi Hirsch Kalisher, a close associate of Mayer Amschel Rothschild in Frankfurt.

Sir Moses Montefiore and Adolphe Cremieux, founder of the Alliance Israelite Universelle, gave added impetus to the new movement. Its goals were greatly publicized by the work of Moses Hess, a close friend of Karl Marx. This is ironic, in view of the fact that the present Soviet Government professes to be ideologically opposed to Zionism. Moses Hess became known as "the father of Zionism." A journalist who was greatly influenced by his writings, Theodor Herzl, was converted to activism, and he is now known as "the founder of the Zionist State." The Encyclopaedia Judaica says that Moses Hess was a Jewish Socialist and nationalist who led the Reform Movement, calling for the colonization of Palestine. His principal work, "Rome and Jerusalem," which received wide circulation, was the book which had great impact on Theodor Herzl.

In 1860, Rabbi Kalisher hosted a secret meeting at his home in Thoru to recap the lessons which had been learned from the Revolution of 1848. This revolution had been intended to topple all the governments of Europe and replace them with Communist governments. It succeeded in only a few isolated instances, such as Venice, where Daniel Manini set up a Communist government. From the Thoru meeting came Kalisher's book, "Drishal Zion," in 1861, and later, Moses Hess' "Rome and Jerusalem." These two works were largely responsible for converting the Jews of Europe to the Zionist program, the political goal of restoring Palestine to the Jewish people.

One of the conspirators present at this 1860 meeting leaked the record of the proceedings to a writer named Maurice Joly. The culprit is reputed to have been one E. Laharane, a confidant of Adolphe Cremieux, head of the influential Alliance Israelite Universelle. A power in French politics, Cremieux had obtained for Laharane the post of private secretary to Napoleon III. Joly later published the proceedings under the title, "Dialogue aux Enfers entre

Machiavelli et Montesquieu," the earliest version of the book now circulated under the title, "Protocols of Zion." The material paralleled much of the text of Kallisher's book, "Drishal Zion," and with the Rabbi's Speech delivered by Goedsche in 1868. It also coincided with the proceedings of the Jewish Synod of Leipzig of 1869. The Kattowitz Conference of Hoveve Zion 1884 also Joincides with the first set of documents which appeared as the Protocols of Zion; the Kattowitz papers had been extracted from the Mizraim Lodge of Paris by one Joseph Schorst-Shapiro. He sold them to a Mlle. Justine de Glinka, who forwarded them to the Russian Ministry of the Interior, where they were received by a Gen. Orgewsky. Shortly afterward, Schorst-Shapiro was murdered in Egypt. The Odessa Conference of Hoveve Zion and B'Nai Moshe, led by Ashed Ginsberg (Ahad Ha-am), and his subsequent stay in Paris In 1894, were followed by the appearance of the Protocols as they are now known; they were published by Philip Stepwoff in Moscow. This essentially was the same set of documents later published by Sergei Nilus in 1905. Extracts of lectures read at B'Nai B'Rith lodges in New York at secret meetings were also extracted and put in the hands of the Russian Consul General in New York. These extracts coincided on all points with the 1895 version of the Protocols and those extracted from the First Basle Congress in 1897. They were also published by B. Butmi in 1901. It was because of these well-established antecedents that the Protocols were denounced as "forgeries," that is, as unauthorized copies.

Because of its well-advertised revolutionary program, Freemasonry has been repeatedly banned by European government - but never in the United States, where it has exercised political power since 1776. It has been repeatedly denounced by the papacy. Holland banned Freemasonry in 1735; Germany in 1738; Zurich in 1740; Berne in 1745. Russia first banned Freemasonry in 1792, again in 1822, and by the Soviet Government in 1922. On April 28, 1738, Pope

Clement VII issued "In eminenti," which condemned Masonry for its naturalism and its demand for oaths. Benedict XIV condemned Masonry in his "Providas" edict, May 18, 1751; Pius VII in "Ecclesiam," September 13, 1821; Leo XIII, "Quo graviora," March 13, 1825; Gregory XVI, "Mirari," August 15, 1832; Pius IX in six separate edicts dating from 1846-1873; Leo XIII, five edicts condemning Freemasonry from 1882-1902. Gen. Pike responded by terming the papacy "a deadly, treacherous enemy" in his letter to the Italian Grand Master Timoteo Riboli. "The Papacy has been for a thousand years the torturer and curse of Humanity, the most shameless imposture, in its pretence to spiritual power of all ages."

Despite these edicts, the Catholic Duke of Norfolk became Grand Master of English Masons in 1730; the Catholic Viscount Montagu, the ninth Lord Petre, who was the head of English Catholics, was also the Grand Master of England from 1772-77. On March 19, 1902, in the fifth of his edicts condemning Freemasonry, Pope Leo XIII said, "Freemasonry is the personification of the Revolution ... whose aim is to exercise an occult overlords hip upon society and whose sole raison d'etre consists in waging war against God and His Church." What a pity that Pope Leo XIII did not know about the Curse of Canaan, or that Freemasonry was simply Satan's rebellion against God, which was being carried on in the twentieth century by his descendants, the Canaanites.

The heads of English Masonry during the nineteenth century were the Duke of Sussex, younger son of King George II, 1813-43; the Earl of Zetland, 1843-70; the Marquess of Ripon, 1870; the Earl of Limerick, 1871; the Prince of Wales, later King Edward VII, 1874; Hugh David Sandeman, of the prominent wine importing family, 1895; Lord Ampthill, 1908; the Duke of Connaught, to 1938. These were all leading aristocrats; the Earl of Zetland married the daughter of the Earl of Scarborough, later appointed Viceroy of Ireland 1889-92; he was the brother-in-law of the Duke of Westminster, the wealthiest man in England; the second Marquess of Zetland, Lawrence Dundas, bore the Sword of State at the coronation of King George VI; he was also Governor of the National Bank of Scotland, chairman of the National Trust, Governor of Bengal; he headed the Round Table Conferences of 1930-32, was Secretary of State for India 1935-40, was admitted to the Order of St. John of Jerusalem, and he wrote the biographies of England's two leading figures, Lord Cromer, head of Baring Brothers banking house, and Lord Curzon, Governor-General of India.

The Marquess of Ripon, George Frederick Samuel, was born at 10 Downing Street while his father was Prime Minister; he became Secretary of War and Secretary for India under Lord Palmerston, and was appointed First Lord of the Admiralty under Gladstone. He was Colonial Secretary 1892-95, Lord Privy Seal in the House of Lords, and leader of the Liberal Party, 1905-08. His name is memorialized in the United States by the Ripon Society, a group of "liberal" Republicans who have exercised considerable influence from behind the scenes on the policies of the Republican Party.

The present Earl of Limerick, Patrick Pery, is deputy chairman of the international banking house, Kleinwort Benson.

The second Marquess of Ripon resigned as Grand Master in 1894 and joined the Catholic Church; he was treasurer of Queen Alexandra's household (wife of King Edward VII) 1901- 1923; he was brother-in-law to the Earl of Pembroke, and he married the widow of the fourth Earl of Lonsdale.

Lord Ampthill's father, Odo W. Russell, served in Lord Palmerston's office from 1850-52; he served with the Florence legation from 1957-70 and was regarded as an unofficial ambassador to the Vatican during those years; he was then sent as Special Envoy to the German Army Headquarters at Versailles during the Franco-Prussian War. He later served as British Ambassador to Vienna and Berlin. The second Baron Ampthill was Grand Master of English Masons from 1908 to his death in 1935. This is the same Russell family which holds the title of the Dukes of Bedford, including Bertrand Russell, the most famous humanist of the twentieth century. The second Baron was born in Rome while his father was serving there; he became president of the Oxford Union; he married the daughter of the Earl of Beauchamp (her father held the title of Lord of the Cinque Ports); his wife was Lady-in-Waiting to Queen Mary; he was also a brother-in-law of the Duke of Westminster; joined the Order of St. John of Jerusalem, and served as Grand Master of the lodge which had been formed at the Bank of England, Lodge No. 263. He wrote the "History of the Bank of England Lodge" and was appointed head of the Masons of Madras, India, before becoming Grand Master of England; he served as private secretary to Hon. J. Chamberlain, Governor of Madras and Viceroy of India.

The backgrounds of these Grand Masters prove that English Freemasonry has always had access to the highest circles of government; Disraeli, a Freemason, became Prime Minister; he referred to "determined men of Masonry," meaning those Masons who were assigned to carry out the crucial tasks of assassination.

One of the Canaanites who became renowned as a leading English economist, and still enjoys wide influence in the United States, was David Ricardo (1772-1823), the third son of Abraham Israel, who was a substantial member of the Jewish community in Amsterdam. Israel emigrated to

London with William III and later became one of the wealthiest members of the London Stock Exchange, where he worked closely with his fellow emigres. His son, David, became an intimate friend of Lord Nathan Mayer Rothschild, speculating heavily in government securities on advice of Rothschild. Together, they profited enormously from the financial coup resulting from early news about the outcome of the Battle of Waterloo. David Israel, now known as David Ricardo, began to write economic dicta intended to become the final word on how much the working class should be paid. He developed a formula which became known as "the subsistence wage," dictating that the worker should never receive more than the bare minimum needed for his subsistence. If his wages were to be increased, the government was charged to take care of it by promptly increasing his taxes (does this sound familiar to any Americans?). The Canaanites in America developed a new twist with the withholding tax, which insured that the worker would never receive his wages in the first place; he would only receive a mutilated portion, from which the Canaanites had already deducted "their" portion. Ricardo's dictum, which also became known as "the iron law of wages," iron meaning that under no circumstances would the worker ever be the beneficiary of any outburst of generosity and be allowed even a small increase, when Rita Ricardo-Campbell, wife of the director of the Hoover Institution, and a direct descendant of David Ricardo, came to Washington as a key member of Reagan's staff, the Reagan anti-Communist, humanitarian Revolution. She became Reagan's advisor on Social Security payments and pensions. Ricardo's economic theories on wages and labor had also been enthusiastically received by Karl Marx, who adopted them as the guidelines by which the slave workers of Soviet Russia are ruled today.

Stephen Knight's book, "The Brotherhood," reveals many interesting details about English Freemasonry. He points out that the Unlawful Societies Act of 1799 required that Freemasons could hold meetings only if the names of the members were submitted to the local Clerks of the Peace; this requirement has never been complied with. Knight says that Queen Elizabeth is the present Grand Patroness of English Freemasonry. One of his most startling revelations is the information that from fifty to seventy per cent of all English judges are Freemasons. Lawyers find that they must join the Freemasons if they expect to get any clients. "The Law Society is one of the most masonic institutions in the world," notes King. Ninety per cent of its members are Masons. This creates great inequities, because the Law Society is the final judge as to who will receive legal aid and who will be denied it. A non-Mason has no chance of receiving legal aid in a suit against a Mason. This is, typical of the Will of Canaan; the secret conspiracy against all who are not members of the tribe.

The Masonic conspiracy which casts a pall over legal procedures in England is but one manifestation of its sinister influence. During the Elizabethan Age, the fascination with the occult appeared in many underground organizations; it now surfaced in the Victorian Age. Witchcraft became widespread, even in the highest circles of society, with its rituals emphasizing mind-altering drugs, plants, and Satanic jewelry. Orgies and blood sacrifices were discreetly carried out in the heart of the London slums, and on remote ancestral estates. One of the more publicized of these groups was the Hermetic Society of the Golden Dawn, founded in 1887 by three members of the Rosicrucian Society. All three were masons of high degree, and well known as cabbalists-Rev. A. F. A. Woodford, Dr. Wynn Westcott, a London coroner, and a Scot named Sam Liddell Mathers. The group was soon joined by William Butler Yeats, the poet, and Aleister Crowley, who was to become known worldwide for his practice of black magic.

The purpose of the Hermetic Society was to worship the Ten Sephiroth, that is the Kabbalah, so that they could then be endowed with magic powers, and could call on supernatural forces as their allies. The members set up Degrees as follows: Neophyte, four degrees; Under Order, four degrees; and the Third Order, four degrees.

Yeats, the leading Irish poet, later claimed that he had joined the group in order to counter the black magic of Crowley with his own white magic. Crowley is famed as the most dedicated Satanist of the twentieth century. He once baptized a toad with the name of Jesus Christ, and then slowly crucified it, reveling in its agonies. He is said to have taken part in 150 ritual murders, most of whom were children. The victims were usually killed with a silver knife. In his "Confessions," he writes, "In Mexico I was known by the name of Beast 666. I had an introduction to an old man named Don Jesus Medina, a descendant of the great Duke of Armada fame, and one of the highest chiefs of Scottish-Rite Freemasonry. My Quabalistic knowledge being already profound by current standards, he thought me worthy of the highest initiation in his power to confer; special powers were obtained in view of my limited sojourn, and I was rushed rapidly through and admitted to the 33rd and last degree before I left the country." Thus the leading Satanist of this century was confirmed as a 33rd degree Mason!

Madame Blavatsky became famous as the organizer of Theosophy. She developed the society after a sojourn in India; the Indian chapters later came under a cloud because of the arrest of its members for the practice of homosexuality. She then moved to Great Britain, where she founded the Theosophical Society there, the precursor of the American group of that name. She also founded the Hermetic Society. Her chief assistant in the Theosophical Society, a cabbalistic organization, was Mrs. Annie Besant, who is also well known as one of the founders of the Fabian

Society in 1884. The co-founders of the Fabian Society were all Freemasons; they were George Bernard Shaw, Lord Haldane, Ramsay MacDonald, and Sidney and Beatrice Webb. The group took its name from the Roman General Fabius, who was celebrated for his deliberate and long-range strategy. The Fabian plan was to wait, as Fabius Cunctator had waited to attack Hannibal, to wait for the right moment. In England, the Fabians proposed to use the Roman general's strategy to gradually impose a tyrannical Socialist government upon the people of England through devious long-range planning. This conspiratorial approach won for the Fabians the nickname, "the Jesuits of Socialism." As part of their strategy, in 1890, Annie Baesant became the chief agitator in the English textile industry, which was centered in Lancashire.

During the 1930s, the Fabians organized a strike force called PEP, the initials of Political and Economic Planning. It was headed by Israel Moses Sieff, the multi-millionaire head of the giant retail empire, Marks and Spencer. In 1931, Sieff distributed a document to leading members of PEP, which was labeled "Strictly Confidential." The program outlined included such items as "Whether we like it or not, the individualist farmer will be forced by events to submit to far-reaching changes of outlook and methods. He will receive instructions as to the quantity and quality of his produce. [This was implemented soon afterward as the Pig Marketing Board. Ed.] He will be less free to make marketing and arbitrary decisions as to his own business ...

Planned economy must clearly-involve drastic increases in inroads upon the right of ownership of land. What is required ... is transfer of ownership of large blocks of land." This program of PEP was later presented as a textbook drawn up by G. D. H. Cole, "Principles of Economic Planning," in 1935. The book featured the compass and the square of Freemasonry prominently emblazoned on the cover, although nothing in the book identified the role of Freemasons in the program.

The wealthy directors of PEP did not intend to transfer ownership of their own large blocks of land, or of the business empires which they controlled. They merely wished to take over large blocks of lands from their competitors, to force ruinous regulations upon their rivals, in short to rob and ruin everyone but their own small coterie of Canaanites.

The most active leaders of PEP were such luminaries as Viscount Astor, Sir Herbert Samuel (Governor of Palestine), Sir Herbert Simon, Sir C. M. Joad, Professor Gilbert Murray, and the Master of Balliol. All of them were Freemasons and members of the Royal Institute of International Affairs, as well. They were closely allied with a group called the World Fellowship of Faiths. The Second International Congress of this group, which met in London in 1936, included among the speakers Canon Barry, Chaplain to King Edward VIII, and ex-Bishop Montgomery Brown. Brown told the audience, "The USSR is just the fore-runner of the International Communist State which will gradually absorb all capitalist States. If any Government, Church, or Institution opposes or stands in the way of the Communist State, they must be ruthlessly overthrown and destroyed. If World Unity is to be attained, it must be through International Communism, which can only be arrived at by the solgan, 'Banish the Gods from the Skies and the capitalist from the Earth.' Then, and only then, will there exist a complete World Fellowship of Faiths." This is a concise statement of the ambitions of the international Canaanite conspiracy. Banish the Gods; Satan's rebellion against God-the Curse of Canaan had not altered its slogans in three thousand years of recorded history.

Rabbi Ben Mozeg told the World Fellowship, "What is certain is that Masonic theology is only theosophy at bottom, and corresponds to that of the Kabbalah ... Those who will take the trouble to examine with care the connection between Judaism and philosophic Freemasonry, Theosophy, and the Mysteries in general ... will cease to smile at the suggestion that the Kabbalistic theology may have a role to play in the religious transformation of the future. It contains the key to the modern religious problem."

Here again, we are offered the solution to all problems by the Canaanites; return to the worship of Baal, brought up to date in the twentieth century, and we enter a religious transformation.

This is the cup of hemlock which the Fundamentalists offer to us.

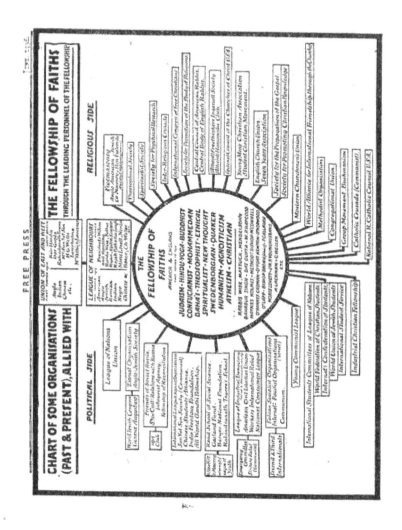

139

.

CHAPTER 5

THE FRENCH REVOLUTION

I t is a grim task for a writer to chronicle the terrible massacres which have been inflicted on the people of Shem. It is even more disturbing to know that even now, the plans have been drawn for even greater and more thorough such massacres of this people. In chronicling the Reigns of Terror of the French Revolution, the Bolshevik Revolution, and the Spanish Revolution, Americans are not being offered another television drama; they are being given a preview of their own future.

To those who travel in France today, the horrors of the French Revolution must seem remote indeed. Enjoying unrivaled cuisine, visiting great chateaux, and viewing the works of art which have made the name of France synonymous with the creation of art, it is difficult to envision that the streets and rivers of this nation once flowed with the blood of innocents, as thousands of women and children were murdered in obscene rites. It is for this reason, perhaps, that even today, tourists, or rather, foreigners, are rarely welcomed in France. At best, they are tolerated in this fair country. Is this not due to a deeply hidden sense of shame, the desire to conceal an unpleasant family secret which causes even innkeepers, traditionally a hospitable lot, to maintain a cool reserve when tourists come in waving their currency like a flag? This is understandable, because the French Revolution, one of the three great orgies of the Canaanite demon-war-shippers during modern history, may have been visited on the French people as a deliberate punishment by God. This punishment would have been in direct retribution for one of the lesser known atrocities of European history, the massacres of the Huguenots during the 16th and 17th centuries.

During the two centuries prior to these atrocities, the people of Shem had wrought great changes in the economic condition of the French nation, transforming it from a medieval state into the most promising industrial empire in Europe. Because of their great energies, intelligence, and abilities, the fairskinned people of Shem had created enormous wealth and economic progress in France. During that period of explosive growth, the France of that day most resembled the Germany of two centuries later, being very productive, extremely inventive, and causing the land to blossom and give forth its fruits. This progress, and its accompanying wealth, was viewed with great envy, and also fear, by the Canaanites who wielded great power in france. As the black nobility, they had furnished the warriors of Normandy who invaded and conquered the British Isles; they constantly conspired to extend their power, and to continue their longstanding war of extermination against the people of Shem. Because of their great power in the highest offices of Church, State, and the Army, the Canaanites began to set the stage for what became known as the Huguenot Massacres. They were able to gain considerable support for their plan from French nobles who were not themselves Canaanites, but who were alarmed at the economic power gained by the people of Shem, which, as they knew, would soon be transformed into political power. They were also enticed by the promises of gold and property to be gained by robbing and killing the prosperous people of Shem.

Because of their blood lust and their constant desire for human sacrifice, the Canaanites were able to turn the Huguenot Massacres into a great orgy of ritual murder.

Children were seized and thrown into pots to be boiled, or fried in great skillets, while crowds stood hooting and reveling in the entertainment. Families were dragged out into the squares in cities and villages to be murdered one by one. No one was spared the terror of the mobs, whether elderly or invalid.

Their property was then divided up among the eagerly waiting instigators of the killings, who would rush on to find other victims.

The physical act of killing whole families in city after city could not remain a secret, and a current of alarm now swept the nation. Many thousands of the Huguenots were able to flee, leaving their possessions behind them, particularly those in the northern districts of France. They were able to make their way across the borders into the Netherlands, where they found that they were hardly welcome. Most of them embarked for the shores of Ireland, and after remaining there for periods as long as one hundred years, they were able to jet sail for the shores of the New World.

It is hardly surprising to learn that the repressive acts against Huguenots began after Catherine de Medici became Regent on the accession of Charles the Ninth. We have already noted that the de Medicis paid for the formulation of the doctrine of secular humanism, when Cosimo de Medici set up the Accademia in Florence, centering its teachings around the Christian Cabala.

The Encyclopaedia Britannica says of Catherine's rule in France, "She introduced Italian methods of government, alternating between concessions and persecution, both alike devoid of sincerity." Catherine began negotiations with Spain to bolster her planned slaughter of the Huguenots; on the 28th of September 1568, she issued the edict which placed the Huguenots outside the protection of the law, an open invitation for the massacres to begin. At this time, they constituted one-tenth of the population of France. Her son, Charles Ninth, realized that his mother's plans would be a catastrophe for the nation, and he opened negotiations with the Huguenot leaders, hoping to avert the slaughter. Catherine true to her black nobility heritage, plotted the massacre to take place while he had the leaders conveniently assembled. The notorious Massacre of St. Bartholomew's took place on the 24th of August, 1572, during which the Huguenot leader, Coligny, and all of the important Huguenots were killed. The Encyclopaedia Britannica notes,

"This date marks a disastrous epoch in the history of France. The Paris massacre was followed by massacres throughout France. One victim was King Charles himself. Overcome with horror at the atrocities Committed by the tragedy of St. Bartholomew's, he expired."

There is a strong possibility that Catherine, knowing of his unwillingness to proceed with the massacre of the Huguenots, and his plans to make concessions to them, may have poisoned him. This, too, would have been in keeping with her black nobility heritage. Charles' successor, Henry II, also died violently; he was assassinated by the monk Jacques Clement, who believed that he, too, would be unwilling to proceed with the massacres of the Huguenots.

The Edict of Nantes, April 13, 1598, was an attempt to reverse the process. It granted the Huguenots a charter guaranteeing them religious and political freedom, but many officials ignored it, and continued the persecutions. The terrible dragonnades (1663-83) saw many Protestants tortured until they abjured their faith. On the 18th of October 1685, King Louis XIV declared that the Edict of Nantes was revoked. As the Encyclopaedia Britannica comments " ...thus was committed one of the most flagrant political and religious blunders in the history of France, which in the course of a few years lost more than 400,000 of its inhabitants, men who, having to choose between their conscience and their country, endowed the nations which received them with their heroism, their courage, and their ability."

It was the revocation of the Edict of Nantes, more than any other single event in history, which set the United States on its future course to greatness. During the American Revolution, and the writing of the Constitution which followed its victory, it was the Huguenots who predominated in every battle and every deliberation. The fortunes of France, on the other hand, sank into a steady decline, from which it has never recovered. Indeed, this nation has subsequently lurched from one disaster to another, not the least of which was the Napoleonic Wars, whose excesses further bloodied the nation of its bravest and best. E. E. Cummings, the American poet, used to remark of Napoleon, "He chopped six inches off of the height of every Frenchman."

Ever since the St. Bartholomew's Massacre, France has fallen back from its once proud history. This, of course, was a great comfort to its historic rival, England, who not only seized the advantages offered by the French decline, but seems to have engineered quite a few of its subsequent misfortunes.

France's birth rate declined, her command of the seas declined, and her rate of invention declined. Most important, she never again won another war. Despite the great military successes of Napoleon, France lost the Napoleonic Wars at Waterloo; she was defeated by the Germans during the Franco-Prussian War and the successive world wars, her foes being halted and turned back only by the arrival of troops from America, many of them of Huguenot descent.

If God may have visited the Reign of Terror upon the people of France as punishment for the massacres of the Huguenots, it was also made inevitable by their absence. With the sober, restraining influence of the Huguenot people removed from France, the way now lay open for every possible excess of the demon-worshipping Canaanites. Sex orgies, financial scandals, and foreign intrigues became every-day occurrences among the high officials of the black nobility, while the kings of France, seeing no alternative to "going with the flow" let license reign. It was not accidental that France was the only country in Europe to undergo a major revolution at this time. It was the only country in Europe in which the central government had allowed itself to be overcome by the desires of the worst elements in the nation.

Every type of heresy flourished in France. Idleness and the pursuit of vice were foremost in the minds of the people, While the economy was being paralyzed by a plethora of lawsuits, some of them litigated generation after generation, which created unrest throughout the nation. As in the United States today, prejudice and bias dictated every decision in the courts, and this favoritism became one of the principal causes contributing to the outbreak of the Revolution.

The rot was very high on the vine. The king's brother-in-law, the Duc d'Orléans, was called Philippe de Égalité because of his close identification with the new forces of "liberation." The Duc had been persuaded by Mirabeau to amalgamate all the Blue Lodges with the Grand Orient of France; at same time, Mirabeau and his mentor, Moses Mendelssohn, persuaded the Duc to make some risky investments, in which, as they had planned, he lost his fortune. By 1780, he owed 800,000 livres. He was forced to sign over his magnificent home, the Palais Royal, to Canaanite lenders. They hired de Laclos to turn it into one of the world's most elaborate brothels. As his aide, de Laclos brought in from Palermo the notorious "Count" Cagliostro, born Balsamo, who had taken his godmother's name. He was a Grand Master of the Rosicrucian Knights of Malta, which he had joined at the age of twenty-three. He now used the Palais Royal as a headquarters for revolutionary propaganda, printing thousands of the most inflammatory pamphlets, with which he flooded Paris. The downfall of the Duc d'Orleans had been carefully planned. Mirabeau had been an habitue of the salon of Henrietta Herz in Vienna and Paris; here he had come under the influence of Moses Mendelssohn, the founder of Freemasonry. He became the principal tool of Mendelssohn and other conspirators, including the Rothschilds, in precipitating the events of the French Revolution. At this same time, the government of England was falling into the hands of Lord Shelburne, the notorious William Petty. The English Prime Minister, William Pitt, had also been maneuvered into a position where he was overcome by onerous debts; Petty and his closest associates paid Pitt's debts and, in return, dictated his subsequent policy decisions. Lord Shelburne was the chief of the British Intelligence Service; as such, he masterminded the course of the French Revolution from London. One of the most persistent legends has been the myth of the Scarlet Pimpernel, a quixotic British aristocrat who risked his neck many times to snatch French aristocrats from the guillotine. If such a person ever existed, he was greatly outnumbered in France by the number of British agents of Lord Shelburne who were to be found there, promoting the most atrocious acts of the Reign of Terror from behind the scenes, in order to make sure that even if the French nation survived the Revolution, it would never again present a threat to the ambitions of the British Empire. This proved to be the outcome.

Mirabeau later was overcome by the developments of the Revolution; in a moment of remorse, he conspired to save

King Louis from the guillotine. To avoid a public trial, he was promptly poisoned by the conspirators, thus sealing his lips against any future revelation of the identity of the true perpetrators of this horror.

In King Louis' final days of power, measure after measure was enacted which served to further weaken the authority of the Crown and fed the appetite of the mob. For instance, the National Assembly resolved to set an example by suppressing slavery. According to the Encyclopaedia Britannica, the measures which they enacted, forbidding any retaliation against slaves, "set the stage for the terrible negro insurrection in Santo Domingo." In fact, the entire white population was slaughtered, being replaced by a black government which is today the poorest nation in the Western Hemisphere. The Assembly also abolished feudal tenure in France, which violated the rights of certain Princes in Alsatia, which had been guaranteed them by the Treaty of Westphalia. Foreign statesmen saw that France was sinking into anarchy, which gave them free rein to pursue their own policies, without fear of any French intervention. King Louis' Minister of Finance, the Swiss banker Necker, was true to his heritage of revolutionary intrigue. He deliberately pursued policies of inflation which caused terrible economic suffering in France, and further inflamed the populace. He is thought to have inaugurated those policies in obedience to certain Swiss bankers who planned to reap great profits from the approaching French debacle. After all, it was no less than Baron Rothschild who advised those who wished to become wealthy that they should "buy when there is blood in the streets."

On the tenth of October, 1789, Talleyrand proposed the confiscation of all the church lands in France. This was thought to be one-fifth of all French land. This was proposed as an economic measure; the famous assignats were issued against these lands, in the amount of four hundred million livres, which was later increased to one billion eight hundred thousand livres. His work done, Necker now resigned and left France in September of 1790. During the ensuing three years of the Convention, more than seven billion livres were issued. Their value fell to one per cent of their face value.

The inspiration for the French Revolution can be traced directly to the doctrine of secular humanism which had been formulated at the Accademia of the de Medicis in Florence, and which were but a modernized version of the Kabbalah. The placing of "human interests" first in all things created the climate which made possible the guillotining of King Louis XVI; after denying God, it was a simple step to deny the authority of a monarch who ruled by divine right. From the Neoplatonic humanism promulgated by the de Medicis came the cults of the Rosicrucians and Freemasonry. Sir Francis Bacon's dictum that "knowledge is power" threw down the gauntlet to the traditional powers of Church and State, which were then cast aside during the Revolution. The Baconian Doctrine logically developed into the Positivism of Comte, who states that "God is only an abstraction--he does not exist; only humanity is real" The Enlightenment of Descartes, surreptitiously aided by the secret alliance between Voltaire and Frederick the Great, both Freemasons, led France into the excesses of the Revolution.

The immediate plans for the French Revolution had been laid at the international convention of Freemasons at Wilhelmsbad in 1781, a gathering later famed as "the Convent." It was attended by seven brothers from England, including Lord Shelburne, who later directed the progress of the French Revolution from London, Lessing, Mirabeau, Dohm, delegates from the French Illuminati, and Knigge, who represented Weishaupt. "The Convent paved the way for the French Revolution" (A. Cowan, "X-Rays in Freemasonry," pp. 67-68). There were some 2000 lodges in

France in 1789, with over 100,000 adepts. The first lodge in France had been set up by Lord Derwenwater of England, paving the way for the later influence of Lord Shelburne and British Intelligence.

French officials soon realized that the assignats which had been issued against the church lands were not negotiable; they could not be used in real estate transactions, because the church lands might be restored, and they would then be worthless; the populace refused to accept them.

Matters were not improved after the Assembly passed laws of varying severity, imposing penalties for refusing to accept the assignats as payment. The penalties ranged from imprisonment to death. The steadfast refusal of the French peasantry to accept assignats in payment for their grain led to their being killed. These killings then unleashed a nationwide Reign of Terror. Like the earlier Massacres of St. Bartholomew's, these atrocities had been foreseen by certain "legislative" acts. The cahiers des doleances denied clerical taxation and benefits, foreswore all their rights to real estate, the church lands having previously been seized, and denied the church any financial privileges. This was followed on August 4, 1789, by the resolutions of the deputies abolishing all privileges of individuals and social groups, inaugurating the formal "dechristianization" campaign, which lasted from May 1792 to October 1794. On the third of August, 1790, Revolutionary France gave full rights to the Jews; the measure was denied for thirteen successive votes, but the Masons forced it through on the fourteenth attempt.

The Assembly itself was split into two rival groups: the Girondins from Bordeaux, who envisioned a modest type of federated Republic; and the Paris Sections, seated high on the left, and thereby called the Mountain. From that day on, revolutionaries have always chosen the Left as their symbolic place. The Mountain consisted of forty-eight sections of the

Paris Commune, led by Marat, and composed of hooligans and criminals. The entire Assembly of 655 members had among its members 405 Masons.

Marat, whose person came to exemplify the excesses of the Revolution, was born in Switzerland of a Sardinian father and a Swiss mother. During the 1770s, he had traveled in Holland and England. In 1772 he published in England a work called "An Essay on the Human Soul," a Masonic work whose emphasis was on Mysticism. A second book, "The Chains of Slavery," published in 1774, continued his radical philosophy. Like the later revolutionary, Karl Marx, Marat always seemed to find support in England for his work, principally among the Masonic Brethren there. He was awarded a degree in medicine at St. Andrews University, and he opened a practice in Pimlico. In 1777, he returned to France, where he became physician to Comte d'Artois, brother of the king. With a salary equivalent to five thousand dollars a year, he lived well. He even petitioned for a coat of arms of nobility. He began to spend more of his funds on publications, financing a radical newspaper, L'Ami du Peuple. Because of this activity, he was soon placed under surveillance. He then resigned from the service of Artois, fleeing to England, where he remained until 1790. Seeing that the revolutionary climate was now ripe for his work, he then came back to France.

An acquaintance described Marat thus: "Marat had the burning eyes of a hyena, marked by spasmodic convulsions of his features, and a rapid and jerky walk." Another description has come down to us: "His countenance was toadlike in shape, marked by bulging eyes and a flabby mouth, his complexion of a greenish, corpselike hue. Open sores, often running, pitted his terrible countenance. He wore no socks, and his boots were usually filthy." His physician, Dr. Cabanes, said, "Eczema, in one of its more revolting and dolorous manifestations ... A suppurating gutter ran from the scrotum to his peritoneum, maddening him with torment. Headaches, pain and fever tormented his spirit. He endured intolerable pains in his arms and legs." Cabanes concluded that Marat was probably in the last stages of syphilis. He usually wore a red bandana over his greasy hair. During the height of the Revolution, he married Susanne Simone in the Temple of Nature, a Rousseau spectacle before an open window. This was the appearance of the creature who spawned the Reign of Terror.

With the power of the Paris Sections behind him, Marat appointed himself the head of a Committee on Surveillance. He then arrested some four thousand people and the slaughter began. It was a Sunday, September 2, 1792, when the first victims, twenty-four priests, were led into a garden, one by one, and beaten to death. Some twelve hundred souls were killed during that September, more than one hundred and fifty being slaughtered at the Carmelite Convent.

The murderers foreswore the convenience of guns, perhaps because these weapons did not exist at the time of their preceptor, Baal. The killers preferred the greater satisfaction of finishing off their victims with axes, shovels, and knives. A chronicler of the time, Philippe Morice, wrote, "The gutter ran red with the blood of the poor creatures whom they were butchering there in the Abbaye. Their cries were mingled with the yells of their executioners, and the light which I had caught a glimpse of from the rue de la Seine was the light of bonfires which the murderers had lit to illuminate their exploits ..." The prisons at Chatelet and the Conciergerie were simultaneously invaded by two trained bands of assassins, who proceeded to kill two hundred and twenty-five victims at Chatelet and three hundred and twenty-eight at the Conciergerie.

An English observer, Dr. Moore, reported that the massacres were the result of cold-blooded planning by certain politicians. "Cannon were fired repeatedly, as a toxin to arouse the populace to their bloody work. Thirty-three boys between the ages of twelve and fourteen were killed at Bicetre." At Salpetriere, girls only ten years old were put to the sword, according to Mme. Roland, who said, "Women were brutally violated before being torn to pieces by these tigers."

In the provinces, the massacres were carried out by lunatics, who seem to have been specially recruited for this purpose. The most notorious of the mass murderers was one Carrier, who was said to be the subject of frequent fainting fits, falling to the floor, foaming at the mouth, and howling and snapping at everyone like an animal. He had an obsessive desire to torture and kill small children, as did his assistant, the hunchback DuRel, a homicidal maniac who delighted in killing children by repeatedly puncturing their bodies with sharpened sticks. These two madmen herded more than five hundred peasant boys and girls into a field outside of Nantes, where they clubbed them to death, with the aid of misfits like themselves who eagerly joined in the slaughter. Carrier was famed for having invented the infamous Noyades in the Loire. Large rafts of victims were floated onto the river, plugs were then removed, and all on board were drowned. Some six thousand people were killed in this manner. Carrier also observed the rites of what came to be known as "Republican marriages." Men and women were stripped, bound together as couples, and thrown into the river. *On attachait deux a deux les personnes de l'un et l'autre sexe, toutes nues et tournées comme pour s'accoupler.*

Another notorious madman, Lebas at Arras, first executed all the rich who fell into his hands, so that he could seize their wine cellars and their jewels. He then set himself up in a requisitioned mansion which overlooked the town square. When there were no more rich to be had, he began to murder the poor, of whom there were many. He had them beaten to death in the square, while he and his friends looked on from overhead, celebrating with orgiastic frenzies. At Lyons, on December 4, 1792, Fouche ordered some two hundred men tied together and shot down with grapeshot just outside the city walls. Robespierre's agent, Achard, was an invited guest at this entertainment; he reported back to his superior, "What delights you would have tasted could you have seen natural justice wrought on two hundred and nine scoundrels! Oh, what majesty! What a lofty tone! It was thrilling to see all those wretches chew the dust. What a cement this will be for our Republic-Held out of doors in Nature's vault!"

The Place Bellcourt contained some of the most splendid mansions in France. They had been designed by Mansart. Fouche had them blown up, one by one.

A visiting English liberal, Helen Williams, described the guillotining of twenty peasant girls from Poitou after they had been taken from the Conciergerie. Soon afterward, Williams herself was thrown into prison. The Terror was genuine, there was no doubt of that. Nor was there any doubt, as Dr. Moore had observed, that it was being carefully engineered by politicians and financiers who intended to profit by it. Speculators poured in from Switzerland and the Rhineland to profit from the ever-changing regulations issued by the Assembly. Having foreknowledge of these measures by the judicious distribution of bribes, the speculators made enormous profits. The climate of terror was increased by the presence of spies everywhere; private agents working for unseen masters; government informers, spies from every faction, and everywhere the demented tricteuses, clad in rags, who often sat in front of the guillotine, shrieking with joy at every head which rolled into the gutter, and constantly screaming for more and more blood. The massacres were carefully organized by the Revolutionary Committees, whose members were selectively chosen by the Jacobin Clubs. The Jacobins were, one and all, Freemasons. During the Terror, the population of France was 650,000; the National Guard alone had some 125,000 members, and there were six thousand members of the Jacobin Clubs. Una Bush, in her important work, "Secret Societies and the French Revolution," wrote, "The Phrygian cap of the Illuminati became the headgear of the populace during the French Revolution; the half-mystical phantasies of the lodges became the habits of daily life."

Those who were not members of the Masonic lodges had no idea of how to comport themselves, or even how to survive; only the Masons profited by and directed every aspect of the Revolution. At the execution of Louis XVI in 1793, an elderly Mason dipped his hands in the royal blood, saying, "I baptise thee in the name of Liberty and Jacques." This was a reference to the Grand Master, Jacques de Molay, who had been immolated by King Philip the Fair. Revenge was now had. Many of the acts committed during the orgy of terror defy belief. The fate of the Princess de Lamballe, a pleasant, middle-aged aristocrat who had escaped from the city, was typical. Driven by loyalty to her mistress, Marie Antoinette, she returned to Paris to administer to her mistress. The Princess was promptly seized by the mob, publicly disembowelled, and her private parts paraded through the city as trophies of the triumph of the Revolution! After the storming of the Guilerriers, a young apprentice fell into the hands of the mob. A great pan was fetched, and a fire built under it. He was then fried in butter, after which the revolutionaries enjoyed a feast.

The cemeteries of Paris became the scenes of nightly orgies, many of them mystical rites which had not been seen on earth since the destruction of the Temples of Baal. Graves were torn open, and the remains used in fiendish rites. All of this had come about because the people of

France were ignorant of the Curse of Canaan, and the Will of Canaan. These horrors, which were beyond the imagination of any sane person, were perpetrated because of the Satanic nature of the Canaanites, who seized on every opportunity to indulge their passion for human sacrifice and cannibalism.

The ideological basis for these atrocities had been enshrined by the National Assembly on August 26, 1789, which formally adopted the Declaration of the Rights of Man. This led directly to the formation of the Revolutionary Tribunal, established March 10, 1793, which then set up the Committee of Public Safety. The initial committee was composed of nine men; it was later increase to twelve, and was led by Marat. He first used the Committee to destroy his chief opponents in the Assembly, the Girondins. On November 1, 1793, he decapitated twenty-one of them in one day. The Girondins principally represented the region of Bordeaux; a young lady from that district, who was of good family, Charlotte Corday, privately resolved to avenge her friends. Because of the agony of his deteriorating skin, Marat now spent most of his time in a bathtub. Corday accosted him there and stabbed him. She was tried and executed that same day. Marat's funeral was turned into another Babylonian orgy, in which large quantities of incense were burned and symbolic paper pyramids, representing his Masonic affiliation, were seen everywhere.

Marat was succeeded by the two other architects of the Reign of Terror, Danton and Robespierre. They, too, were soon to be destroyed by the monster which they had unleashed upon the nation. A great Festival of Reason was held at the Cathedral of Notre Dame. Mercier's account describes "the infuriated populace dancing before the sanctuary and howling the Carmagnole (the Song of the Revolution). The men wore no breeches (the sans culottes); the necks and breasts of the women were bare. In their wild whirling, they imitated those whirlwinds, the forerunner of tempests, that ravage and destroy all that is in their path. In the darkness of the sacristy, they indulged in the abominable desires that had been kindled in them during the day ... the mob howled for worship of Virtue instead of that Jew slave and his adulterous woman of Galilee, his mother."

Blasphemy was the hallmark of the Revolution, not merely the fury which brought about the slaughter of hundreds of priests, but also the urge to degrade and defame that which was greater than themselves. At the Clootz Convention, a militant atheist, one Hebertist, declared, "A religious man is a depraved beast. He resembles those animals that are kept to be shorn and roasted for the benefit of merchants and butchers."

After the death of Marat, Robespierre achieved his peak of power, being named President of the Convention. To celebrate his elevation, he organized a great celebration, the Festival of the Supreme Being, on June 8, claiming it signified the rebirth of God. In "The Life of Robespierre," G. Renier writes, "On the 28th of July, 1794, Robespierre made a long speech before the Convention ... a philippic against ultraterrorists ... uttering vague general accusations. 'I dare not name them at this moment and in this place. I cannot bring myself to entirely to tear asunder the veil that covers this profound mystery of iniquity. But I can affirm most positively that among the authors of this plot are the agents of that system of corruption and extravagance, the most powerful of all the means invented by foreigners for the undoing of the Republic. I mean the impure apostles of atheism, and the immorality that is at its base.' " Renier comments, "Had he not spoken these words he might still have triumphed!"

Because he had threatened to expose the Illuminists behind the Revolution, Robespierre had doomed himself. At that very moment, his archenemy and deadly rival, Fouche, was passing the Law of 22 Prairial, which provided in Article 16 "no defense for conspirators." At the Assembly of 9 Thermidor, Robespierre was not allowed to speak, or to defend himself against his accusers. Soon afterward, he was arrested at the Hotel du Ville. In the struggle which ensued, he was shot in the jaw. He was dragged away to the Conciergerie, still adorned in his costume for the Festival, a skyblue coat and jonquil breeches. Twenty-two of his supporters were first executed; then Robespierre himself was led to the guillotine. Before throwing him down before the guillotine, the famous executioner, Samson, deliberately ripped the bandage from Robespierre's jaw. Spectators said he screamed like a slaughtered animal before the blade mercifully descended.

The third leader of the Reign of Terror, Danton, also was soon led to the guillotine, and Paris slowly began to return to normal. The inevitable reaction, which was called the White Terror, soon began. It culminated in the famous 18th Brumaire, a date cited with hatred and anger by revolutionaries ever since. On the 18th Brumaire, Napoleon took power, and the Revolution was over.

A further development of the French Revolution was the unleashing on the world of a new formula for mankind's control, the social sciences. This technique was developed by an imprisoned aristocrat, Comte de Saint Simon, during his Imprisonment in the Luxembourg. While awaiting trial, he amused himself by developing his vision of a new social system, one which would be developed purely on scientific principles instead of political realities. From his concept came the entire socialistic system of "social welfare," which proved to be a necessary tool for imposing socialism by the governments of many countries.

The Terror had offered a great opportunity for the Canaanites to indulge their inhuman desires. They now hated Napoleon with all the passion of which they were capable, because he had taken away their delights. After his downfall, they saw to it that he was slowly poisoned to death with administration of arsenic in his food. This was proven one hundred fifty years later by examination of his hair, which showed heavy concentrations of arsenic. The poison had been administered to Napoleon on the island of St. Helena by a trusted agent of the Rothschilds. To further satisfy their lust for revenge, these same conspirators later murdered his young son, the Duke of Reichstadt.

It was the Duke of Brunswick himself (known as "Aaron" in the Illuminati) who delivered the last word on the French Revolution: "A secret sect working within Freemasonry had brought about the French Revolution and would bring about and would be the cause of all future revolutions." Monsignor Dillon, writing in 1885, offered a further comment: "However subversive the doctrines of the Grand Order may have been - and undoubtedly were - it was not Freemasonry itself but Illuminism which organized the movement of which the French Revolution was but the first manifestation."

The great French historian, Hippolyte Taine, wrote: "Liberty, equality, fraternity! Whatever the great words with which the Revolution was ornamented, it was essentially a transference of property."

The successful conclusion of the Napoleonic Wars found the Rothschilds in unchallenged control of that property. They held the Congress of Vienna to celebrate their great victories. Von Gentz, secretary to Prince Metternich, pointed out that there never really was a Congress of Vienna; the Rothschilds merely dictated the signing of the Final Act, in June of 1815, to the four great powers. Von

Gentz comments, "The real purpose of the Congress was to divide among the conquerors the spoils taken from the vanquished."

The Congress of Vienna was formally headed by Lord Castlereagh, Foreign Minister of Great Britain, and his half brother, Lord Charles Stewart, who was serving as Ambassador Plenipotentiary to Vienna. Lord Aberdeen, Lord Cathcart, and Lady Burghe, a niece of the Duke of Wellington, also represented Great Britain. Princess Thurn und Taxis arranged nightly meetings in her drawing room between Talleyrand and the Czar of Russia. During these meetings, Talleyrand routinely betrayed the French people. Nearly all the royalty of Europe was present in Vienna for the Congress. They gathered at the Opera House for a special concert by Beethoven, which he conducted.

Because England was the victorious power, the world supremacy of British naval power was accepted without question by the members of the Congress. An important piece of business was the passage of Acts on March 20 and March 29, 1815, which permanently guaranteed Swiss neutrality. These acts not only ensured that Switzerland would continue to be the nation where the revolutions of the world could be plotted, but also that the ill-gotten gains of those revolutions would be guaranteed safe deposit and insurance against being repossessed by the victims of robberies.

Lord Castlereagh later addressed the House of Commons in this report on the Congress: "The Congress of Vienna was not assembled for the discussion of moral principles, but for great practical purposes, to establish effectual provisions for the general security." One of these provisions was Nathan Mayer Rothschild's setting up a Special German Committee at the Congress to work out a grant of rights to German Jews. This provision was inserted into the final Act, which was then advertised as establishing "equilibrium in Europe," the famed doctrine later known as "the balance of power." In fact, British Intelligence, led by Lord Shelburne, had operated the entire French Revolution from London as a Masonic plot to rid England of its oldest and most historic rival. After 1815, France never again mounted any threat to the British hegemony. It was not a balance of power at all; it was the triumph of the Hegelian system.

The Bourbons had now become a weak and ineffectual ruling family: Lord Castlereagh formally restored them to the throne in the Treaty of Paris, only because they would be an important contributing factor to France's future weakness.

Castlereagh, Marquis of Londonderry, was now considered the most powerful single politician in the world. He was the godson of Lord Camden, who, with Lord Shelburne, had lent large sums to Britain's Prime Minister, William Pitt; thereafter they were able to control him for their own devious purposes. Lord Shelburne, William Petty, was denounced by Edmund Burke as "a Cataline or Borgia in morals," which was undoubtedly true. Henry Kissinger openly modeled his own diplomatic techniques on those of Lord Castlereagh. In his book "A World Restored," which he dedicated to McGeorge Bundy (of the Brotherhood of Death), Kissinger wrote, "There are two ways of constructing an international order; by will or by renunciation; by conquest or by legitimacy." The "world restored" to which Kissinger dedicated his career was, of course the continuation of the Rothschild World Order which had been established at the Congress of Vienna. His idol, Lord Castlereagh, apparently had some second thoughts about the consequences of his diplomacy. He returned to London from Vienna believing that he had achieved a great personal triumph both for himself and for his country. On later examining the actual results of the

Congress of Vienna, he belatedly realized that he had
delivered the entire continent of Europe into the hands of
the Rothschilds. On the 12th of August, 1822, he had an
emotional audience with King George IV, informing him,
"Sire, it is necessary to say goodbye to Europe." He then
went home and cut his throat, slashing his artery with a
small penknife.

This story has even more interesting significance today. A
principal partner of the Rothschilds in their worldwide
wheeling and dealing is the financier, Sir James Goldsmith.
He is married to the daughter of the present Marquis of
Londonderry, the descendant of Lord Castlereagh. This is
Goldsmith's third marriage. He first married Isabel Patino,
heiress to the great tin fortune, when she was only twenty
years old. She died mysteriously. Goldsmith then married
the niece of the Comte de Paris, the Bourbon Pretender to
the Throne of France. He later married the descendant of
Lord Castlereagh.

In the forty years since Mayer Amschel persuaded the
Elector of Hesse to let him invest his fortune (the money
paid him by King George III for the Hessian mercenaries
who were intended to crush the American revolutionaries
and maintain control over the American colonies), the
Rothschilds had come a long way. They had parlayed the
Elector's money into a worldwide fortune of their own.
Until that stroke of good luck, they had been by no means
the most important family in the Frankfurt moneylending
hierarchy. There had been a considerable Jewish contingent
in Frankfurt-on-Main since 625 A.D. In 1265, a covenant
was signed which allowed them to remain. However, in
1614, the Judengasse was sacked. Some 1390 Jews were
living there at that time. In 1615, the gates of the Judengasse
had been posted with the warning, "Under the Roman
Imperial Majesty and the Holy Roman Empire's Protection."
In 1715, there were some 415 families in the Judengasse, of

whom 109 were moneylenders; there were also 106 hardware dealers; the remaining families were engaged in second hand clothing or fruit businesses. Of the twelve wealthiest families there in 1715, the Speyers were the richest, having a fortune of 604,000 florins; then came the Goldschmidts, the Wertheimers, the Haas family, etc. No. four the list were the Rothschilds, with 109,375 Florins. Exactly one hundred years later, the Rothschilds were the masters of Europe, dictating the terms at the Congress of Vienna. They then requested a noble coat of arms with a royal coronet, featuring the Leopard of England and the Lion of Hesse. This request was denied in 1817, but after a tremendous financial pressure was brought to bear on the government, it was finally granted in 1822. The following year, the Rothschilds took over all of the financial operations of the worldwide Catholic Church. Of the head of the family, Sir Nathan Mayer Rothschild, the Dictionary of National Biography noted: "The influence of his firm and himself compared with that of the-Bank of England; after the death of Sir Moses Montefiore Rothschild may almost be said to be the generally authorized, leader of the Jews of the world."

The success of the French Revolution, which was really a coup d'etat, was due to the reorganization of the Freemasons in France. The original French Lodge had only three degrees; the 33 degrees of the Ancient and Accepted Scottish Rite, the revolutionary degrees, were then introduced; this guaranteed the success of the conspiracy. After the Revolution, the Supreme Council of the Order generally met in Paris. The Jewish Lodge of Frankfurt, *L'Aurore Naissante*, the Rising Dawn, had been authorized by the Grand Lodge of Paris in 1808. The Scottish Rite always dates its official documents in the Hebrew months. On September 18, 1885, the Bulletin of the Grand Orient of France openly called for the destruction of the Catholic Church. In 1886, the International Congress of the Grand

Orient continued the call to arms with the battlecry "War on God!" The political battleground of Freemasonry was then concentrated in Italy, hence the call for war against the Catholic Church. There was no subsequent Italian Revolution, as had occurred in other countries, notably France, because the area was too diffuse; the only central enemy in Italy was the power of the Church. The Italian "liberators," Mazzini and Garibaldi, were the leading Masons in the Lodges. Here again, they were merely carrying out the instructions of British Intelligence. It was no less a personage than Lord Sackville who had introduced Freemasonry into Italy, in 1733. The British influence was dominant when Lord Palmerston, with the assistance of Cavour, guided the "liberators" in their capture of Rome and their placing the Pope under arrest.

The ascension to power in France of Louis Napoleon, later known as Napoleon III, was a further triumph of the Canaanite conspirators. Louis Napoleon had been born to Queen Hortense in 1808. Her residence in Paris was also the headquarters of the House of Rothschild; it later became the private residence of James de Rothschild; the building was torn down in 1968.

General Spiridovich, an authority on the period, states unequivocally that it was common knowledge that Napoleon III was a Rothschild. Napoleon III was also a well known member of the Carbonari, a group of Italian noblemen who were the leaders of the Guelphs, or black nobility, in Europe. The Alta Vendita was the Supreme Director of the Carbonari, whose orders had to be obeyed on pain of death. When Louis Napoleon was proclaimed Emperor in 1851, the Carbonari moved quickly to consolidate their gains in Italy. An international Masonic group led by Lord Palmerston, and which also included Kossuth, Lemmi and others, had met in London in 1860 to plan their strategy for seizing absolute control in Italy. When Garibaldi occupied Naples, a group of English Masons was on hand to aid him.

Despite his Canaanite origins, Napoleon III deeply offended the world order when he organized his coup d'etat in December, 1851 and seized power in France. To atone for his breach of discipline, his son, the Prince Imperial, was later murdered. No less a person than Gambetta, former premier, whose secretary was Adolphe Cremieux founder of the Alliance Israelite Universelle, said, "The providential death of the Duke of Reichstadt [the son of Napoleon I] has been the penalty for Brumaire [when Napoleon I seized power]. I swear to you that December 1851, [Napoleon III's coup d'etat] will be punished also." In 1879, the Prince, then twenty-three years old, joined a British expedition against the Zulus, because he had been proscribed in France. He developed a mysterious fever on the boat to Africa, but recovered. He was then assigned an aide, Lt.--------, a Freemason, who later persuaded him to go eleven miles past the bounds of prescribed reconnaissance, where they set up camp. When the Prince mounted his horse (during an attack), the strap broke; it had been cut in half, although it was a new leather strap. He died from seventeen javelin thrusts from the Zulus. Adrien Paillaud recounts this story in "La Mort du Prince Imperial," Paris, 1891. Paillaud wrote, "At the time of the Prince's departure from France for England, a Freemason Republican Deputy said, 'You will never see him again [the prince]. I don't pretend to be a prophet, but, believe me, the Prince will be killed in Zululand.' The Deputy was a close friend of Gambetta. On May 19, 1879, a radical paper announced that the Prince had been killed. A Masonic Lodge at the Cape had sent word to Paris; however, on that day the Zulus had failed to appear. On a later expedition, the Prince was killed, on June 1. This remarkable circumstance was noted in a highly successful play, 'Thy Wife of Claudius,' by Alexander Dumas in Paris. The hero' Daniel says, 'The Diaspora has not scattered us;

on the contrary, it has extended us in all directions. In consequence, we enmesh the whole world in a net, so to speak.'"

CHAPTER 6

THE AMERICAN REVOLUTION

The history of the United States properly begins with its "discovery" by Columbus in 1492, if we ignore the numerous voyages which had been made to this land by adventurers for some one thousand years. King Henry VII granted Letters Patent to John Cabot (a Genoese named Giovanni Caboto) on March 5, 1646, and to his three sons, Lewis, Sebastian, and Santius. The Cabots were given the right to possess all the "towns, cities, castles, and isles" which they might discover. Cabot landed at Labrador May 2, 1647. His descendants became important leaders in New England.

The first body of laws for the new land, The Mayflower Compact, had been signed by the passengers on the Maynower on November 11, 1620, as follows: "In the Name of God, Amen. We, whose names are underwritten, the Loyal Subjects of our dread Soverign, Lord King 'limes, by the Grace of God, of Great Britain, France, and Ireland, King, Defender of the Faith, &c.

Having undertaken for the Glory of God, and Advancement of the Christian faith, and the Honour of our King and Country, a Voyage to plant the first colony in the northern Parts of Virginia; Do by these Presents, solemnly and mutually in the Presence of God and one another, covenant and combine ourselves into a civil Body Politick, for our better Ordering and Preservation, and Furtherance of the Ends aforesaid; And by Virtue hereof do enact, constitute, and frame, such just and equal, Acts, Ordinances, Acts, Constitution, and Offices, from time to time, as shall be thought most meet and convenient for the general Good of the Colony; unto which we promise all due Submission and Obedience. In WITNESS whereof we have hereunto subscribed our names at Cape Cod the 11th of November, in the Reign of our Sovereign Lord King James of England, France, and Ireland, the eighteenth and of Scotland the fifty-fourth.

Anno Domini 1620. Signed, William Mullins and others."

11 John Dee, *General and rare memorials*, 1577, title-page

Thus, the first legal agreement or constitution in the New World was followed in 1661 by a Declaration of Liberties, dated June 10, 1661, in General Court, which included: "2. The Gouvernor & Company are, by the pattent, a body politicke, in fact and name. 3. This body politicke is vested with power to make freemen ... " This Declaration is an important document in the history of this nation, because It announced that we now possessed the power of sovereignty, that is, the right to make freemen. On October 2, 1678, the colonists boldly announced that "the laws of England are bounded within the fower seas, and doe not reach America."

Of the colonies, Virginia was said by the scholar J. R. Pole to be the most like England. This was probably because it was the most Masonic of the colonies. It was ruled from London by the Lords of Trade, formerly known as the Board of Trade, by the London Company and the Virginia Company, and the law by which they ruled was Admiralty Law. (p. 59, "Royal Government in America," Leonard Woods Labaree, Yale, 1930.) In 1723, LL Gov. Drysdale of Virginia enacted a 40 shillings tax on each slave brought into the province. A protest against this tax immediately arose from the principal English slave dealers, The Royal Africa Company, consisting of "divers merchants trading in Africa," the South Nun Company, and the Liverpool Corp. "the Mayor, Aldermen, and Merchants of the ancient and loyal Corporation of Liverpool." English common law ruled in the courts; it omitted all evidence from the record.

It was this free ranging spirit of the colonists, many of them originating as Huguenot refugees from France, which early on gave rise to fears in London that the New Land might still prove to be a tractable province of the British power. From the outset, many of the settlers in America considered themselves to be independent in reality, if not politically. London was a faroff presence, and in most cases, the settlers were left to their own devices. The people of

Shem had now found their Promised Land, where they could build the type of civilization they requried, and where they could raise their families, free at last from the dread Canaanites and their addiction to human sacrifice and cannibalism.

However, the Canaanites had not lost sight of their prey, far off though they might be. They had the formula for controlling any people, the subversive organization of the Masonic Order of Canaanites. The Encyclopaedia Judaica notes that Moses M. Hays was appointed inspector general of North American Masonry in 1768. Benjamin Franklin had been Grand Master in Philadelphia since 1731. Hays soon brought the Scottish Rite into the United States, introducing it at the Newport Lodge in 1780. The Franklin Masonic organization had been authorized by Lafayette, who later backed Benito Juarez in the Mexican Revolution. Until the onset of the Scottish Rite, a rival organization set up by the Duc d'Orleans, the Swiss bankers, and British Intelligence, Franklin had been the chief Masonic organizer in the colonies. By 1785, fifteen lodges of the Illuminati had been set up in America. They were led by a group of New Yorkers, who included Clinton Roosevelt, Charles Dana, Governor DeWitt Clinton, and Horace Greeley. Roosevelt later wrote an influential book, "The Science of Government as Founded on Natural Causes," which became the textbook for the implementation of Illuminati programs in America.

The American Revolution differed substantially from the revolutions in France, Spain, and Russia. It was not a local uprising against oppressive masters. Rather, it was the takeover of property by those who had worked to develop it, and who felt they owed nothing to the absentee landlords, the British Crown. The Revolution was largely free from the mobs, Reigns of Terror, or the atrocities usually associated with Canaanite Masonic controlled uprisings. Nevertheless, the same British master of espionage, Lord Shelburne, who had run the French Revolution from London, now contrived to place many of his agents in crucial positions among the American revolutionists. These agents appeared on the seen during critical times and were presented as able and daring patriots. Just as the Swiss bankers had influenced the French Court by placing their agent, the financier Necker, in a key position to precipitate an economic depression, so Lord Shelburne maintained a decisive role in the manipulation of the American forces during the Revolution. The most famous of these was Benedict Arnold, whose name remains synonymous with treason. Arnold was merely the most visible officer in a much larger network which had been set in place by the Mallet-Prevost family, the single most important name in Swiss espionage. Augustine Prevost became Grand Steward of the Lodge of Perfection which was set up in Albany in 1768. Solomon Bush became Masonic deputy inspector general for Pennsylvania in 1781, and Abraham Forst of Philadelphia was named deputy inspector general for Virginia in 1781. On October 5, 1785, the Masonic records note that "Brother Augustine Prevost, a Prince of the Royal Secret, was a visitor." In retrospect, we find that Masonic agents moved freely back and forth between the British zones and the areas controlled by the Americans throughout the Revolution. During one battle, an English regiment lost its Masonic valuables. These were promptly returned by General George Washington under a flag of truce, and escorted by a guard of honor. After the battle of Yorktown in 1781, a great banquet was given at which British, French, German, and American Masons all sat down and celebrated together.

The Prevost family in Geneva, Switzerland, was one of the most powerful members of the ruling Council of 200. The aforementioned General Augustine Prevost, Prince of the Royal Secret, commanded British forces in North America throughout the Revolution; his brother, Mark

Prevost, was his second in command. They wrote the orders for Major Andre, who "ran" the Benedict Arnold treason operation. Being caught in the act, Andre, the son of an influential Swiss merchant banker, could not be saved. He was hanged by the Americans who had captured him. America's most famous traitor, Benedict Arnold, went the postwar years comfortably in England. General Augustine Prevost's son, Sir George Prevost, was commander of the British forces in North America during the War of 1812.

At the conclusion of the Revolutionary War, most Americans believed that they had won their independence from Great Britain. They were now free to perfect an instrument of government which would guarantee them and their posterity independence in perpetuity. The result of the convention of the people of Shem was the Constitution of the United States, a remarkably simple but incredibly comprehensive document. It guaranteed them their independence primarily because it deliberately excluded the Canaanites from participation in the government. It was a genuinely racial document, written by and for the fair-skinned people of Shem. Its provisions were explicitly drawn to be applicable to no one else. Because it was written as a Shemitic document, which had been drafted to provide for the security of the Shemitic people, any future alteration or dilution of this "original intent" of the Constitution would be an anti-Shemitic act. The primary purpose of the Constitution of the United States was to protect the free citizens from any intrusion by an arbitrary, tyrannical, Canaanite government agency. The subsequent gradual erosion of these provisions of the Constitution and its subtle alteration to permit and encourage attacks on the free citizens of the United States by a demoniacal Canaanite centralized government, constitutes a most grievous racial and religious assault against the people of Shem. Thus, all subsequent alterations of this Constitution, which were enacted with this purpose in mind, form an unwarranted and flagrant attack inspired by the desire to commit racial and religious persecution, with the ultimate purpose of the total genocide of the people of Shem.

During the ensuing two hundred years, all of the arguments for and against the Constitution, as presented in our courts of law, and most particularly, in the Supreme Court of the United States, have been worthless, because they have refused to mention the explicit purpose of the Constitution, the protection of the people of Shem from racial and religious persecution. Many scholars freely admit that the Constitution was written to limit the powers of government, and to guarantee freedoms to the people, but because these discussions never mention just who these "people" are, the discussions never approach reality. Certainly the Constitution cites certain basic "rights," but these rights apply only to the people of Shem. It is impossible to cite the Constitution in discussing the rights of Papuans or Slavs, because this document was never intended for such applications. What the Canaanites have succeeded in doing is to warp or stretch the Constitution of the United States until its original intent, which was explicitly expressed in its language, has now been expanded to encompass all the peoples of the world; our present-day Constitution is nothing more nor less than a Charter of the United Nations, and this is precisely how the American judges now "interpret" the Constitution. Each such interpretation is not only an act of high treason, but it is also an act of aggression against the people of Shem. The state Constitutions were also explicit in their dedication to the Christian religion of the people of Shem. The Constitution of North Carolina, 1776, required, "That no person who shall deny the Being of God or the truth of the Protestant religion ... shall be capable of holding any office or place of trust for profit." This provision remained in force until 1830. The Constitution of Delaware, 1776, required that "Every officeholder had to declare faith in Jesus Christ."

The ratification of the Constitution of the United States was soon followed by the first in a long series of attempts to subvert it. This was the Edwardean Conspiracy, headed by Timothy Dwight, president of Yale. The conspirators were Calvinist clergymen and professors, that is to say, Cromwellians, akin to those who had committed regicide in England and beheaded King Charles I. They now proposed to make short shrift of the new Republic. They were aided by venal politicians, whom they easily controlled through bribery and blackmail. This plot had as its goal the nullification of the First Amendment. By bribery and intrigue, they planned to establish the Calvinist church as the officially authorized, and state subsidized, religion in each state. We have previously pointed out that the founder of this religion, Cauin, or Cohen, had set up a theological autocracy in Switzerland which promptly killed or imprisoned anyone who dared to criticize its acts of oppression. Cauin had then exported this diabolical "religion" to England, where its excesses devastated the entire country. The Edwardean Conspiracy was exposed by an Anglican clergyman, Rev. John Cosens Ogden, who published in Philadelphia in 1799 the results of his findings, "A View of the New England Illuminati, who are indefatigably engaged in destroying the Religion and Government of the United States." Although this book first appeared in 1799, it could be republished today with virtually the same text. It would only need to be updated by including the names of the current conspirators. We know the name of Timothy Dwight as one of the three organizers of the Russell Trust at Yale, also known as Skull and Bones, or the Brotherhood of Death. The same small band of conspirators has figured in every plot to destroy the American Republic.

The exposure of this conspiracy did not deter the plotters, who soon followed it with another, the Essex Junto of 1804-1808. The principal conspirators were born in or near Essex County, Massachusetts, hence the name of the plot. They worked closely with agents of British Intelligence in Boston to bring about the secession of the New England states from the United States. These Judases were no haggard, bomb-carrying revolutionaries; they were from the leading merchant and banking families of New England. Their leader was Massachusetts Senator George Cabot, a direct descendant of the Genoese Cabot who had been commissioned by King Henry VII, and who had landed in Labrador almost two centuries earlier; other conspirators were Judge John Lowell, ancestor of the Bundy family of the Ford Foundation and other leading agencies; the Higginsons, Pickerings, Parsons, and Judge Tapping Reeve, of Litchfield, Connecticut, who happened to be Aaron Burr's brother-in-law. The conspiracy had been fueled by the efforts of a leading British Intelligence operative, Sir John Robison, who worked closely with the Aaron Burr network. After President Thomas Jefferson was informed of the details of the Essex Junto, the malefactors reluctantly abandoned their dream of an early breakup of the Union, and then dedicated themselves to a longer-range strategy, which culminated in the Civil War.

The British Secret Intelligence Service had been funded by Lord Shelburne to promote the interests of the East India Company, the Bank of England, of which it became the primary intelligence network, the banking families Hope and Baring, and their Swiss allies, the bankers Prevost and de Neuflize. Their most able supporters in the United States were John Jacob Astor and Aaron Burr. Astor was treasurer of the Grand Lodge of New York from 1798-1800. In 1800, he was given free entry into all ports of the world which the East India Company had brought under their control. This gave him a tremendous financial advantage over his competitors. In return for this favorable treatment, he provided the financial backing for the plot to replace

President Thomas Jefferson with Aaron Burr, after Jefferson had exposed the plot of the Essex Junto.

Throughout the Revolutionary War, Burr had worked as a double agent, reporting daily to British forces from West Point. Burr later became attorney for the Astor interests, drawing up their contracts and doing commercial work for the East India Company. He routinely fixed elections in the New York area through his connections with the Masonic lodges. He had founded the Society of St. Tammany in New York City in 1789. It was set up symbolically with thirteen tribes, each of whom had a Grand Sachem at its head; the entire network was supervised by one Grand Sachem at the headquarters. This became the famous --or infamous-- Tammany Hall, which controlled the political structure of New York City for many years, rife with corruption and favoritism. It was never anything but a subsidiary of the Masonic lodges, of whom it was organized in open imitation.

The head of the Masons in New York in 1783 had been rand Master William Walter, a British Army general. With the withdrawal of the British troops, he turned his leadership over to Robert Livingston, whose family connections included the Lees of Virginia and the Shippens of Philadelphia (who were prominent in the Benedict Arnold scandal; Arnold had married Peggy Shippen). Robert Livingston was installed as Grand Master of the New York Lodge in 1884; his brother Edward was Mayor of New York. With these powerful allies supporting him from behind the scenes, Burr was able to conclude many successful financial deals. He easily obtained a charter for the Manhattan Company, with his registered purpose a plan to provide water for the city. No mains were ever built. Instead, he used the charter to start a bank, the Manhattan Company. This was later taken over by the investment firm of Kuhn, Loeb, Co., New York representatives of the

Rothschilds. Today, it is the Chase Manhattan Bank, flagship of the Rockefeller fortune.

Burr became Vice President in 1801, under Thomas Jefferson, who was President. Burr succeeded in persuading President Jefferson to appoint the Swiss banker, Albert Gallatin as Secretary of the Treasury. Gallatin's family were prominent members of the Ruling Council of 200; his cousin was none other than the notorious Jacque Necker, whose financial policies had precipitated the French Revolution. Burr and Galatin now set about to implement policies which would wreck the young Republic. They distributed bribes of gold along the frontier to Indians and renegades, so that they would murder the settlers; Gallatin then deliberately provoked the Whiskey Rebellion, the first insurrection against the government.

On July 11, 1804, Burr shot Andrew Hamilton at Weehawken, New Jersey. He then had to flee from New York. John Jacob Astor gave him $40,000 to help him on his way, and later added another $70,000; these were enormous sums at that time. Burr fled to Philadelphia, where he conferred with Colonel Charles Williamson of British Intelligence. Two towns in New York, Williamson and East Williamson, are named after this British agent. This conference resulted in a letter from British Ambassador Anthony Merry to the London office: "I have just received an offer from Mr. Burr, the actual Vice President of the United States, to lend his assistance to His Majesty's Government in any matter in which they may think fit to employ him, particularly in endeavouring to effect a separation of the western part of the United States from that which lies between the Atlantic and the mountains, in its whole extent. His proposition on this subject will be fully detailed to your lordship by Col. Williamson, who has been the bearer of them to me, and who will embark for England in a few days." This amazing document was unearthed many years later by the historian Henry Adams. It is one of the most startling evidences of high treason by an elected official of the United States which has ever surfaced in any record. It was written on August 4, one month after the killing of Alexander Hamilton.

The British plan for setting up a separate western nation in competition with the United States received a fatal setback when Napoleon sold the Louisiana Territory to the United States.

Nevertheless, the plan was further pursued by Edward Livingston, who had been given $21,000 by John Jacob Astor to go to Louisiana, where he became Grand Master of the Louisiana Lodge. Burr was later tried for treason in Richmond, Virginia. His attorney was Edmund Randolph, former Grand Master of Virginia; the case was heard by Chief Justice John Marshall, then Grand Master of Virginia. Although overwhelming evidence of Burr's guilt was presented, he was acquitted by Justice Marshall. It was a Masonic field day. Burr then traveled to London, where he informed customs officials, "The reasons for my visit are known to Lord Melville [Henry Dundas, chief of special operations, British Intelligence Service] and Prime Minister Canning." Burr then became an opium addict, enjoying the pleasures of the pipe with such luminaries as Jeremy Bentham and the Jardine family.

Burr's accomplice, Edward Livingston, was later installed as Secretary of State by President Andrew Jackson; soon afterward, Livingston was formally installed as Grand High Priest of the Masons of the United States, which prompted ex-President John Quincy Adams to address to him his famous "Letters on the subject of Masonry." These Letters noted that "Masonic oaths of secrecy made it impossible for anyone to hold an office of public trust."

Lord Shelburne and the agents of British Secret Intelligence service continued their plots against the Republic of the United States, aided by those traitors most aptly described In Disraeli's term, "the determined men of Masonry," men whose sale loyalty was to the cause of restoring the Temple of Solomon, and the placing of the wealth of the entire world therein. Their dedication to secrecy received a considerable setback when one of their members, a Captain William Morgan defected and published a book describing some of their secret rituals. They immediately murdered him. The case caused a nationwide sensation. An Anti-Masonic Party was formed, which for some years was headed by a Congressman from Pennsylvania, Thaddeus Stevens, who later played an important role as head of the Radical Republicans in Congress after the Civil War. At the national convention of the AntiMasonic Party in 1832, Stevens delivered the principal address. He informed the assembled delegates that Masons held most of the important political posts in the United States through intrigue. He denounced the Masonic Order as "a secret, oath-bound murderous institution that endangers the continuance of Republican government." Stevens later sponsored legislation in the Pennsylvania legislature, a Resolution of Inquiry, to investigate the desirability of making membership in the Order a cause for peremptory challenge in court, when one and not both principals in a suit were Masons. He would have excluded all Masons from the jury in criminal trials where the defendant was a Mason, and would have made it unlawful for a judge belonging to the Order to sit in a trial where a Mason was involved. The resolution was barely defeated. Stevens then sponsored a resolution demanding that Masonry be suppressed, and secured a legal inquiry into the evils of the Order. He spoke in Hagerstown, Maryland, on the propostition that "Wherever the genius of liberty has set a people free, the first object of their solicitude should be the destruction of Free Masonry." He succeeded in electing an

Anti-Masonic Governor of Pennsylvania, but after this victory, the vigor of his Anti-Masonic crusade waned, and he gradually abandoned it.

The great problem of any public opponent of Freemasonry, such as Thaddeus Stevens, was the great secrecy of the Order, with death penalties invoked for any members who violated its secret agenda or its international loyalties. From the year 1776, Freemasonry has been an omnipresent international government operating treasonably from within the United States, and it has exercised those powers ever since. Because of its secrecy, an opponent has insuperable difficulties in presenting to the people any detailed information about its conspiratorial activities. Since the murder of Captain William Morgan, no American Mason has dared to expose its stealthy operations. The present writer had for some thirty years focused on the conspiratorial activities of the leading international bankers, without realizing that governing their every action was their primary involvement with and commitment to Freemasonry. Only the discovery of the Curse of Canaan, and the subsequent Will of Canaan, forced this writer to the reluctant conclusion that behind every financial conspiracy was the demonic attachment to a Satanic cult, which manifested itself through the operations of Freemasonry.

The emblems of this cult are boldly emblazoned on the Great Seal of the United States and on our Federal Reserve notes (unpaid debts of the American people). The words "Annuit Coeptis" announce the birth of "Novus Ordo Seclorum," the New Order. The Canaanites have even appropriated the Great Pyramid of Gizeh, built by Shem, as their emblem. However, to demonstrate that they have not yet put into operation the final phases of their conspiracy, they show the top of the pyramid missing, indicating that "the lost word" of Freemasonry is still absent. The "eye" represents the Great Architect of the Universe, a cabbalist concept; it is enclosed in a triangle, which is the symbol of magic. The thirteen steps refer to Satan, Belial, and rebellion, which cabbalistic gematria assign to the thirteen colonies, thirteen stripes, thirteen olive leaves, thirteen arrows on the seal, and the thirteen letters of "E Pluribus Unum," all of which emphasize the importance of the number thirteen in any enterprise which is controlled by Freemasonry. It reminds them of their war against Christ and his Twelve Disciples. The eagle is represented as the symbol of Rome, the historic enemy of the Canaanites, whom they can never forget, the adversary who razed their capital, Carthage, and who sought to control their bestiality through the administration of laws (the fasces). Consequently, all Freemasons must be vigorously anti-Fascist, that is, they must place themselves against the rule of law. The eagle has nine tail feathers, representing the Inner Circle of Nine in the Illuminati, and also the number of degrees in the York Rite; the thirteen stars represent the Seal of Solomon.

The Great Seal, which is replete with these symbols of Freemasonry, was designed by Benjamin Franklin, Thomas Jefferson, Churchill, and Houston, all of whom were Freemasons. The eagle's right-wing has thirty-two feathers, the number of the ordinary degrees in the Scottish Rite; the left wing has thirty-three, the additional feather symbolizing the 33rd degree, which is conferred for outstanding service to Masonry.

To detail all of the Masonic emblems with which the Great Seal is rife would require more space than we need to give; these esoteric hidden meanings show that the combined number of feathers in the two wings of the eagle is sixty-five; in gematria, this is the value of the Hebrew phrase "yam yawchod," "together in unity," which is cited in Psalm 133:1. "Behold, how good and pleasant it is when brothers dwell together in unity!" The five-pointed stars represent the Masonic Blazing Star and the five points of fellowship. The All Seeing Eye has a cabbalistic value of seventy plus three plus two hundred, the value of the phrase "eben mosu habonim," "the stone which the builders refused," which is familiar to all Royal Arch Masons; it also represents the value of Hiram Abiff, the architect of King Solomon's Temple.

CHAPTER 7

THE CIVIL WAR

The Civil War was the most tragic blood-letting of the people of Shem in recorded history. This people, religious refugees from Canaanite oppressors and massacres in Europe, succeeded in establishing in the United States the most productive society in the world. Their Constitution had unleashed the great talents of this people to do God's work on this earth. Of course, Satan's people, the Canaanites, were livid with hatred and envy. If there is one passion which America has always excited in the world, it is the passion of envy. The United States was the most admired nation in the world, because its Constitution guaranteed to its legal citizens the unfettered right of personal liberty, something which no other nation could offer to its people. In the States of the South, the people of Shem had carved from the wilderness productive plantations and impressive manor houses, built in the tradition of Greek Neo-Classicism, and expressing their conviction that this was the only way that they wished to live on this earth. Like the ancient Greeks, the people of Shem had slaves to attend to their daily needs, the descendants of Canaan, on whom the Curse of Canaan had been pronounced, and which committed them to that status.

Despite the efforts of the people of Shem to maintain their slaves in a healthy and comfortable environment (from an economic standpoint alone, this was an absolute requirement, because the bulk of their operating capital was invested in them), the existence of these slaves became their

Achilles heel, which the Canaanites cleverly used as the weapon with which to mount an attack against them. There were many contemporaneous records attesting to the kindly treatment of the slaves, such as the observations of Samuel Phillips Day, special correspondent for the London Morning Herald, who wrote, "On Sunday, June 8, 1861, in Asheville, Kentucky, I took a drive with some friends. Judge of my surprise, reader, when I found almost the entire Negro population abroad; some parading thoroughfares, and others riding about in carriages! They were dressed so showily and so finely, and appeared so happy and contented, that I was virtually forced to exclaim, 'Surely these people are not slaves!' The response was, 'Certainly they are.' Some of the women wore lace shawls and gold watches and looked (only for their colour) like London duchesses going to a ball. The men too were well attired. I reflected for a moment on the condition of British laborers and London needlewomen ... the contrast was too painful to dwell upon ... The thought flashed across my mind that there was nothing so very wicked in slavery after all --that it possessed a bright side as well as a dark side."

Samuel Phillips Day's comments were well-taken; it is doubtful if any Southern plantation owner would have treated his slaves as badly as the average British workingman was treated by his brutal black nobility landowners and factory operators. It was no accident that world Communism, Fabianism, and other desperate remedies were born, not in the slave quarters of the South, but in the working class districts of London and Manchester. However, the daily life of the slaves in the South, as observed by many travelers, was obscured for all time by the relentless promotion of a single book, Harriet Beecher Stowe's "Uncle Tom's Cabin." Even today, any black who dares to say that perhaps we are not as badly off as our brethren in the jungles of Africa is hooted down as an "Uncle Tom." Only warfare to the death is recommended by the militant Masonic activists; propaganda, invasion, and civil war - these are the only accepted remedies for the "injustices" visited upon the blacks. It was no accident that Harriet Beecher Stowe's book became the greatest best seller of its time - it was tirelessly promoted throughout the entire nation, in the most successful book promotion campaign in our history. The force which promoted "Uncle Tom's Cabin" was the same force which, as early as 1799, sought the dissolution of our Constitutional Republic, which had continued its efforts in the Essex Junto, and which found its final fruition in the Civil War.

Despite repeated provocations from the Canaanites in the North, the Southern States proved remarkably tractable, freely making concessions to demands which were intended only to force them into war. The Missouri Compromise, written in 1820, was accepted even though it prohibited slavery in the new state. It did restrict voting privileges to "free white male citizens," thus excluding women, slaves, and Indians from exercising the ballot. In 1849, the people of California adopted a constitution which prohibited slavery. The Compromise of 1850 provided that the prohibition of slavery should be left up to the individual States, thus thwarting the Canaanites in their attempts to make this problem an excuse for federal intervention and a cause of war between the States.

It is a matter of historical record that the Civil War was precipitated by the action against Fort Sumter in South Carolina, across the bay from Charleston. This opening of hostilities can be traced directly to the power of the Scottish Rite in Charleston, which is known officially as "the Mother Lodge of the World." It was founded by Moses Lindo as the King Solomon Lodge. Lindo had a monopoly on the indigo trade, a much-needed dye similar to the "phoenicia" or purple dye which had been the principal monopoly of his Canaanite ancestors, and who changed their name from

"Canaanite" to "Phoenicians" because of this monopoly. According to the Encyclopaedia Judaica, other founders of the King Solomon Lodge included Isaac and Abraham da Costa (da Costa was one of the leading names among the Maranos). In 1793, the cornerstone of a new synagogue, Beth Elohim, was laid in Charleston according to the Rite of Freemasons. Charleston is also known as the cradle of Reform Judaism in America (we have previously noted that this movement originated in Frankfort-on-Main with the Rothschilds, and that it has culminated in the successes of World Zionism). The Charleston cemetery dates from 1764.

Other organizers of the Charleston Lodge included Stephen Morin, 25th degree, Inspector for North America, who had been initiated into the Rite of Perfection in Paris in 1761; Henry A. Francken, deputy inspector general for North America, 25th degree, initiated in Jamaica in 1762; Augustine Prevost (later commander of British forces in North America during the Revolutionary War), 25th degree, initiated in Jamaica in 1774; Moses Michael Hays, 25th degree, initiated in Boston in 1767 as deputy inspector general for North America; John Mitchell, 25th degree, initiated in Charleston, named deputy for South Carolina; B. Spitzer, deputy for Georgia; Moses Cohen, 25th degree, initiated in Philadelphia in 1781; A. F. A. de Grasse Tilly, 25th degree, initiated in Charleston 1796.

John Mitchell had been residing in Philadelphia during the Revolutionary War; through his Masonic connections, he had himself named as Deputy Quartermaster General of the American Army, although, he remained in Philadelphia throughout the British occupation! He and his co-worker, Benedict Arnold, were later tried on charges of corruption, stemming from their illegal diversions of Army supplies, but here again, because of their powerful Masonic defenders, they were acquitted.

Mitchell later moved to South Carolina.

Count Alexander de Grasse (Tilly) was the son of the French Admiral who aided George Washington in the defeat of the British forces at Yorktown. The opposing forces then sat down for a cordial Masonic banquet. De Grasse later set up Scottish Rite Supreme Councils throughout Europe; he was later named Supreme Commander of France. He played the crucial role in promoting insurrectionary activity in South Carolina, which culminated in the firing on Fort Sumter. Another member of the Charleston Lodge, James Moultrie, was the principal figure behind the Nullification Crisis in South Carolina during the 1820s and 1830s. He was named Grand Secretary General of the Scottish Rite for all of the Southern states.

During the nineteenth century, Masonic agitators traveled about the world, inflaming the populaces with passionate cries for "liberation," and "the Rights of Man." Unfortunately for those who were deceived by these manipulations, the only rights they were pursuing were the rights of Masonic Canaanites to battle and exterminate the people of Shem. Every other consideration was subordinated to this primary goal. As a result, every nation which was lured into the "Rights of Man" trap became an absolute dictatorship whose officials used their powers to destroy the people of Shem, their demonic goal, and part of their Satanic rebellion against God. As Grand Master, Lafayette directed the Juarez revolution in Mexico; in South America, Bernardo O'Higgins and Simon Bolivar, both of whom were Masons, led the revolutionary forces against Spain in country after country. Since the Spanish governments in these countries were also Catholic, these revolutions proved to be an integral part of Masonry's openly declared war against the Catholic Church.

In Italy, Mazzini and Garibaldi led the atheistic revolutionary forces which culminated in the arrest of the Pope and the establishment of "unification" in Italy in 1860. From the outset, this Masonic uprising was planned and financed by British Secret Intelligence Service, and directed by Lord Palmerston, Foreign Minister of the British Empire. When Louis Kossuth, the Hungarian revolutionary, visited the United States, Masonic organizations throughout the country planned large scale demonstrations and victory banquets for him. It is doubtful that any visitor to these shores has previously or since been lionized to the extent that Louis Kossuth was received. Even today, there are still many buildings and avenues in American towns throughout the country which are named after Kossuth, memorializing this leader of Freemasonry.

In 1845, Mazzini originated the Young America movement in the United States. Although primarily active in rural areas as a farmer's movement, it was directed by Mazzini to play an active role in the growing abolitionist movement, which he also directed. His friend, William Lloyd Garrison, who later wrote the Introduction to Mazzini's authorized biography, became the most inflammatory of the abolitionist propagandists. He called his newspaper "The Liberator." Garrison started this paper in 1831. From the outset, it was liberally financed by unnamed backers, who saw to it that free subscriptions to "the Liberator" were distributed throughout the Southern states. The State of Georgia was moved to offer $500 reward for Garrison's arrest or for the detention of any member of his American Anti-Slavery Society. Garrison frequently went to London for conferences with Mazzini on the strategy of the abolitionist movement. They usually met at the offices of the well-known London solicitor, William Ashurst. Few Southerners have ever heard the name of Mazzini, and even fewer know that this fiery Masonic revolutionary was the actual instigator of the Civil War. He is privately known among the cognoscenti (or Gnostics) as the godfather of the anti-slavery campaign in the United States.

This abolitionist propaganda caused widespread resentment throughout the South. On December 16, 1835, the State of South Carolina issued a formal resolution on the matter: "Resolved, that the formation of the abolitionist societies and the acts and doings of certain fanatics calling themselves abolitionists in the nonslaveholding states of this confederacy, are in direct violation of the obligations of the compact of the union, dissocial, and incendiary in the extreme."

Note that in 1835, South Carolina used the term common until after the outcome of the Civil War, a confederacy of states associated under the provisions of a compact, the Constitution of the United States. The abolitionist propaganda did constitute a direct invasion of the Southern States and as such was an undeclared state of war; it was also, as the South Carolina Resolution pointed out, a direct violation of the terms of the compact. Nevertheless, this invasion by propaganda continued, until it was at last followed by the direct military invasion of the Civil War.

Despite the fact that slavery existed in the Southern States under the direct authority of the Biblical Curse of Canaan, the war against the people of Shem was conducted without mercy by the invading Canaanites, who faithfully followed the precepts of their founder in the Will of Canaan, "hate your masters, and never tell the truth." The ideological successor to the Edwardean Conspiracy and the Essex Junto in the New England states was a curious, pseudo-religious cult, often called "the New England religion," but also known as Unitarianism and Transcendentalism. It was a direct spawn of the demonic cult of Baal, as adapted through the centuries by such "liberalizing" and "humane" influences as Pythagoreanism, NeoPlatonism, and secular humanism (which had been bought and paid for by the banking family, the de Medicis). The "New England religion," quite simply was the latest modern heresy preached against the people of Shem. The cult was directed by Rev. William Channing; one of his principal assistants was a teacher named John Brown, the son of the infamous revolutionary who was to die on the gallows for the insurrection at Harper's Ferry. This cult survives today principally in the preachings of some who call themselves "Fundamentalists." These renegades preach the doctrine of the Will of Canaan, and they work avidly for the final defeat and extermination of the people of Shem. These "Transcendentalists" did not bother to conceal the fact that they took the basics of their "religious" doctrines directly from the Cabala, preaching that each person has an oversoul, and that there is no final authority in any religious matter, thus invalidating the entire Bible and the pronouncements of God. Their true leaning was always dominated by Oriental despotism, and their doctrines originated in the Far East. Consequently, their first line of attack was the overthrowing of the Constitution of the United States, the principal safeguard of the people of Shem; their campaign resulted in the adoption of "amendments" which totally invalidated the original intent of this Constitution. This is the basis of decisions of federal judges in federal courts today, always against the people of Shem, always strengthening the stranglehold of Oriental despotism over our captive people.

At one point, the leader of the abolitionists, William Garrison, publicly burned a copy of the Constitution, calling it "a Covenant with Hell"! The abolitionists repeatedly denied that there was any authority for slavery in the Bible, thus ignoring the Curse of Canaan (Genesis 9:25) and many other commandments. They also worked desperately to forestall the peaceful emancipation movement in the South; the gradual freeing of the' slaves, which had been led by Thomas Jefferson, had received widespread approbation among the plantation owners. They welcomed emancipation because they had come face to face, with the economic reality which has made a shambles of the Communist empire, that without incentives and the promise of ultimate gain, few people were willing to do more than the absolute minimum of labor to survive. Economic growth was impossible in this situation. Emancipation was not merely a humanitarian measure; it was welcomed by the plantation owners because they faced ruin due to the daily demands of maintaining their increasing slave populations. Thomas Jefferson was an outstanding example; despite his brilliant career, he died bankrupt. He tried crop after crop in desperate attempts to make Monticello a profitable enterprise; in every case, he was defeated by the mounting expenses of caring for his slaves.

The "religious" assault on the Constitution of the United States, the compact which had been drafted by the people of Shem in order to protect their religious freedom, now took a more ominous turn. In 1857, the financial leaders of the Canaanite powers, the House of Rothschild, assembled to celebrate the wedding of Lionel's daughter, Leonora, to her cousin, Alphonse, son of James de Rothschild of Paris. At this gathering, Disraeli said, "Under this roof are the heads of the family of Rothschild-a name famous in every capital of Europe and every division of the globe. If you like, we shall divide the United States into two parts, one for you, James, and one for you, Lionel. Napoleon shall do exactly and all that I shall advise him" (p. 228, "The Rothschilds," by John Reeves).

The tragic Civil War which the Canaanites planned and executed against the people of Shem in the Southern states actually began in 1859, with the invasion of the South by the homicidal maniac, John Brown. The abolitionists had already spent millions of dollars to promote slave rebellions in the South, but this expensive propaganda had very little effect.

As Day and other observers had reported, the slaves were leading very comfortable lives. After this tactic failed, it became obvious to the conspirators that an actual military invasion was the only solution to their campaign. The merchant bankers of New England, who were directly controlled by the Rothschilds, were now instructed to finance a military attack against the South. Their instrumentality was the already well-known terrorist, John Brown. He was financed by a group famed as "the Secret Six," which was composed of "Thomas Wentworth Higginson, Rev. Theodore Parker, Dr. Samuel Gridley Howe (married to Julia Ward, from a wealthy banking family who later wrote "Battle Hymn of the Republic"), Franklin Benjamin Sanborn, George Luther Stearns, and Gerrit Smith. Smith had been John Brown's first financial angel. He was the son of the business partner of John Jacob Astor (East India. Company, the opium trade, and British Intelligence). His mother was a Livingston; he was related to the Masonic leaders, Edward and Robert Livingston. Smith was the largest landowner in the State of New York, holding a million acres, which included land he had given to John Brown in 1848. Smith's total contribution to John Brown's military raids and other radical causes came to more than eight million dollars, a tremendous' sum in those days. Rev. Theodore Parker typified the "religious" inspiration of the abolitionist movement; his mother was a Stearns, and he married into the Cabot family. He was educated at the Harvard Divinity School, and he became a leading Transcendentalist and Congregationalist minister. He was always an "activist" in the Masonic tradition. In 1854, he had been indicted by a grand jury for inciting an attack on a courthouse where a runaway slave was being detained. He was an active member of the Vigilance Committee, and he was the principal organizer of the Secret Six to finance John Brown's raid. He later became an expatriate, living in Europe. He died in Florence (birthplace of secular humanism).

Thomas Wentworth Higginson, of the leading New England banking family, was from Newburyport, Massachusetts, the birthplace of Albert Pike, who became the national leader of American Masonry. Higginson actively assisted Rev. Parker in the attack on the courthouse and engaged in many other illegal and nefarious activities. His cousin married Theodore Roosevelt.

Samuel Gridley Howe and his wife, Julia, founded and edited a fiery anti-slavery newspaper, "The Commonwealth." Like so many of the Canaanite agitators in the United States, Gridley was descended from Calvinist revolutionaries; his ancestor was an officer in Cromwell's army, John Ward of Gloucester, who later fled to the United States to avoid punishment for the atrocities he committed under the banner of Cromwell. Franklin Benjamin Sanborn was a leading disciple of Rev. Parker and Ralph Waldo Emerson.

The Senate ordered his arrest in 1860. He had been the principal agent for John Brown in New York since 1857. George Luther Stearns married into the Train family. He was the leader of the Free Soilers, the anti-slavery agitators in the state of Kansas; their depredations gave rise to the term "Bloody Kansas." He donated large sums to John Brown and bought a farm for the terrorist and his family. The chief agent for Stearns in Kansas was Martin Conway. Originally from Baltimore, Conway was sent to Kansas to lead the Free State forces there; he later became the first Congressman from Kansas. On October 11, 1873, he fired three shots at Senator Pomeroy, wounding him. Conway was taken to St. Elizabeth's Hospital, where he was judged hopelessly insane. He later died there.

Other leading New Englanders deeply involved in the planning of uprisings in the South included Samuel Cabot; he paid for $4000 worth of rifles which were sent to John Brown's forces in Kansas. The guns were used to massacre entire families during John Brown's orgy of terrorism. The Cabot Bank later provided $57,000 for John Brown's military expenses. There is no record that it was ever repaid, or that any attempt was made to collect it. It was a donation to the cause of terrorism, a familiar technique of bankers. Other financial supporters of John Brown included John Murray Forbes, a wealthy railroad builder (his mother was a Perkins), who served on the Republican National Committee.

Between 1827 and 1843, the plans of the conspirators received a temporary setback with the emergence of the AntiMasonic Party as a national force. This political movement threatened to expose the entire conspiracy as a Masonic operation. From its outset, the Anti-Masonic Party was handicapped by its inability to penetrate the shroud of secrecy which veiled every act of the conspirators. Without direct evidence of this conspiracy which could be presented in court or laid before the people, they soon lost their popular support. In fact, they were soon infiltrated by the very conspirators whom they sought to expose, and they were rendered impotent! Albert Pike later boasted that "The Anti-Masonic Party actually was of great assistance to us." After its dissolution, Freemasonry never again faced any organized opposition in the entire United States. Those who mention this subject are quickly discredited as "poor overwrought fools" and paranoid "Know-Nothings" who see Masons behind every tree. In most cases, they are quickly consigned to the nearest lunatic asylum, a la Soviet Communism's handling of its "dissidents. "

For some years prior to the outbreak of the Civil War, the Young American Masonic conspiracy had been active in the Southern states, laying the groundwork for the approaching Civil War. A native New Yorker, John A. Quitman, moved to Mississippi and married into a wealthy Southern family. He was given the warrant to form a

Scottish Rite organization in Mississippi. On February 1, 1848, the Freemason magazine of Boston carried the notice that Brother John Quitman, who was now a Major General in the United States Army, had been inaugurated as Sovereign Grand Inspector General of the 33rd degree. All Southern Lodges were now ordered to obey him. Quitman had also become one of the most outspoken leaders of the secessionist movement in the South; this movement was now firmly controlled by the Masonic Canaanite conspirators. Quitman also sponsored a plan to annex Mexico, and financed an invasion of Cuba by mercenaries. He had been elected Governor of Mississippi, when he was indicted in New Orleans for his part in the planned Cuban invasion, and he was forced to resign from that office. Here again was the deep involvement of a leader of the Scottish Rite, the revolutionary arm of Freemasonry, in planning wars and revolutions throughout the world. The ideological leader of the Cuban invasion was one Jane McManus, who had last been heard from as the girl friend of the revolutionist, Aaron Burr.

In order to build popular support for his Presidential campaign, Senator Stephen Douglas, Lincoln's opponent, hired one George Sanders, 'a Young America agent, to edit the Democratic Party Review. Sanders is identified in Who's Who by profession as a "revolutionist." The American political agent of the Hudson Bay Company, he had worked for the Bank of England, and as United States Consul in London, he had worked closely with Mazzini. London was at that time the world headquarters of Masonic revolutionary movements. Sanders soon devoted the pages of The Democratic Party Review to lauding the efforts of Mazzini and other Masonic agitators.

In 1853, Killian H. van Rensselaer, one of the New York "patroons," or hereditary landlords, opened the Western Headquarters of the Scottish Rite in Cincinnati, Ohio. At the same time, another secret organization, the Knights of the Golden Circle, began its operations in Cincinnati. The organization, which, as usual, was well-financed, soon enlisted and trained some 100,000 members in paramilitary tactics. These members spread throughout the Southern States; they formed the nucleus of what would become the Confederate Army during the Civil War. Most Southerners neither envisioned nor prepared for an armed struggle with the North. The "Southern" cause was always directed and promoted by "Northern" infiltrators. The stage was now set for the Civil War.

The nation was further polarized by the Dred Scott case. Scott, an elderly and infirm Negro who was financially supported by his owners, was pushed into a direct legal confrontation, amply financed from New England merchant bankers funds. The case went to the Supreme Court. Listed in the court records as "Dred Scott v. Sanford, 19 Howard 393," the matter was decided in an opinion by Chief Justice Taney dated March 6, 1857. "The question is simply this; can a negro, whose ancestors were imported into this country, and sold as slaves, become a member of the political community formed and brought into existence by the Constitution of the United States, and as such become entitled to all the rights and privileges, and immunities, guaranteed by that instrument to the citizen? .. The words 'people of the United States' and 'citizens' are synonymous terms, and mean the same thing ... 'the sovereign people' ... The question before us is, whether the class of persons described in the plea in abatement comprise a portion of this people and are constituent members of this sovereignty? We think they are not, and that they are not included, and were not intended to be included, under the word 'citizens' in the Constitution, and can, therefore, claim none of the rights and privileges which that instrument provides for and secures to citizens of the United States. On the contrary, they were at that time considered as a subordinate and inferior class of beings, who had been subjugated by the dominant race, and, whether emancipated or not, yet remained subject to their authority, and had no rights or privileges but such as those who held the power and the government might choose to grant them ... In the opinion of the Court, the legislation and histories of the times, and the language used in the Declaration of Independence, show, that neither the class of persons who had been imported as slaves, nor their descendants, whether they had become free or not, were then acknowledged as a part of the people, nor intended to be included in the general words used in that memorable instrument ... They had for more than a century before been regarded as beings of an inferior order; and altogether unfit to associate with the white race, either in social or political relations; and so far inferior that they had no rights which the white man was bound to respect; and that the negro might justly and lawfully be reduced to slavery for his benefit ... This opinion was at that time fixed and universal in the civilized portion of the white race. It was regarded as an axiom in morals as well as in politics, which no one thought of disputing, or supposed to be open to dispute; and men in every grade and position in society daily and habitually acted upon it in their private pursuits, as well as in matters of public concern, without doubting for a moment the correctness of this opinion ... There are two clauses in the Constitution which point directly and specifically to the negro race as a separate class of persons, and show clearly that they were not regarded as a portion of the people or citizens of the Government then formed ... the right to import slaves until the year 1808 ... and the States pledge to each other to maintain the right of property of the master, by delivering up to him any slave who may have escaped from his service ... the right of property in a slave is distinctly and expressly affirmed in the Constitution ... the Circuit Court of the United States had no jurisdiction in this case, and could give no judgment on it... Its judgment for the defendant must, consequently, be reversed, and a mandate issued directing the suit to be dismissed for want of jurisdiction."

The Chief Justice of the Supreme Court paid dearly for this decision. His name has almost entirely been erased from the legal history of this nation; he was repeatedly threatened with house arrest during the Civil War by President Lincoln, and after the war, his two elderly daughters, shunned as prospective brides, eked out a precarious existence as government clerks at the very bottom of the pay scale, always on the verge of complete destitution.

After the Dred Scott decision, events moved rapidly toward an actual military confrontation, with the Knights of the Golden Circle taking their places throughout the Southern states. John Brown then attacked Harper's Ferry, an incident which was intended to set off a slave uprising throughout the South. The anticipated popular revolution failed to materialize, and Brown was captured and hanged. To this day, he remains a martyr in the cabbalistic circles of New England, the Fundamentalists. Their ideological leader, Ralph Waldo Emerson, wrote, "He makes the gallows as Glorious as the Cross." Emerson later promoted John Brown as "a new Saint in the calendar."

In order to arouse provocation for the Fort Sumter attack, Lincoln now dispatched heavy reinforcements to the fort. Even his Secretary of War, Seward, objected to his move, suggesting instead that Fort Sumter be yielded peacefully to the state of South Carolina. Lincoln himself was eagerly anticipating the approaching bloodbath and would hear of no compromise. He is known to have suffered from hereditary insanity, which did not come from the Lincoln family, for they were not his actual forebears. His mother, Nancy Hanks, being homeless, had been taken in as a charitable act by the Enloe family; she was thrown out by Mrs. Enloe after she had become pregnant by

Abraham Enloe. Ward H. Lame, Lincoln's law partner, later wrote a biography of Lincoln stating that Lincoln was of illegal parentage, and referring to his real father as Abraham Enloe. The Yorkville Enquirer, April 8, 1863, noted that Lincoln's mother, Nancy Hanks, was "a single woman of low degree [Canaan means 'low'. Ed.] ... generally reputed to have from one-eighth to one-sixteenth Negro blood in her veins, and who always associated with Negroes on terms of equality." The Atlanta Intelligencer in 1863 noted of his vice president, Hannibal Hamlin, who had been named after the historic leader of the Canaanite forces of Carthage, Hannibal, that Hamlin was identified by State Senator Hon. John Burham, of Hancock County, Maine, who lived in the area and knew of Hamlin's ancestry. The Senator reported that Hamlin's greatgrandfather was a mulatto, who had married a Canadian woman; his grandfather during the Revolutionary War commanded a company composed only of mulattoes, Negroes, and Indians under Generals Sullivan and Green. This Captain Hamlin is recorded as having embezzled the funds sent to pay his troops; he also was said to have stolen wine and other supplies. The father of Hannibal Hamlin's father lived in Paris, Maine, and had a brother named Africa. When Hannibal Hamlin was born, one of his uncles peered into his cradle and exclaimed, "For God's sake, how long will this damned black blood remain in our family?"

In Louisiana, John Slidell, who was also a New Yorker, was the leader of the state's secessionist party; his second in command was one Judah P. Benjamin. Slidell was the Masonic protege of the Grand Master, Edward Livingston, also of New York, a key member of the Aaron Burr treason apparat. Benjamin, from the West Indies, was a British subject. He was hired as a law clerk by Slidell. He later became the Secretary of State in the Confederate Government. After the Civil War, he was permitted to leave the United States without hindrance, and he lived his later years in splendid luxury as one of the highest paid Queen's Counsels in London, while his former superior, Jefferson Davis, languished in a federal prison, burdened with heavy chains.

In Texas, the secessionist conspirators were blocked for a time by Sam Houston, a Virginian who was the founder of Texas. Houston ruled that the secessionist efforts were illegal. The conspirators then succeeded in deposing Governor Houston by a "rump" election, which was similar to the tactics which the Cromwellians had used to condemn King Charles I in England. The conspirators then claimed that their secessionist delegates had received 40,000 votes, as compared to only 10,000 for Houston's supporters. This was later cited as the "popular" support for the "insurrection," as the action taken by the Southern states was later termed. The Confederacy was officially established at Montgomery, Alabama, chaired by Scottish Rite Supreme Commander Howell Cobb. He was ably assisted by Scottish Rite backers from the Charleston Mother Lodge and representatives from other Masonic groups.

Thus the American people were maneuvered into a Civil War which they neither envisioned nor desired. They were manipulated by Masonic Canaanite conspirators working together in the Northern and the Southern states. The resulting bloodbath proved to be the greatest disaster ever suffered by the people of Shem. The great civilization which they had spent some two hundred years building in this land was now swept away, "Gone with the Wind"; the Constitution which they had written to protect their existence as the people of Shem was scrapped, being replaced by "Amendments" which reduced them to the status of serfs, while giving the Canaanites total power to set up a tyrannical dictatorship.

Nevertheless, the anticipated division of the United States into two small, weak countries, each to be easily controlled from the European headquarters of the Rothschilds, failed to take place. At one point, the massing of French and Spanish troops in Mexico seemed to doom the future of the United States, and to bring about the division which the Rothschilds desired. However, the Czar of Russia, a great leader of the Shemite people, learned of the plan. He immediately dispatched two of his fleets to the United States, one which landed at San Francisco, which was commanded by Admiral Lesowsky, and the second squadron, which arrived in New York harbor, commanded by Admiral A. A. Popoff. Needless to say, these names are not encountered by students of American history. However, the presence of these Russian fleets served to preserve the Union. James de Rothschild was left without his anticipated empire in Mexico, while Lionel was forced to forego his control over the Northern states. Because of these good offices on behalf of the Union, the Czar was later murdered by Rothschild agents, and Russia was condemned to be turned over to the atrocities of the demonic Canaanite revolutionaries.

The Civil War ravaged the Southern states, while leaving the North untouched. The civilization of the people of Shem was in ruins. Once again, as during the Revolutionary War, hordes of German mercenaries moved through the South. Southern ladies reported that their homes had been put to the torch by Union soldiers who could speak only gutteral English. Yet these horrors were only a harbinger of what was to come. The defeat of the underfinanced and poorly prepared Southern states had been a foregone conclusion, as they were overrun by the numerical and financial superiority of the Northern states. Their defeat was followed by an unrivaled brutality toward the vanquished population. For generations afterward, Southern families suffered genetic diseases directly attributable to the starvation forced upon them by their conquerors; such formerly unknown illnesses as scurvy, rickets, gum disease, and other diseases gave rise to the depiction of the Southern people which is still universal in the New York owned and controlled publishing industry, movies, and television, the Joads of Tobacco Road. However, no explanation of their pitiful condition is ever offered.

The 1949 World Book states under the title "Reconstruction," "This plan was unmatched in history for its generosity to the defeated foe." This is typical of the anti-Southern bias of the publishing industry; no Southern writer can be published in New York unless he depicts his fellow Southerners as alcoholic womanizers and homosexuals. In fact, this "generosity" consisted of military occupation for many years after the war, ruinous taxation, systematic starvation, and brutal military courts in which the Southern people found it impossible to obtain justice (the same system is largely in place today).

In his First Inaugural Address, Lincoln had clearly stated, "I have no purpose, direct or indirect, to interfere with the institution of slavery in the states where it exists. I believe I have no lawful right to do so, and I have no inclination to do so."

Despite this pledge, on January 1, 1863, Lincoln issued his Emancipation Proclamation. It had actually been previously written on September 22, 1862; Lincoln had prepared the first draft as early as July, 1862. Lincoln excused his action as due to "military necessity," and therefore warranted by the Constitution. No court challenge was ever made to this claim. On the same day that Lincoln issued this proclamation, the Illinois State Legislature, hardly a hotbed of Southern reactionaries, issued a formal denunciation of the proclamation: "Resolved, that the emancipation proclamation of the President of the United

States is as unwarrantable in military as in civil law; a gigantic usurpation, at once converting the war, professedly commenced by the administration for the vindication of the authority of the Constitution, into the crusade for the sudden unconditional and violent liberation of three million Negro slaves ... The proclamation invites servile insurrection as an element in this crusade - a means of warfare, the inhumanity and diabolism of which are without example in civilian warfare, and which we denounce, and which the civilized world will denounce, as an ineffaceable disgrace to the American people."

The key word in the Illinois Legislature's Resolution is "diabolism." Perhaps someone in the Legislature realized that this was the triumph of the Will of Canaan, a celebration of the demonic concepts of the Canaanites. They have celebrated it ever since.

The Masonic Canaanite forces throughout the world hailed the Emancipation Proclamation as a great victory for their program of worldwide revolution. Garibaldi, at that time the most famous Masonic leader and revolutionary in the world, signed a Proclamation from Italy to Lincoln saying, "weal to you, redeemed sons of Ham." Whether Garibaldi knew of Lincoln's actual origins is not known. Certainly he hailed him as a fellow revolutionary. A little-known incident of the Civil War was Lincoln's offer to Garibaldi to take the commander in chief's post of the armies of the United States in 1861; he repeated the offer in 1862. Garibaldi had considered it seriously, but was forced to decline because of other commitments.

European writers generally were appalled at the excesses committed by the Union troops and the Lincoln administration during the war. The great French writer, Alfred de Vigny, had written to a Southern lady on September 10, 1862, "Those abominable acts of cruelty perpetrated by the Northern armies in New Orleans remind one of the invasion of the Barbarians, of Attila's Huns, or even worse than the Vandals. I well understand your hatred for those depraved and ferocious men who are drowning in blood the whole of your beloved country ... A wise state is not one that resorts to brute force, to murder and fire in order to find a solution to the complex problems of states' rights. It is a question that should have been settled in public debate."

A public debate was just what Masonic Canaanite conspirators did not want; they managed to avoid it each time the issue came up. The Times of London, October 21, 1862, editorially commented, "Is the name of Lincoln to be classified in the catalogue of monsters, wholesale assassins, and butchers of humanity? ... When blood begins to flow and shrieks come piercing through the darkness, Mister Lincoln will wait until the rising flames tell that all is consummated, and then he will rub his hands and think that revenge is sweet." The Times did not know this, but Lincoln's entire political career was dedicated to the revenge of the Canaanites against the fair-skinned people of Shem, those who were always to be considered his enemies because of the color of his skin. The Civil War was merely the latest campaign in a battle which had been surreptitiously waged during the past three thousand years. After Lincoln's assassination, the Radical Republicans in Congress moved to impose even more Draconian measures against the defeated South. The Southerners had offended the basic principle of Masonic Canaanism, that is, Oriental despotism; any refusal to obey the command of the dictatorial central government must automatically be followed by the severest punishment. No matter that the Constitution of the United States had been written by the people of Shem, or that it guaranteed them their States rights; no matter that the federal government was legally confined in its authority to the District of Columbia by statute; no matter that no federal authority could enter any state except by express request of the state legislature. All of this was systematically violated, and now the violated ones were to endure even greater punishments.

Hordes of carpetbaggers followed the Federal troops into the Southern states like avid camp followers; Federal courts and Federal insane asylums were now set up in the states for the first time, in flagrant violation of the Constitutional prohibitions against them. Now ensued a series of "legal" measures which were hailed by the revolutionary Mazzini, who was known as "the prophet" by Masonic organizations throughout the world. Mazzini enthused to the Northern conquerors, "You have done more for us in four years than fifty years of teaching, preaching, and writing by your European brothers have been able to do!" These measures effectively scrapped the Constitution. A hastily written "Civil Rights Act" was rushed through Congress. President Andrew Johnson immediately vetoed it, noting that the right to confer citizenship rested with the several states, and that "the tendency of the bill is to resuscitate the spirit of rebellion." Indeed, many of the measures enacted by the Radical Republicans were deliberately intended to provoke the Southerners into open resistance, so that they could then be exterminated by the overwhelming superiority of the military forces quartered in their states. The Civil Rights Act was passed over Johnson's veto, as were other similar measures.

The Federal troops now ordered that "conventions" be held in the Southern states, which were akin to the conventions called by the perpetrators of the French Revolution. These conventions were ordered to do three things: (1) nullify the ordinance of secession; (2) repudiate all Confederate debts; and (3) declare slavery abolished. Collier's Encyclopaedia notes that these Constitutional conventions held in the Southern states were composed of

(1) scalawags (renegade Southerners); (2) carpetbaggers; and (3) Negroes. The World Book lists them in slightly different order, as blacks, carpetbaggers, and scalawags. These conventions set up Radical Republican governments in the Southern states, which were nothing more than occupation governments, set up by military force. From 1868-1870, the Southern states were once again represented in Congress, but only by delegates chosen by these three groups. Collier's notes that after Grant was elected President in 1868, "It was important to maintain Radical Republican governments of the southern states because these corrupt organizations provided votes for the Republican Party. Largely for this reason, the Fifteenth Amendment was passed by Congress and its ratification made a condition for readmission to the Union for Virginia, Mississippi, Texas, and Georgia. The Reconstruction governments in the South could only be sustained by force."

Thus Collier's makes a definitive statement about the Fifteenth Amendment, that it was passed by blackmail of the Southern states, and that it was merely a political ploy of the Republican Party to maintain its political power. The reason that these brutal and alien state governments of the Masonic Canaanites could only be sustained by force was because of their unwavering hatred and brutality toward the people of Shem. Military and Federal courts whose dicta can be enforced only by martial law can hardly be welcomed by any people. The military occupation of the South was similar to the present military occupation of East Germany, Czechoslovakia, and other European nations by the Soviet armies. An alien ideology was imposed on a defeated people by brute force. The Thirteenth Amendment to the Constitution of the United States was enacted in 1865 by martial law. The Fourteenth Amendment was enacted in 1868 by martial law. The Fifteenth Amendment was enacted in 1870 by martial law. Military occupation of the Southern states did not end until 1877, twelve years after the end of the Civil War. The occupation was maintained throughout those years solely as a punitive measure, in the hope of starving to death the last white survivors of the Civil War.

Thus we find that the Thirteenth Amendment, enacted in 1865, during military occupation, abolished slavery; the Fourteenth Amendment, which changed the status of citizenship in the United States, was enacted in 1868 during the military occupation; and the Fifteenth Amendment, dictating voting procedures, was enacted in 1870 during the military occupation. These amendments were similar to orders issued by the Soviet commanders today in East Germany or in Czechoslovakia. In 1868, when the Fourteenth Amendment was ratified, Great Britain was still shipping boatloads of political prisoners to the Swan River in Western Australia as slave labor. Many of them were "Irish politicals," who were deported to wipe out popular resistance to the British occupation of Ireland.

The Civil Rights Act of April 9, 1866, stated, "Be it enacted, that all persons born in the United States and not subject to any foreign power, excluding Indians not taxed, are hereby declared to be citizens of the United States." This Act nullified Art. 1, Sec. 2, Cl. 3 of the Constitution defining "free persons"; even so, the Civil Rights Act continued the exclusion of "Indians not taxed" from citizenship. This Act also excludes all members of the Masonic Order from citizenship, because they are subject to a foreign power.

The state of martial law under which these three amendments to the Constitution were ratified was authorized by the First Reconstruction Act, dated March 2, 1867: "Whereas no legal State governments or adequate protection of life or property now exists in the rebel states," the ten Southern states were thereby divided into five military districts. President Johnson vetoed the bill on the same day, noting that "The bill places the people of the ten

States therein named under the absolute domination of military rule but each State does have an actual government." Johnson further noted that the commanding officer is "an absolute monarch," which was a clear violation of the provisions of the Constitution. He also said, "This is a bill passed by Congress in time of peace [the war had been over for two years]." He further noted the absence of "either war or insurrection" and that laws were already in harmonious operation in the Southern states. Johnson concluded his veto message as follows: "The Constitution forbids the exercise of judicial power in any way but one- that is, by the ordained and Established courts." Thus Johnson excluded the exercise of military courts in the Southern states.

The Second Reconstruction Act, dated March 23, 1867, established military control over voting in the Southern states. Free elections, anyone? President Johnson again vetoed it the same day. "No consideration could induce me to give my approval to such an election law for any purpose, and especially for the great purpose of framing the Constitution of a State." The bill was passed over his veto.

The Third Reconstruction Act, dated July 19, 1867, extended even greater powers to the military commanders of the Southern states. It provided that no military officer in any district shall be bound by any civil officer of the United States. By giving absolute power to the commanding officer, the Third Reconstruction Act confirmed that the Southern states were under absolute martial law, an important point to be brought up in a Constitutional challenge to the validity of the Thirteenth, Fourteenth, and Fifteenth Amendments. There is also the legal point to be made that if these amendments were and are illegal, having been enacted under martial law, all of the subsequent amendments to the Constitution are also invalid, since they not only are not numbered correctly, but they also must be considered as having been enacted according to the provisions of these three amendments, which changed the requirements for citizenship and voting rights!

The Fourth Reconstruction Act imposed even greater voting restrictions on the militarily occupied Southern states.

Because he opposed the four Reconstruction Acts, which were patently unconstitutional, the Radical Republicans moved to impeach President Johnson and remove him from office. This has been a favorite tactic of those who have been defeated at the polls, as Presidents Nixon and Reagan were later to discover. The move to impeach Johnson lost by only one vote. The Radical Republicans had passed the four Reconstruction Acts only because they had previously taken the precaution in July of 1866 to reduce the number of justices on the Supreme Court from ten to seven, fearing that President Johnson might appoint justices who would uphold his opinion of the Reconstruction Acts. Such is the "law of the land." In April, 1869, after Grant had been elected President, the Congress again increased the number of justices to nine, which remains the number today. Congress subsequently denounced Presidents for their attempts to "pack" the Supreme Court, a privilege which seems to be reserved for themselves. Grant appointed justices who unanimously ruled to uphold the unconstitutional Reconstruction Acts. As Chief Justice of the Supreme Court, Salmon P. Chase, the New York banker, resisted all challenges to the Reconstruction Acts by the captive Southern states, declaring that these Acts were indeed "constitutional." From 1830 to 1860, he had been renowned in Ohio for his work in aiding fugitive slaves; he was called "the attorney general for runaway slaves." He later founded the Chase Bank, which is now allied with Aaron Burr's Manhattan Company to form the Chase Manhattan Bank.

The Radical Republicans in Congress were led by the fiery Thaddeus Stevens, a lawyer from Pennsylvania who, through judicious investments in real estate, had become the largest taxpayer in Gettysburg. He was a grotesque cripple, clubfooted, described by his contemporaries as "fox-featured, with hollow voice and a permanent pout." He was bald from the effects of some disease, and wore a chestnut colored wig. For many years his only companion had been his mulatto mistress, one Lydia Smith; he died in her bed.

The military occupation was the principal force upholding the depredations of the carpetbaggers in the Southern states. They had swarmed in to quickly amass huge fortunes in land by having the property of the impoverished Southerners confiscated, they being unable to pay the ruinous increases voted by the scalawag legislatures. During Reconstruction, six million acres in the state of Mississippi were sold for back taxes. The scalawag legislatures embarked on great spending sprees, running up huge state debts to the bankers. During Reconstruction, the state debt of Louisiana increased from fourteen to forty-eight million dollars; in South Carolina from seven million to twenty-nine million; in Florida from a mere $524,000 to five million dollars. The Fairfield Herald in South Carolina wrote editorially, November 20, 1872, "Reconstruction ... a hellborn policy, which has trampled the fairest and noblest of states, our great statehood beneath the unholy hoofs of African savages and shoulderstrapped brigands-the policy which has given up millions of our freeborn, high-souled brothers and sisters, countrymen and countrywomen, of Washington, Rutledge, Marion, and Lee, to the rule of gibbering, louse-eaten, devil-worshipping barbarians, from the jungles of Dahomey, and perpetuated by buccaneers from Cape Cod, Memphremagog, Hell, and Boston." Note that even a Southern editor knew about the devil-worship of the Canaanites. Amazingly enough, this was written during the military occupation, or rather, during its close. The descendants of the carpetbaggers now own all of the Southern press, and such an editorial cannot be read anywhere in the South today.

The military occupation of the South was further reinforced when President Grant passed the aptly named Force Act of 1870. This act suspended habeas corpus and placed total power in the hands of the military occupiers of the Southern states. His Enforcement Acts of 1871 put Congressional elections in the South under the control of federal authorities, a method which was revived in the 1960s and 1970s, when federal authorities again invaded the Southern states to place elections under their supervision. These were the auspices under which the Constitution of the United States was rewritten and nullfied. In 1877, twelve years after the end of the Civil War, twelve years after the Thirteenth Amendment was ratified, nine years after the Fourteenth Amendment was ratified, and seven years after the Fifteenth Amendment was ratified, President Hayes withdrew the federal troops from the Southern states.

The scalawag looting of the impoverished South was typified by the career of Franklin Israel Moses Jr. in South Carolina. His father had been appointed Chief Justice of the Supreme Court of South Carolina during the period of Reconstruction, serving in that office from 1868-1877. Significantly, he ended his term when the federal troops were withdrawn. In 1866, Moses Jr. began to publish a newspaper, Sumter News, which enthusiastically endorsed all four of the Reconstruction Acts. He was elected as Speaker of the House by the "Loyal League," a scalawag group. For more than a decade, he spent millions of dollars in lavish living, money which he accumulated by accepting bribes in office, and by filing bogus state pay vouchers for hundreds of nonexistent state employees. He also dealt heavily in fraudulent state contracts. He purchased a $40,000 mansion (the equivalent of $10 million in today's money), and was renowned as the biggest spender in South Carolina. With the withdrawal of federal troops, which zealously protected the "rights" of such scoundrels, he came under scrutiny for his criminal acts. In 1878, to avoid prosecution, he fled to Massachusetts, where he finally died in 1906. Throughout the remainder of his life, he was known as a dope addict and confidence trickster. The Moses saga is redolent of the aroma which attended every act of the scalawags and carpetbaggers in the South.

In "The Tragic Era" by Claude Bowers, one of the many books which have documented the excesses of the Reconstruction period, Bowers writes on p. 29, "... in Louisiana, Sheridan rattling the sword, was spluttering epithets in an attempt to save the Radicals he served from the destruction they merited ..." Bowers describes the Reconstruction as "Cromwellian," an apt description. The revolution in the South which it served to introduce was in essence a Cromwellian interpretation of the Masonic Canaanite Order. The mockery of election laws and indeed of the legal system under Reconstruction was remarkably exposed by Bowers when he wrote of the Durell episode. A conservative group had elected John McEnery as Governor, but an illegal returning board had ignored his election and given the Governorship to his opponent, W. P. Kellogg, without even counting the votes, although a legal returning board had already certified the election of McEnery. Bowers writes, "The drunken Federal Judge Durell, with the trembling fingers of inebriety, had written his midnight injunction against the legal returning board, and instructed U.S. Marshal Packard, the Republican manager, to take possession of the State House ... The next morning, the besotted judge declared the lawful board illegal and restrained it from counting the election returns." Bowers noted that "the audacity of the crime rocked the Nation." Terming Durell a "drunken tyrant," Bowers chronicles the widespread protest against his vicious act. Today, the name of Durell is still despised in the State of Louisiana as a synonym for federal judicial tyranny. Durell was typical of the besotted Oriental despots, acting with the backing of federal troops, as they still do today, who use the Constitution of the United States as toilet tissue while they crush the people of Shem under the heels of their judicial Masonic Order of Canaanite tyranny. It is the Durells who have made the federal courts the most hated institutions in American life today, in 1987, just as Durell caused them to be despised in 1872.

Because of the depredations of such scalawags as Durell and Moses, the defeated Southerners had lost more than $500 million in cash during the Civil War, the result of their patriotic purchases of Confederate bonds, which were repudiated one hundred per cent by the scalawag legislatures. Only their land holdings were left. Almost half of their assets were computed in their holdings of slaves, and these were now gone. Much of their land was now confiscated, due to heavy taxation imposed by the authority of the federal troops. Of a total population of sixty million, the ten Southern states had suffered five and one-half million casualties, roughly ten per cent; one-fourth of the male population was dead or incapacitated by 1865. It would seem impossible for even the people of Shem to go on after such losses, yet survive they did, even though the cruel twelve years of the Reconstruction Period was designed to ensure that none of them would survive.

It is a fact of law that legislation enacted during periods of martial law is valid only during the period for which martial law is declared and sustained. Amazingly enough, the Thirteenth, Fourteenth, and Fifteenth Amendments have never been challenged on this basic premise of law. The Thirteenth Amendment abolished slavery, even though President Johnson informed Congress that they had no power to interfere with slavery; the Fourteenth Amendment changed the requirements for citizenship, even though Congress had no power to act on this question. Johnson urged the Southern states to reject the Fourteenth Amendment; he vetoed the four Reconstruction Acts, showing that the executive branch of the government was unalterably opposed to the excesses of the Radical Republicans in Congress.

The Oxford Companion to Law states, "In the Middle Ages, martial law meant law administered by the Court of the Constable and the Marshal - it now means law applicable by virtue of the Royal Prerogative to foreign territory occupied for the time being by the armed forces of the Crown."

Thus the federal troops who occupied the Southern states were exercising a Royal Prerogative, which had nothing to do with the Constitution of the United States - hence President Johnson's veto of the Reconstruction Acts. It was the exercise of absolute power over the population by a military officer who was directly responsible to the President. No martial law has been imposed in Great Britain since the seventeenth century. "Martial law may, exceptionally, be established within the State itself, in substitution for the organized government and administration of justice, when a state of war, or rebellion, an invasion, or other serious disturbance exists; in that event, justice is administered by its martial and military law tribunals."

There cannot be two governments exercising the same authority in the same area; when the military governments were established by the Reconstruction Acts in the ten Southern states from 1865 to 1877, no other government had sovereignty in those states; thus no legislation could be enacted except under the umbrella of martial law; therefore, when martial law ended, all legislation enacted under martial law was void.

Black's Law Dictionary says of martial law, "military authority exercises control over civilians or civil authority within domestic territory. Ochikubo v. Bonesteel, D.C.Cai. 60 F supp. 916, 928, 929, 930."

Webster's Dictionary says of martial law, "From Mars, Roman God of War. Law applied to all persons and property in occupied territory by the military authorities." The Oxford English Dictionary says of martial law, "1548 Hall Chron. HenIV 7b. He ... caused dyvers lustie men to appele divers older men upon matters determinable as the common law of the court marcial." OED further states of martial law, "That kind of military government of a country or district, in which the civil law is suspended and the military authorities are empowered to arrest all suspect persons at their discretion and to punish offenders without formal trial. 1537 Hen VIII. Let, Dk Norfk St Papr ii 537 ... The cours of our lawes must give place to the ordinaunces and estates marciall, our pleasure is that you shall cause such dredful executions to be done on a good nombre of thinhabitantes o euery towne, village and hamlet that have offended in this rebellion and they may be a ferefull spectacle to all other hereafter, that wold practise any like matter." The OED quotes Wellington as saying in 1851, on military law in Hansard, "Martial law was neither more nor less than the will of the general who commands the army. In fact, martial law meant no law at all."

Thus these three amendments to the Constitution were ratified while the ten Southern states were under martial law, and "had no law at all." The Force Acts, the four Reconstruction Acts, and the Civil Rights Act were all passed by Congress while the Southern states were not allowed to hold free elections, and all voters were under close supervision by federal troops. Even Soviet Russia has never staged such mockeries of the election procedures!

The Congress in 1987 went even further in changing the requirements for citizenship. The Washington Post, March 17, 1987, reported that Congress was now offering sales of citizenship for $185 each, with a bargain rate of $420 for entire families! It is expected that some two million aliens will purchase these bargain citizenship offers. The only requirement is that they be criminals, that is, that they be present in the United States in open violation of the laws of the United States. It is the greatest threat to the people of Shem since President Carter persuaded Castro to let him have many thousands of Cuban homosexuals and criminally insane Marielitos to import into the United States. The ensuing nationwide crime wave has terrorized our cities. The Carter-Castro deal openly violated our entire mandated immigration procedures.

There are two inescapable conclusions to be drawn from this record-first, that the Thirteenth, Fourteenth, and Fifteenth Amendments, which drastically changed qualifications for citizenship in the United States, voting rights, and other fundamental matters, were ratified while the ten Southern states were under martial law, and their rightful governments had been superseded by military force; and two, that legislation passed during periods of martial law effectively ends or is automatically repealed when martial law ends and the troops are withdrawn. The Reconstruction governments, which, as Collier's notes, could only be sustained by force, ended when that force was withdrawn.

Thus these amendments to the Constitution have had no legal status since 1877, when President Hayes withdrew the federal troops from the Southern states. These amendments are and have been invalid since 1877.

CHAPTER 8

THE STATE OF VIRGINIA

The tentacles of the Masonic Canaanite octopus are nowhere more deeply embedded than in the State of Virginia. Known to American tradition as the "Mother of Presidents," it is reputed to have set the standards of Southern living and culture. In actuality, Virginia is a degraded, backward state which from the beginning of history had been invaded and overcome by "the determined men of Masonry." Since the Civil War, the state has been run by a succession of Masonic carpetbaggers, and later invaded by a host of millionaires, most of them Masons, who bought out and evicted the last of the old families of Virginia, the legendary "First Families of Virginia" from their historic homes. In most cases, these showplaces have been turned into advertisements for the type of decor which is featured in "Better Homes and Gardens."

The state of Virginia is dominated by three large residential areas, the northeast, which is a bedroom community for the federal government workers in Washington, D.C.; the Richmond axis, which is totally dominated by the burgeoning state bureaucracy, and the Norfolk area, which is dominated by a huge naval base-and the defense bureaucracy. Thus the state is merely a vassal of the bureaucracy. On close examination, its much vaunted "culture" vanishes like the morning mist. Its "great" writers consist of two wealthy dilettantes, James Branch Cabell and Ellen Glasgow, whose unreadable, and unread, books languish on library shelves until they are mercifully disposed of at garage sales.

These two Establishment figures made little or no impression on the literary world. Cabell churned out some eighteen volumes about an imaginary place which he called "Poictesme"; its significance apparently was known to no one but himself. Virginia's literary tradition was buried with Edgar Allen Poe. In the twentieth century, young writers and artists flee the state like chain gang refugees fleeing across a fetid swamp, before their talents are irrevocably damaged and poisoned by the noxious vapors emitted by Virginia's prison-like estate, the result of its domination by the bureaucracy. These young people never return; thus Virginia nourishes the cultural life of other states, but never its own.

As in the most fearful days of the Reign of Terror during the French Revolution, the state of Virginia is overrun by hordes of agents and spies, most of whom have no idea that they are actually being "run" by the British Intelligence Service, which totally controls the top officials of the state. The FBI maintains its training school at the Marine base at Quantico, Virginia. Here they are taught techniques for following "subversives," who in most instances turn out to be anyone who professes a belief in the Constitution of the United States. The CIA also has its massive Babylonian headquarters at McLean, Virginia, as well as various training schools and "safe houses" throughout the state, closed off areas such as Vint Hill and other sacrosanct preserves. These agencies maintain a close liaison (read control) over the state and local police agencies throughout Virginia. The rube policeman finds it very exciting to be told that he can keep watch while FBI or CIA agents burglarize, or "black bag," the home of "dissidents," stealing whatever they might suppose to be valuable in framing him with a criminal charge or committing him to a mental institution. Some of the things which they take, of course, are simple "valuables," which enrich the private purse of the agents. Although there have been thousands of such incidents in the past fifty years, only a few cases challenging these strange intruders have ever come before the controlled courts, where they are promptly dismissed as "paranoia" by the compliant judges.

The state also has large numbers of spies in such agencies as the State Liquor Control Board, the Department of Taxation, and other agencies whose zeal stems directly from the worst days of the Reign of Terror. During the Byzantine Empire, the Emperor used the profits from his liquor and wine monopoly to pay for his enormous household expenses. In the state of Virginia, a local Byzantine Emperor, Senator Harry Byrd, who was then Governor, rammed through the ABC Law in 1933 in a typical Virginia plebiscite; it was later found to have been copied from the statute setting up the Soviet Liquor Trust in Russia! The patronage and the profits from the Liquor Trust have since become the mainstay of the Party Machine. The stateside network of ABC agents terrorizes small businessmen with their carefully developed Gestapo-like tactics and constant surveillance.

Any unfavorable report means the loss of the business, after the all-important "license" is suspended. This power creates an ideal political climate for totalitarian control, continuous shakedowns, which are euphemistically called "contributions," either to the political machine or to "collectors" who promise to pass the funds along to the proper parties. Whether this ever occurs is not traceable in any way. With these profits, Byrd built the largest per capita State Socialist bureaucracy in the United States, which effortlessly perpetuated his machine rule throughout his long political career. To maintain the illusion of a "two-party democracy," Byrd usually allowed token opposition in political campaigns for state offices, but he never permitted any serious opponent to challenge his reign. As a result, he never had to campaign, nor did he have to spend the millions which had been raised to pay his campaign expenses. He routinely filled the state offices with look-alike Byrd stooges, elderly, soft-spoken, white-haired, and hard-drinking men who spoke slowly and carefully, with the Old South modulations of a wool-topped keeper of the men's room at an exclusive country club.

Byrd himself was merely the heir to a longstanding previous corruption. After the Civil War, the carpetbaggers had swarmed into Virginia, seizing the pitiful remnants of property from the defeated and impoverished Virginians. The corruption reached its apogee in 1893, when control of the state legislature was purchased openly, as at a cattle auction, by Senator Thomas Martin. Martin had long been the lawyer for the Morgan-Behnont interests in Virginia, and represented their substantial railroad holdings, the Chesapeake and Ohio Railroad, and the Norfolk and Western Railway.

Congressional testimony showed that J. P. Morgan and Kuhn Loeb Co. between them controlled ninety-two per cent of all the railroad mileage in the United States. Both of them were fronts for the Rothschild interests. The funds advanced for that purpose by the Morgan-Behnont interests (Behnont was the Rothschild's authorized representative in the United States) were used by Martin in 1893 to buy nine members of the legislature for $1,000 each; this gave him complete control of that body. His assistant in this bribery was William A. Glasgow, Jr., the chief counsel for the Norfolk and Western Railway. Martin's chief ally in controlling the state legislature was his able assistant, Senator Hal Flood, grandfather of Senator Byrd. With such political prospects before him, young Harry Byrd left school at the age of fifteen. In 1919, Martin died, and Byrd took over the machine. He ruled it with an iron hand for more than half a century. Politically, Byrd had access to all the funds he needed to control the state, that is, the political slush funds which Rothschild agents routinely dispensed throughout the United States to maintain their control of the nation. The funds came from Kuhn, Loeb Co. in New York, the largest banking house handling Rothschild investments in America. Byrd had been born in Martinsburg, West Virginia; a classmate there had been one Lewis Lichtenstein Strauss. Strauss later became an itinerant shoe salesman. With the advent of World War I, he suddenly showed up in Washington as "secretary" of the U. S. Food Administration, being named assistant to Herbert Hoover, a longtime Rothschild agent who had been named by them as director of their family firm, Rio Tinto. After World War I, Strauss was named a partner in Kuhn, Loeb Co.; Byrd, with Strauss' money behind him, became Governor of Virginia. Strauss bought a large estate at Brandy Station, Virginia, scene of the last cavalry charge in the United States. He continued his long association with Byrd during their years together in Washington. When Byrd retired, Strauss became his son's campaign manager.

After Martin's domination of the state of Virginia for some thirty years, Byrd was in place to take power, just as Stalin was waiting when Lenin mysteriously fell ill and died. For the next fifty years, Virginia suffered from what was not humorously called "the Byrd blight," while Byrd's lifelong financial sacrifices to serve his country in the Senate brought him a vast family empire of orchards, warehouses, banks, newspapers, and stock portfolios. All of this had been gained since he entered the Virginia Senate in 1915. The Byrd millions historically were sweated from cheap labor, which shed some light on why he converted vast areas of Virginia into hopeless regions of poverty; at the same time, neighboring states such as North Carolina enjoyed unparalleled prosperity. The Byrd blight, which resulted in the famous rural poverty area known as Appalachia, ensured the Byrd empire an ample supply of cheap labor; he and his minions bitterly fought government efforts to intervene with their various programs. Byrd refused to allow federal funds to be spent in Virginia unless he retained absolute control over their allotment; they were to go to his political supporters; none other need apply. Byrd realized that dispensation of federal funds would bring a horde of federal supervisors into his domain, while he fought to remain in position to name every recipient of these funds, guaranteeing himself future support from those who had received "the Byrd largesse."

Although he was always dependent upon contributions from the agents of the Rothschilds, Byrd's machine remained politically unassailable because of the statewide network of Masonic lodges, which had been in place for some two hundred years. They controlled every business and every state and local office in each of the Virginia counties and hamlets. No one could expect any advancement or preferment, or even a bank loan, without Masonic approval. Historian Allen Moger writes that "Byrd's power amazed observers"; "it was explained by friends as an association of like-minded men." Moger does not tell us what the like minds were committed to, or that they were "the determined men of Masonry." Moger's book, "Virginia: Bourbon to Byrd," University of Virginia, 1968, does not even mention Masonry in the index! Not only that, but Moger only mentions the Federal Reserve Act twice en passant, with no credit given to the fact that this bill was originated in the House by Carter Glass of Lynchburg, co-authored by Senator Owen of Lynchburg, and signed into law by President Woodrow Wilson of Staunton. In fact, the Virginian, Woodrow Wilson, left an unsurpassed legacy to the nation; he gave us the income tax, World War I, and the Federal Reserve Act. No other President can claim to have saddled his unfortunate fellow-countrymen with so many crushing burdens.

While Byrd kept the state of Virginia in poverty, the newspapers kept the state in ignorance. Having been totally taken over by the Masonic Order of Canaanites, they carefully refrained from printing anything that Byrd's Pravda (or Truth) would disapprove. No censorship was necessary; every editor and reporter in the state knew what was required of their unbiased journalism. The "federal" area, the northeast bedroom community bordering Washington, was dominated by the Washington Post, the family property of the Meyer family. Eugene Meyer, partner of Lazard Freres international bankers, had purchased the paper cheaply, and gradually drove all of his competition out of business. The political activist, Lyndon LaRouche, also operated in the Washington area. He was allowed free rein until he published a story that "the black widow," Katharine Graham, daughter of Eugene Meyer, had killed her husband, Philip Graham, to prevent him from giving the Post to his current girl friend. Shortly after LaRouche printed this story in his newspaper, 648 federal agents swarmed down on his headquarters at Leesburg, Virginia, seizing all of his documents and carting many of his assistants off to jail. If they were looking for Philip Graham's death certificate, the ostensible reason for the raid, they didn't find it; the concerned agencies had steadfastly refused to release it, or to even let anyone see it. If LaRouche had had any doubts about the power behind the Washington Post, he was soon enlightened; his entire operation seemed to have been shattered.

Byrd himself traditionally laid down the party line for the state in his chain of newspapers, which was run from Winchester. A survey by professors of journalism ranked the state of Virginia 49th in the nation in the record of its press' public service campaigns. Byrd's papers, like most of the other Virginia newspapers, were generally considered "the end of the road" by the profession because of their lower pay and working conditions. Most Virginia publishers,

Masons to the man, conformed to the image which Byrd cultivated, and aspired only to be accepted into the local "squirearchy." At the same time, they continually printed editorials cynically denying that there had ever been a "Byrd machine" in the state of Virginia!

The eastern press of the state is totally dominated by Media General, a conglomerate which had been put together from the Richmond newspapers and a Norfolk publication. The Richmond papers had strong scalawag and carpetbagger connections; after World War II they showed powerful CIA direction. Their chairman, Joseph Bryan, had served in Naval Intelligence during World War I, and as chairman of the 5th Federal Reserve district. To prove his stellar liberal credentials, he was appointed to the board of overseers of Harvard University. His son married into the Standard Oil fortune, the Harkness Davidson family. He is also a director of the Hoover Institution, a supposedly rightwing think tank, and a member of the exclusive Bohemian Club of San Francisco. The senior vice president of Media General is James A. Linen IV. Formerly vice president of the National Enquirer, which is widely reputed to be a CIA or a Mafia operation, or both, he is the son of James A. Linen III, the longtime publisher of Time Magazine. James A. Linen IV is also chairman of the American Thai Corporation, which operates in the marketing area of the drug empire known as "the Golden Triangle," an area which has been dominated by the CIA for years. The founder of ass (later the CIA), William J. Donovan, was appointed Ambassador to Thailand in 1953.

For many years, Richmond Newspapers had as its chairman of the board Paul Manheim, partner of Lehman Brothers in New York. The Lehmans made millions during the Civil War, when they operated as agents and fixers for both belligerents, moving easily back and forth through the zones of war. Paul Manheim was also a director of Bankers

Trust in New York, and Paramount Pictures in Hollywood. His brother Frank Manheim, also a partner of Lehman Brothers, was a director of Warner Brothers. They exercised financial control over these giant studios during the years when the producers relentlessly churned out leftwing pictures; this could not have been done without their approval.

The passing of Harry Byrd brought no significant change to the iron hand which ruled Virginia; the same officials of the Masonic Order of Canaanites continued to exercise absolute power. The state became even more depressed, its people even more discouraged, and increasingly suspicious of each other, mired in self-hatred and gloom. The Byrd excrescence was merely the twentieth century manifestation of a cancer which has rotted life in Virginia since the earliest settlement. Vernon Stauffer's definitive work, "New England the Bavarian Illuminati," reproduces a speech made by Rev. Jedediah Morse, delivered at Charleston on April 25, 1799, from which we excerpt: "It has long been suspected that secret societies, under the influence and direction of France, holding principles subversive of our religion and government, existed somewhere in this country ... I have, my brethren, an official, authenticated list of the names, ages, places of nativity, professions &c. of the officers and members of a Society of Illuminati (or as they are now more generally and properly styled Illuminees) consisting of one hundred members, instituted in Virginia, by the Grand Orient of France ... The date of their institution is 1786 ... " Morse then translated a letter in French for the benefit of the audience, from the French Master to the Virginia disciples, "At the East of the Lodge of Portsmouth in Virginia, the 17th of the 5th month, in the year of (V .. L.) True Light 5798: The (R .. L. .Pte .. Fse ..) respectable French Provincial Lodge, regularly appointed under the distinctive title of WISDOM, No. 2660 by the GRAND ORIENT OF FRANCE. TO The (T .. R .. L. .) very respectable French Lodge, the Union, No. 14, constituted by the Grand Orient of New York. S .. F .. V .. TT .. CC .. and RR .. FF." These abbreviations are apparently a secret code. The letter goes on to report the establishment of two new Masonic workshops in Petersburg, Virginia, and in the East of Port de Paix in the Island of St. Domingo. It closes with the salutation, "May the Grand Architect of the Universe bless your labours, and crown them will all manner of success. P .. L .. N .. M .. Q .. V .. S .. C .. TT .. CC .. and TT .. RR .. FF .. By order of the very respectable Provincial Lodge of Wisdom, Guieu, Secretary." Morse declared that there were at that time at least seventeen hundred Illuminati in the United States, "systematically conducting the plan of revolutionizing this country ... The changes which they can produce by secret influence and intrigue, the novel arts which they can thus exhibit before the eyes of men, are doubtless to be efficacious means of teaching men the new system of philosophy, which sets at defiance, and condemns all old and settled opinions, by which the governments of nations and the conduct of individuals have heretofore been directed."

Thus we find from Rev. Morse's investigation that the state of Virginia had long been infiltrated, and was being "run" as a colony by the French Illuminati. All the while, the people of Virginia supposed that they had a state government composed of dedicated politicians who wished only to serve this state. This has never been the case. The secret society has always been in control. From the outset, the Masonic Canaanites in Virginia always seized the highest offices. The career of Edmund Randolph aptly illustrates this point. The Winchester Lodge No. 12 was established by the Grand Lodge of Pennsylvania in 1768. (Winchester was the lifelong headquarters of Harry Byrd during his fifty-year rule of Virginia; he owned the Winchester newspaper.) The Grand Lodge of Virginia was established at Williamsburg, which was then the capital of Virginia, on October 13, 1768, and is said to be the oldest Grand Lodge in America. The first Grand Master of the Grand Lodge of Virginia was John Blair. At that time, he was the Acting Governor of the Commonwealth of Virginia. On October 27, 1786, Edmund Randolph was unanimously elected Grand Master of the Grand Lodge of Virginia. He was at that time the Attorney General of the State of Virginia. From that day on, the legal system of Virginia has been continuously in the hands of the Masonic Order. On the day after his election as Grand Master, Edmund Randolph signed the charter of the Staunton, Virginia, Lodge, which became Lodge No 13. The number 13, as we have pointed out, is of tremendous significance in the Masonic Order. Lodge No. 13 has played a pivotal role in the conduct of state affairs ever since. In fact, the Supreme Court of Virginia set up its offices in Lodge No. 13's Masonic Building.

Edmund Randolph had an outstanding career, moving easily from one high office to another, as usually occurs when one has the world power of the Masonic hierarchy behind him. His path was considerably smoother after he joined the Williamsburg Lodge of the Ancient Order of York Masons at the age of 21, in 1774. A few months later, he was given the signal honor of being named aide de camp to General George Washington himself. The following year, he was named the first Attorney General of the State of Virginia. He was named Deputy Grand Master of the Grand Lodge of Virginia in 1785, and he then laid the cornerstone of the new Masonic Lodge in Richmond. The next year, he was named Grand Master. Not only was Edmund Randolph symbolic of Masonic power; he and his family also represented the traditional power of the British Crown in the colonies. His father, John Randolph, was King's Attorney, as had been his grandfather, Sir John Randolph.

Edmund Randolph's father, a leading Tory, proved his loyalty to the King by leaving Virginia with the departing

British Governor, Lord Dunmore, and returning to England with him. He never came back to America, yet his son played a crucial role in writing the Constitution! Edmund Randolph was adopted by his uncle, Peyton Randolph, after his father's defection; his uncle was also King's Attorney. Peyton Randolph was also a Grand Master of the Masonic Order; he was soon named first President of the First Continental Congress. Thus we see that the British power in the colonies, wielded through its King's Attorneys, was also wielded through the members of the Mason Order, the York Rite which traditionally was headed by a member of the royal family. Peyton Randolph had no children; Edmund inherited his vast estates.

Not only was Edmund Randolph's loyalty to the American cause overshadowed by his father's defection, he himself showed strong signs of loyalty to England. Thomas Jefferson reported that when Patrick Henry delivered his famous speech, "Give me liberty or give me death," it was Edmund Randolph and his law professor, George Wythe, who leaped to their feet, shouting "TREASON!" Later, Edmund Randolph and Patrick Henry almost fought a duel during their quarrel as to whether Virginia should join the Union. Governor George Clinton of New York, a member of the Illuminati and a leading Mason, offered Randolph a deal to join with New York in opposing the ratification of the Constitution. Instead, Randolph kept quiet on the matter, and was rewarded by Washington with the post of the first Attorney General of the United States; Washington then appointed him the second Secretary of State, after Thomas Jefferson resigned. Virginia was the tenth state to ratify the Constitution; New York was the eleventh.

It was Edmund Randolph who actually was the unseen hand behind the writing of the Constitution. A convention had been called to amend the Articles of Confederation to the point where they would be accepted by the states.

Instead of doing this, Edmund Randolph, who was then Governor of Virginia, cleverly steered the delegates to the idea of writing a new set of laws, the Constitution, as a federal entity which would incorporate the states. He sprang the agenda for this new cause of action upon the delegates with no previous warning, and soon persuaded them that this would be the best course to pursue. Thus it was the Grand Master of Virginia, Edmund Randolph, in league with Aaron Burr and British Intelligence, who foisted on the nation the concept of a federal government which could rule over and above the sovereignties of the states. All of our subsequent political trials, including the Civil War, stemmed from this Masonic conspiracy, which perfected the technique of ending the sovereignty of the several states, and placing them under the Masonic Oriental despotism of a central federal government.

This was done as a typical Masonic Canaanite conspiracy. The "Records of-the Federal Convention" show the Virginia contingent to consist of "His Excellency George Washington, George Wythe, Gov. Edmund Randolph, John Blair, James Madison, George Mason, and James M. McClurg. Blair was former Grand Master of the Grand Lodge of Virginia; Edmund Randolph was the present Grand Master.

George Wythe read the rules which were to be followed during the convention. On May 29, 1787, the stipulation was made "that the federal government could not check the quarrels between states, nor a rebellion in any state having constitutional power nor means to interpose according to the exigency."

Gov. Edmund Randolph then opened the proceedings by launching an all-out attack on the Articles of Confederation. "He observed that the confederation fulfilled none of the objects for which it was framed. [He then listed them; we quote number 5.] 5. It is not superior to state constitutions. Thus we see that the confederation is incompetent to anyone object for which it was instituted. Our chief danger arises from the democratic parts of our constitution." Randolph then raised the specter of lack of defense, claiming that the states had no defense against attack, and calling for a plan of national defense. He ignored the fact that the states had just concluded a successful revolt against the greatest military power in the world. As part of the Masonic conspiracy, Randolph used this specter to foist on the convention a new constitution, which established a national legislature, a national executive, and a national judiciary, thus creating what had never been desired or envisioned by the other delegates, a supreme federal power having control of the several states.

As is often the case with prominent Masons, Randolph's public career was marred by repeated scandals, due to his involvement with alien powers. He had become deeply involved with the Illuminati adventurer, Edmond Genet, who had been sent as the first French Ambassador to the new Republic. Genet landed at Charleston on April 8, 1793, to be enthusiastically greeted by his fellow Masons of the Charleston Lodge, the Mother Lodge of the World. Genet immediately began to act as a conquering general, issuing commissions and letters of marque to his Masonic colleagues.

When he arrived in Washington, instead of presenting his credentials immediately to President Washington, as protocol required, he ignored him. Instead, Genet gave a great banquet, during which he received demonstrations and deputations like, a visiting monarch. During the ceremonies, the symbolic red Phrygian cap of the Illuminati revolutionaries was reverently passed from table to table. Observers soon noted that "the high-handed insolence of Genet grew from day to day more intolerable." Thomas

Jefferson, who was then Secretary of State, was daily besieged with demands that Genet's credentials be rescinded, and that he be asked to leave the capital. Jefferson refused these demands. As they increased, and more pressure was brought to bear on him, Jefferson, rather than act against a Mason, resigned as Secretary of State. Washington appointed Edmund Randolph to succeed him. In 1794, Genet was busily organizing an army to invade Florida and Louisiana and to seize these territories from Spain. This was a key element of a Masonic plot to set up a separate republic on the borders of the thirteen colonies, and possibly later, to invade and reconquer the United States for England.

When he was informed of these military objectives of Genet, President Washington had no alternative but to order Secretary of State Randolph to seize Genet's credentials and have him removed. Incredibly, Randolph failed to act on this direct request of the President. To protect Genet, he delayed the procedure. However, Genet was a member of the Girondist faction in France, which had now been defeated by Marat; he was ordered recalled, and a new ambassador, Joseph Fouchet, now arrived from France. President Washington also issued a proclamation halting Genet's proposed expedition against Florida and Louisiana. This document, dated February 21, 1794, was also held back by Randolph to aid Genet. On March 24, exasperated by Randolph's repeated delays, Washington personally issued the proclamation himself. Meanwhile, Genet had gone to Charleston, where he was hailed as a conquering hero by the members of the Charleston Lodge, including Stephen Morini, Abraham Israel, Isaac and Abraham da Costa, Samuel de la Motta, Israel Delieben, and Abraham Alexander.

In August 1795, dispatches by Fouchet to France were seized by privateers; the papers found their way back to

President Washington. These diplomatic papers contained a number of documents which clearly implicated Edmund Randolph in financial deals with fouchet, showing evidence of bribery and treason. Once he had seen these papers, President Washington had no alternative but to demand Randolph's resignation. He is the only Secretary of State who had to resign under such charges. Randolph never again held public office, although he lived thirty-eight years after his disgrace, dying in 1813.

After Edmund Randolph sent in his resignation, the accounts of the Secretary of State showed that $49,000 was missing from the funds of the department. A later Treasury Department investigation showed an additional $61,000 was missing, for which Edmund Randolph was solely responsible. Thus the Grand Master of Virginia Masonry left office under a cloud of accusations of bribery, treason, and embezzlement. This was hardly surprising in a man who had sworn to rebel against God, and to impose the demon worship of Baal on his unsuspecting fellow-citizens. The missing government funds were never recovered.

Edmund Randolph devoted his later years to the practice of law. Because of his Masonic connections, he never wanted for clients. He also worked for years on the writing of a massive History of Virginia, which he began in 1786, and finally completed in 1810. For some reason, he made no attempt to have it published. The manuscript was stored for many years at Staunton Lodge No. 13, and was finally published by the University of Virginia Press in 1970. Although it is a well-researched and factual work, it does not contain a single reference to Freemasonry or to the part which this organization played in controlling the state from behind the scenes.

During his legal career, Edmund Randolph received considerable publicity because of his defense of two controversial criminals, George Wythe Sweeney and Aaron Burr. Sweeney was the nephew of George Wythe, who is generally regarded as the father of the legal profession in the United States, because of his long tenure as professor of law at the College of William and Mary in Williamsburg. His pupils included Thomas Jefferson, Edmund Randolph, and many other political figures. Like his close friend, Edmund Randolph, George Wythe's commitment to the cause of the Revolution was always suspect. It was Wythe and Randolph who had shouted "Treason!" at Patrick Henry. In 1793, George Wythe, sitting as Judge of the Chancery Court of Richmond, ruled against Americans and awarded British creditors full payment from Virginia debtors on all loans predating the Revolutionary War, holding them to the full valuation of the loans. Many Virginians demanded that Wythe be lynched because of this Tory decision, although it was more likely a Masonic one.

Wythe had a young wife who died after only one year of marriage; she was but sixteen. Henry Clay then became secretary to Wythe at Chancery Court and for some years was like a son to him.

Wythe's housekeeper, a slave named Lydia Broadnax, became his consort, and he had a son by her, whom he set free. Dr. John Dove reported the subsequent events in a document now known as "Dove's Memorandum": "Wythe had a yellow woman by the name of Lydia who lived with him as wife or mistress as was quite common in the city. By this woman he had a son named Mike." In 1806, Edmund Randolph was called in by Wythe to write a codicil to his will, providing that some of his stock in the Bank of Virginia be left to his son, Mike. Wythe had a grandnephew named Sweeney who was to be his principal heir. Wythe claimed that the nephew had been stealing from him, and he called Randolph in to write a second codicil leaving Mike the remainder of his bank stock. In fact, Wythe's decision was prompted by his passion for the youth, who for some time had been serving him as a catamite, according to the Curse of Canaan.

Through the natural aging process, Lydia, who was about the same age as the now venerable Wythe, was no longer a satisfactory bed partner. Wythe, still lusty beyond his years, now began to satisfy himself with his handsome mulatto bastard. Overcome by his passion for the youth, he made his fatal mistake. The tradition of the Old South was that an owner might sire as many mulatto children as he wished, they being a desirable commercial commodity, and the lighter-skinned, the higher the price; an equally powerful tradition was that such offspring could never inherit money or property. They were often left some clothing, perhaps a gold watch, but the owner was never expected to award them status by willing them large sums of money or land holdings.

Because he violated this fundamental principle, Wythe was murdered by his rightful heir. Wythe's will provided that if Mike preceded him in death, Sweeney would receive the entire estate. Sweeney prepared coffee for his granduncle and Mike, and laced it heavily with arsenic. They both died in agony. Sweeney was charged with murder, and much damaging evidence was presented against him; that he had purchased arsenic, and testimony from Lydia that she had seen him put something in the coffee. Nevertheless, Edmund Randolph, who defended Sweeney, won acquittal by jury. Thus George Wythe, the father of the legal profession in the United States, had a personal history rife with miscegenation, homosexuality, and murder by arsenic poisoning. Here again, we can only conjecture that much of the later antics of the legal profession in America would prove to be equally colorful if its true history could be revealed to the public. Wythe had violated a basic principle by which his society lived, and so his murder went unpunished. The scene is worthy of a turgid drama in ancient Rome, perhaps to be set to music by Verdi; an aging aristocrat resolves to leave his estate to his compliant catamite, and is promptly poisoned by an angry relative. Somehow, one is not surprised to find that the principal actor in this sweaty drama is also the acknowledged founder of the legal profession in America.

Edmund Randolph made another appearance to defend a noted criminal; after he had delayed government action against Edmond Genet, Genet was finally deported. The plot to set up a rival republic in Louisiana was then taken over by the Masonic leaders Edward Livingston and Aaron Burr. Burr was finally brought to trial for treason in sensational proceedings which were conducted in Richmond, Virginia. Here again, the Masons brought in their former Grand Master, Edmund Randolph, to defend Burr. Not surprisingly, the sitting judge was Chief Justice John Marshall, who was at that time Grand Master of the Lodge of Virginia. Burr was acquitted. Indeed to have convicted him, one would have needed the strength to defy the entire Masonic Canaanite conspiracy in the United States. No such person appeared.

The amazing acquittal of Burr by his Masonic fellow-conspirators has been repeated thousands of times in the Virginia courts. Stephen King reports in "The Brotherhood" that in England, from fifty to seventy per cent of all judges are Masons, and that ninety per cent of the members of the Laws Society (corresponding to our Bar Association) are Masons. The legal system in the United States, from all appearances, has an even higher preponderance of Masons. Thus we have no federal, state, or local courts; we have only Masonic courts. The result is that judicial decisions on Rules of Evidence, motions for or against discovery, and other legal procedures, are decided solely on the basis of whether they will aid or injure a Mason involved in the suit. The

Masonic Handbook commands (p. 183-184): "Whenever you see any of our signs made by a brother Mason, and especially the grand hailing sign of distress, you must always be sure to obey them, even at the risk of your own life. If you are on a jury, and the defendant is a Mason, and makes the grand hailing sign, you must obey it; you must disagree with your brother jurors, if necessary, but you must be sure not to bring the Mason in as guilty, for that would bring disgrace upon our order."

It was for these reasons that Congressman Thaddeus Stevens sponsored a resolution demanding that Freemasonry be suppressed, denouncing it as "a secret, oath-bound, murderous institution that endangers the continuance of Republican government," and further demanded that being a Mason would be cause for peremptory challenge in court, and made it unlawful for a Mason to sit as judge in a trial involving another Mason. For years, thousands of Americans have been puzzled by the odd decisions rendered in our courts. They do not know what has taken place; the victims of these injustices have no way of knowing that they have been subjected to the arrant assumptions of an Oriental despotism masquerading under color of law; that no justice can be administered if the Judge has taken an oath under penalty of death to always rule in favor of a brother Mason. But, asks the doubter, what if both parties in a lawsuit are Masons, and the judge is a Mason what then? In that case, my friend, the case will be judged on its merits. However, if a non-Mason is a party to the suit, he is bound to lose.

The Handbook continues: "You must conceal all crimes of your brother Masons..., except murder and treason, and these only at your own option, and should you be summoned as a witness against a brother Mason, be always sure to shield him. Prevaricate, don't tell the truth in this case, keep his secrets, forget the important parts. It may be perjury to do this, it is true, but you are keeping your obligations."

This writer knows of cases where a Mason was called into a case to commit perjury against his own brother, in order to defend a fellow Mason. This writer has been involved in many lawsuits in which subornation of perjury by Masonic lawyers was the order of the day; altered records, legal documents which the clerks of the court denied ever receiving even though they had been personally handed to them, judges who do not bother to even read the motions filed by a non-Mason, and important documents supporting his charges which are stolen from his home, including copies of checks, receipts, and other vital papers. The Will of Canaan instructs these criminals, "Never tell the truth," and they are faithful to Canaan's admonition. This is justice as it is handed out in a legal system which is dominated by Masons, and Virginia is one of the prime offenders. This writer has frequently sent in complaints against Masonic lawyers and judges to the United States Attorneys; in every case, the Department of Justice replied to documented evidence of blackmail and extortion, "You should hire a private attorney." In other words, find yourself a Masonic lawyer and take it from there. The Masonic Handbook says, "If you cheat, wrong, or defraud any other society or individual, it is entirely your business. If you cheat government even, Masonry cannot and will not touch you; but be very careful not to cheat, wrong, or defraud a brother Mason or lodge. Who ever else you may defraud, live up to your [Masonic] obligations."

This again is merely a restatement of the Will of Canaan. The Virginia courts are particularly vicious in the legal procedures involving pretrial discovery, or questioning of the opponent. In many civil lawsuits, this writer has seen his discovery demands ignored by the opponent without penalty, but in every instance, when the opponent and his

Masonic lawyers make the most outrageous demands upon this writer, the judge never fails to place him under court order to provide whatever the opponent requests. In a recent suit in which this writer sued to recover substantial embezzlement of the proceeds of his history of the Federal Reserve System, the embezzler had his attorneys place this writer under court order to produce all of his expense accounts and income tax returns for the past thirty-three years! When he could not do so, he was faced with an indeterminate jail sentence, with the alternative offered by the lawyers that he could turn over the entire bank account of proceeds from the sale of his book. This was done; the result of thirty-five years work went to an unprincipled person who had had the foresight to hire two of the most influential politically connected law firms in Virginia to defend him. In any case, this writer, not being a Mason, had no expectation of obtaining justice in any American court, and he never has.

The American system of jurisprudence, as practiced, is the enshrinement of a system of Oriental despotism to compel non-Masons to accede to enslavement by Masons. This system, which has no relationship to the Constitution of the United States, derives its authority from the Hindu law book of Manu, "The whole world is kept in order by punishment." This is the complete opposite of the law of the people of Shem, as enshrined in the Anglo-Saxon common law, and which is based on the assumption that because men are basically good, they should never be compelled to do any act against their will.

Karl Wittfogel exposes the system in his work, "The Hydraulic Society," in which he defines our legal system as a system of Oriental despotism which is based on the government's control of water supplies, their subsequent allotment of these supplies to favored adherents, and the condemning of everyone else to suffer from lack of water for agricultural endeavors or home needs. Thus government agencies have made great strides-in seizing control of water, the latest being the Virginia bureaucracy's desperate effort to place all rural wells under state control, and to meter them, charging the farmer for the water on his own land! This Soviet plan is frenetically supported by agricultural "experts," colleges, and other bureaucrats.

The ensuing disrespect for law and order creates a climate in which the citizen no longer can believe or trust anyone or any official. This produces desperation, which in turn will soon produce social change. We have reached the apogee of cynical manipulation of our legal system by perjurers and criminal conspirators acting on the instructions of their Masonic Canaanite order. Either we will restore the rule of law, or these Oriental despots will reduce us all to serfs obedient to their every command. To walk into a courtroom in Virginia and hear the snickers of the Masonic lawyers and judges, contemptuous of anyone who has not had the foresight to enlist themselves in their sinister conspiracy, is to realize the final degradation of a once proud state and its people. The dignity of the office of Governor of Virginia may be measured by the fact that it was once purchased by a DuPont heiress as a birthday gift for her husband. She later explained at a Capitol tea, "I wanted to get him some antique furniture for his birthday, and when I shopped around, I found that the Governor's chair was the cheapest thing on the market!"

An Ohio businessman who had settled in Virginia found that he needed a certain measure passed by the state legislature in order to protect his enterprise. He nervously asked a prominent Virginia landowner, "Can I look for someone down there who needs some financial assistance?" "Don't be ridiculous!" snorted his friend. "You couldn't buy a single one of those people. They were all bought and paid for before they got there!"

The Byrd legacy lives on in the iron control maintained over every aspect of life in Virginia, the press, state and local governments, education, and the Masonic control of the court system. The carpetbagger tradition was upheld in the area when two wealthy carpetbaggers, Rockefeller of New York and Robb of Texas and points west, encountered no difficulty in purchasing office. Rockefeller bought the Governorship of West Virginia (which had been illegally torn from Virginia territory during the Civil War). Robb became Governor of Virginia, after claiming descent from one John Lewis, who fled from Ireland after committing murder. As a handsome young Marine officer, Robb had caught the roving eye of President Lyndon Johnson, who later married him off to his daughter. Thus Robb became the beneficiary of the Johnson millions, which, like the Byrd empire, had been amassed during a lifetime career of dedicated service to the public. As Governor, Robb created his own revolution, ruthlessly firing Virginians with good records, and replacing them with blacks and feminists. Their socialist policies created havoc in many departments, most notably in the department of corrections, where widespread prison riots destroyed Robb's hopes of higher public office. As part of his Canaanite scheme to further degrade Virginians, he offered $1,000 in cash to any black who would enroll in Virginia schools, but there were few takers. With the state of Virginia in shambles as the result of Robb's policies, the Republican Party was a shoo-in to regain the state offices. Knowing they would lose anyway, the Democrats decided to run a black as Lieutenant Governor, the first such candidate for statewide office. Amazingly enough, the Republican national leaders then instructed the Virginia Republicans not to mount a campaign in opposition, claiming that they might be interpreted as being "anti-black." The Republicans abandoned their campaign, and the surprised Democrats easily won, with no opposition. They immediately imposed a $426 million tax increase on all Virginians; the Republicans had been firmly opposed to any tax increase. It was estimated that each vote for the Democrats in this election would cost the unfortunate taxpayers in Virginia an additional $1,000 per year.

In this recital of Masonic power and its incumbent operations in the state of Virginia, we have not wished to slight any other state. In New York, Illinois, and other states, the Masonic conspirators dictate the choice of political candidates, how they will be financed, and whether they will be elected. The criminals are committed to maintaining Masonic control through their demoniacal Babylonian monetary system, which gives them absolute power; they control every aspect of the economic system through their techniques of taxation and interest. Every act of government is legislated with this program in view.

In 1967, this writer issued a public appeal to the people of Virginia, titled "Fifty Years of Shame," which concluded with the demand: "5. Restoration of the government of Virginia to the people of Virginia. Abolition of all Soviet-type trusts such as the ABC Board and restoration of free enterprise and small individually-owned businesses. Soon the Byrd era will only be a dark stain on the history of this fair state. Let us work together to achieve the Virginia that we love, the Virginia that we want, the Virginia of our great traditions!"

Despite statewide distribution of this appeal, the craven and demoralized citizens of Virginia feared to make a single response.

CHAPTER 9

THE WORLD WARS

lbert Pike had promised his Masonic allies in Europe that they would have three world wars to consolidate the world power of the Canaanites. We have now seen two of those world wars, and, as promised, the first world war was to set up a Communist regime, the second world war was to raise it to the status of a world power, and the third world war is planned to destroy both Communism and Christianity in a great orgy of annihilation. This coming war is intended to be the final death knell of the people of Shem; after its conclusion the Canaanites will reign unchallenged throughout the world.

The two world wars which have already taken place in the twentieth century have been nothing more than wars of extermination, as proven by the fact that most of the onslaught has been directed against women and children. The millions of young men of Shem who have been killed in these wars did not have an opportunity to marry and begin families. All of this was done according to the plan of the Canaanites. Working behind the scenes for many years to place their agents in positions of guidance and power in the various nations of the world, they have been able to carry out their own designs, often in direct violation of the interests of the nations which they have infiltrated. Of all countries, this has been most true-of the United States. It is difficult to think of a single act of foreign policy in the past fifty years which the Washington agencies have directed as a benefit to the American people. By achieving dominant roles in all factions and parties in the United States, the Canaanites have faced no serious opposition in planning and executing their programs. As a result, the wars and revolutions of the twentieth century have been nothing more than great celebrations before the image of Baal, large scale human sacrifices in such numbers as the world has never seen. The emphasis on the massacres of women and children are twentieth century updated observances of the child murders and immolation of women which marked the festivals of Baal more than three thousand years ago. This will come as a shock to those scholars who have labored patiently for decades in the hopes of finding some logical explanation of the two past world wars, some economic or political cause which they have sought as a prospector might patiently toil through the arid hills of the west, seeking the Lost Dutchman's Mine. The Lost Dutchman's Mine has not been found; neither have the scholars discovered any logical cause of World War I and World War II. Let us, then, attempt to end their quest, and allow them respite.

In the Boer War, for the first time in a war conducted by a major European power, the British used concentration camps, starvation and disease as the crucial weapons to subdue the enemy. These atrocities were directed by Sir Alfred Milner, a Rothschild agent who had founded the Round Tables (which later became the Council on Foreign Relations). The stakes were high; the Rothschilds needed the enormous capital represented by the gold and diamond riches of South Africa to finance their final drive for world power. Because of these riches, South Africa remains one of the world's principal areas of contention today. The furor about "apartheid" and "racial problems" provides a convenient cover for the real struggle of the Rothschilds to protect their diamond holdings, DeBeers, and their gold hoard, Anglo-American Corporation. The Rothschilds have also managed to pick up a few billion dollars by speculating in the South African rand. Due to their worldwide media campaign, they drove the rand down from $1.45 to 25¢.

The Babylonian monetary system relies on a strong central government, that is, a non-representational Oriental despotism, which in turn is dependent on its continual financing by a strong central bank. The central bank exercises power by obtaining a monopoly on the entire money and credit of the people; it then uses this power to loot the nation through enormous expenditures.

The Rothschilds established central banks throughout Europe, as one of the plums which fell to them after their victory over Napoleon. They then programmed these central banks to launch the nations of Europe on a costly and ruinous "arms race," even though no nation in Europe had any plans for attacking any other nation. It was a time of continuous peace. By the year 1886, it was apparent that these nations could no longer survive these enormous expenditures; they must either collapse into internal revolution, or embark on fullscale external war.

The European economies staggered on for nearly three decades, with no relief in sight. These were the years, we might recall, which have been termed the "Golden Years" of Europe. Art, music, and Cultural institutions flourished in spite of the Canaanite conspiracies. However, it was soon to be thrown on the block. The way out of their dilemma was granted by a curious American, of undefined origins, a dour academic who convinced the bankers of Wall Street that he was their man. Woodrow Wilson was elected President, and he signed the Federal Reserve Act into law. A few months later, World War One was under way.

During the years immediately preceding the World War, there was a continuous outflow of emigrants from Europe to the United States. They had found that "the Golden

Years" were not golden for those who had no gold. The masters of the Order, the Canaanites, floated from country to country and from great estate to great estate on a sea of champagne, but for most Europeans, life was brutal and short. They did not flee "the good life"; they were searching for it.

At a millionaires' club on Jekyl Island, Georgia, in November, 1910, the problem of financing a world war was resolved. Paul Warburg, of Kuhn, Loeb Co., and Henry P. Davison, of J. P. Morgan Co., met with Senator Nelson Aldrich (after whom Nelson Rockefeller was named) to secretly draft a plan for an American central bank. Seventy-five years later, it is impossible to find any Establishment scholar or historian who has ever heard of the Jekyl Island meeting. They earn their comfortable salaries by concealing from the public what has taken place.

The people of Shem had always opposed a central bank, fearing its power over them. Now the Congressmen, led by Congressman Charles A. Lindbergh, Sr., waged a gallant struggle against the power of Wall Street money. The Wall Street money won. On December 23, 1913, a significant year in Masonry, Wilson signed the Federal Reserve Act into law. The American people were now poised for a great roller coaster ride, up and down from depression to prosperity and back again, and from world war to world war.

The actual planning for the outbreak of World War I had been in operation for some years. The fuse was to be lit by the assassination of Archduke Ferdinand, the heir to the throne of the Austro- Hungarian Empire. His murder was carried out at Sarajevo on June 28, 1914. Within a few weeks, the nations of Europe were at war.

Surprisingly enough, the approaching fate of the archduke had been widely known for some time to

European politicians, including the Archduke himself. Cassell's "The World War," p. 45, quotes Count Ottkar Czernin, the Austrian Foreign Minister: "A fine quality of the Archduke was his fearlessness. He was quite clear that the danger of an attempt to take his life would always be present, and he often spoke quite simply and openly of such a possibility. A year before the outbreak of war, he informed me that the Freemasons had resolved to kill him." This is not as startling a revelation as it may seem. The Masonic Order of Canaanites has always relied upon murder and assassination as the key elements in its march to world power; many royal heads have fallen before their lust for vengeance.

On July 11, 1914, Horatio Bottomley published in John Bull a document obtained from the Serbian Legation in London, dated April 14, 1914, which was found to be in "crude Spanish," and which was decoded to reveal an offer of two thousand pounds for "eliminating" Ferdinand.

Prof. R. W. Seton-Watson, in his book, "Sarajevo," p. 127, notes that "crude Spanish is really the dialect employed by the Jews of Salonika, and that the man who hawked this document round several London newspaper offices and was eventually accepted by the sensation-loving Bottomley, was a Salonikan Jew. This suggests some connection with the Committee for Union and Progress, which had centered in the Jewish lodges of Salonika until the expulsion of the Turks eighteen months previously, and whose course was actively hostile to Serbia."

Rt. Hon. W. F. Bailey, in his book, "Jews of the War Zone," p. 227, notes that "The Jews of Bosnia are named 'Spagnolo'."

C. H. Norman notes in "A Searchlight on the World War," p. 42, that "the originals were worded in Spanish. It is within the writer's knowledge [as he was connected with an endeavor to form an English Lodge of the Grand Orient, from which he withdrew on learning of the real nature of this confederacy against European safety] that the language used by the Polish Dept. of the grand Orient for communication with its agents in the Balkans is Spanish."

Ambassador Gerard, in his book "My Four Years in Germany," p. 137, notes, "I was able to converse with some Serbians in the first days of the war in their native tongue, which, curiously enough, was Spanish."

In fact the language was not Spanish, but a language defined in the Encyclopaedia Judaica as "Ladino," also known as "Latino," "a Judeo-Spanish spoken and written language of Jews of Spanish origin after expulsion in 1492 by Ferdinand and Isabella [The execution of Ferdinand may have been a symbolic revenge for this historic event. Ed.]." The Encyclopaedia Judaica notes various forms of Ladino: "Oriental Ladino" spoken in Constantinople and Smyrna, and "Western Ladino" spoken in Salonika, Bosnia, and Serbia. Many of the refugees from Spain settled in Serbia, where they ever afterward conversed in their private tongue, Western Ladino. Pozzi's book, "Black Hand Over Europe," notes of "A Mr. Stevens, who spoke Spanish, whose job was to shoot the murderers at Sarajevo after they had performed the assassination, so that they could not reveal the plot."

These revelations bear out the insistence of Albert Pike to Mazzini some forty years earlier to involve the nations of the world in three world wars. Grant Richards, in "The Cause of World Unrest," 1920, p. 144, comments on the Committee for Union and Progress: "Indeed, I can go so far as to say that the Union for Progress was practically born in the Masonic Lodge called 'Macedonia Risorta' established by the Salonikan Jew, Emannuele Carass ... though Freemasonry was forbidden in Turkey, there were two lodges in Salonika under the Grand Orient of Italy." Mathias Erzberger, in "Experience in the Great War," stresses that the Grand Orient of Italy was completely under the control of the Grand Orient of France; he refers to the transfer of 700,000 francs from Paris to Rome between the Grand Orients on behalf of the Jewish charitable trust, Alliance Israelite Universelle; this is the funding which was provided for the assassination at Sarajevo.

McCurdy's "The Truth About the Secret Treaties," 1925, quotes on page 45 the article published in 1914, "After Vivordan," by Ljuba Jovanovitch, president of the Serbian Parliament and Minister of Education, "I do not remember if it were the end of Mayor the beginning of June when one day, M. Pashitch told us that certain persons were preparing to go to Sarajevo, in order to kill Franz Ferdinand, who was expected there on Vivordan, Sunday, June 28th. He told this much to us and others, but he acted further in the office only with Stefan Protitch, then Minister of the Interior; this was prepared by a society of secretly organized men. Protitch and the whole cabinet of Serbia knew of the plot. King Alexander, the Russian Minister Hartwig, and the Russian military attache Artmanov were in on the plot. M. Pashitch's nephew was a member of the Black Hand; he was the link between Protitch and the conspirators. The agent of the Black Hand in Sarajevo was Gatchinovitch. The Black Hand where the murder plans had long been laid was known by and encouraged by the government of Serbia. Printzip confessed that it was through Ciganovitch that they had been referred to Major Tankositch, supplied with weapons, and given shooting lessons.

After the Salonika trial, the Pashitch government sent Ciganovitch, as a reward for his services, to America with a false passport under the name of Danielovitch. After the war, Ciganovitch returned and the government gave him land near Usakub, where he then resided ... Dimitryevitch, who was chief of intelligence, who led in the assassination of King Alexander and the Queen in 1903, was executed in Salonika in 1918 to silence him about Sarajevo."

Thus there were many persons, both conspirators and highly-placed government officials, who knew well in advance of the coming assassination of Archduke Franz Ferdinand. Probably no one among them wished to interfere with the plot, because of the certainty of immediate retaliation.

There were many Freemasons in government circles throughout Europe who also must have been informed of the plot; no doubt they awaited the outcome with great anticipation. Once Ferdinand had been eliminated, it was but a matter of a few days to launch the Great War. Lord Grey, British Foreign Minister, wrote in his book, "Twenty-five Years," v. 2., p. 25, "If matters had rested with him [the Kaiser], there would have been no European War arising out of the Austro-Serbian dispute." This would seem to deny the oft-repeated charge that it was Kaiser Wilhelm who insisted on the war; it also may explain why he was never tried as "a war criminal," despite repeated demands that such a trial be held. Such statements as Grey's (who, after all, was his "enemy") would have exonerated him.

Lord Fisher, First Lord of the Admiralty, stated in the London Magazine, January 1920, "The nation was fooled into the war." This statement would also bely the "war guilt" of the Kaiser.

The urgency to involve the United States in direct participation in World War I was required so that the Canaanites would acquire the necessary authority to inflict even more oppressive laws against the people of Shem. In 1916, fifty-four per cent of the American people were of German origin: a vote to make German the official language of the Republic had failed by only one vote during the formation of the Republic. During the first hundred years of this nation, German was the only language to be heard in many areas. A poll in 1916 asked of the American people, "If we should enter the war, would you choose to go in on the side of Germany, or of England?" An overwhelming majority responded that they preferred to enter the war on the side of Germany. This was hardly surprising; England's policies, her interference, and her continual attempts to destroy the American Republic were no secret to the American people, despite the efforts of our historians to gloss over or cover up these campaigns. Pro-British groups such as the Pilgrims, the English Union, and other well-financed operations in the New York area poured forth British propaganda, but it had little or no effect on the rest of the nation.

There was as yet no conceivable reason for the United States to involve itself on behalf of either belligerent. No threat was ever presented against any of its territory; therefore the desired result had to be achieved by the usual devious means. The firm of J. P. Morgan, which had originated in London as George Peabody and Company, had made large loans to England from the enormous sums made available by the operations of the newly-launched Federal Reserve System. J. P. Morgan headed the Federal Advisory Council, which met with the Federal Reserve Board of Governors. A veteran of the Jekyl Island meeting, Paul Warburg, was Vice Chairman of the Board of Governors. Everything seemed well in hand.

William Jennings Bryan, who had campaigned against the Cross of Gold on which the international bankers planned to crucify the American people, now led the "Keep Us Out of War" movement. On February 3, 1917, he addressed a mass meeting of five thousand people in New York. The entire procedure would be repeated in 1940, as if by rote, and with the same outcome; we would go into the war.

We did not lack for religious leaders to urge us into this "godly" war. This was a great blasphemy, because it was really a ritual celebration of Baal's orgy of human sacrifice. Frank North, president of the Federal Council of Church of Christ, declared, "The war for righteousness will be won." Clergymen were instructed in propaganda to promote the Liberty Loans by special banking officers of the Second Federal Reserve District (New York). Bishop William Alfred Quayle shrieked that "Germans have ravished the women of Belgium, Serbia, Roumania, Poland; Germans murdered the passengers of the Lusitania; Germans poisoned wells, crucified inhabitants and soldiers, and denatured men and boys."

All of this was part of a well-financed propaganda campaign on the part of British agents. As usual, the government of the United States was being "run" by the British Secret Intelligence Service. The propaganda was intended to be purely inflammatory, and no accusation was too wild to be denied a front page coverage in the American press. Alfred Ponsonby's book, "Falsehood in Wartime," E. P. Dutton, 1928, was one of a number of books which later exposed the fantastic lies which were used to incite Americans to go to war against Germany. Ponsonby's book was dedicated to his friends, the Marques of Tavistock and the 'historian Francis Neilson. On p. 17, Ponsonby writes, "General von Hutier of the 6th German army, 'The method of Northcliffe at the Front is to distribute through airmen a constantly increasing number of leaflets and pamphlets; the letters of German prisoners are falsified in the most outrageous way, tracts and pamphlets are concocted to which the names of German poets, writers, and statemen are forged.' On p. 19, "*Tant que peuple seront armés les uns contre les autres, ils auront des hommes d'etat menteurs, comme ils auront des canons et des mitrailleuses.* As long as the peoples are armed against each other, there will be lying statesmen, just as there will be cannon and machine guns."

One of the most notorious propaganda coups of World War I was the German "Corpse Factory," the Kadaver. On April 16, 1917, the Time reported that "The Germans are distilling glycerine from the bodies of their dead, burning of bodies for fat, turned into lubricating oils, powder from bones; the story proved to be a popular one and was repeated for weeks afterward in the Times (London). On October 22, 1925, the Times belatedly blamed General Charteris for the story, which had proven to be the greatest propaganda falsehood of all time. Charteris, in a letter to the Times, November 4, 1925, denied any involvement with the story.

Relying heavily on faked documents and doctored photographs, British agents deluged credulous American journalists with "hot copy." The result was that American mobs began to attack elderly German shopkeepers, blaming them for the "atrocities" committed in Europe. In most instances, these shopkeepers were the most staid, as well as the most patriotic, residents of their areas. The principal vehicle used by Woodrow Wilson to justify his declaration of war against Germany was "submarine warfare" against American shipping; the keystone of this claim was the sinking of the Lusitania. In fact, the German government had published warnings to Americans in the New York press, advising them not to travel on the Lusitania, because it was known to be carrying munitions. George Sylvester Viereck showed this writer the actual clipping of this ad, which he had kept in his files. To this day, the United States government has refused to admit that the Lusitania was carrying arms, consigned to the British Army. In its issue of November, 1920, the Nation quoted D. F. Malone, Collector for the Port of New York as stating that the

Lusitania carried 4200 cases of Springfield rifle cartridges on its manifest, consigned to the British government. The Wilson Administration had refused permission for Malone to publish this report. When Sen. LaFollette referred to it, they attempted to have him expelled from the Senate. Malone stated that he would testify in defense of LaFollette, and the attempt was dropped. Later records revealed that there were 5400 cases of ammunition on the Lusitania.

The World War was satisfactorily concluded with some fifty million persons having been slaughtered, most of them prime representatives of the people of Shem. With this happy result, the Masonic Order of Canaanites decided to go for one hundred million victims in their next outing. For this purpose, they assembled the most sinister members of the world's Masonic lodges at the Versailles Peace Conference. As Ezra Pound later pointed out over Radio Rome, "The real crime is ending one war so as to make the next one inevitable." Woodrow Wilson became famous as the originator of the Fourteen Points and the League of Nations; in fact, he merely read from the script which had been prepared for him. The Fourteen Points and the other agenda of the Versailles Peace Conference had previously been drawn up at a secret meeting of the Grand Orient of France and the International Masonic Conference at their headquarters, 2 Rue Cadet, Paris, on June 28-30, 1917.

The Versailles Peace Conference actually consisted of a three-tier system, each distinct from the others. The first was the public conference, highly visible, attended by swarms of reporters from all over the world, and extensively reported; the second tier was the secret conferences of the Big Four, who met privately to compare notes and go over their instructions from their hidden masters; the third tier was the nightly Masonic conferences, known only to a chosen few, at which the actual decisions of all agenda at the Conference were discussed and decided upon. The ministers of the victorious Allied Powers were well-treated for their cooperation. Woodrow Wilson himself returned to America with private gifts of one million dollars in gold and precious gems to ensure his efforts on behalf of the League of Nations. When he realized that the Congress would never approve this dismantling of American sovereignty, he was haunted by the fear that he might have to return these bribes, and he suffered a nervous breakdown, from which he never recovered.

Accompanying the Wilson delegation to Paris was an array of Wall Street bankers, among them Bernard Baruch, Thomas Lamont of the J. P. Morgan firm, and Paul Warburg, of Kuhn, Loeb Co. When they arrived in Paris, Paul Warburg was pleasantly surprised to find that his brother, Max Warburg, was the head of the General delegation. At Wilson's side was his longtime adviser, Colonel Edward M. House and House's son-in-law, Wall Street lawyer Gordon Auchincloss.

Secretary of State Robert Lansing was accompanied by his two young nephews, John Foster and Allen Dulles. They were direct descendants of the Mallet Prevost Swiss intelligence families, which had installed the Scottish Rite in the United States. A definitive work on John Foster Dulles, "The Road to Power," by Ronald Pruessen (published by Macmillan) fails to mention Freemasonry in the entire book. The Dulles brothers were later to play crucial roles in setting up the Hitler regime in Germany, preparing the way for World War II, and respectively as Secretary of State and founder of the CIA in the postwar period. Allen Dulles remained a director of the Schroder Bank, which handled Hitler's personal funds; Dulles consigned many millions of dollars to the Schroder as "covert" funds for the CIA. No accounting was ever made.

Another disappointment for Woodrow Wilson at Paris was his resolve to achieve fullscale diplomatic recognition for the bloodsoaked Bolshevik terrorists in Russia, a goal which was fervently shared by the Prime Minister of England, Lloyd George. They were dismayed to find that other European diplomats, fearing Communist insurrection in their own countries, were adamant that no recognition be given to Soviet Russia. Bemoaning their defeat as a victory for "bigotry and intolerance," Wilson and Lloyd George turned to other affairs on the agenda. Their program to make the next war inevitable was considerably eased by Bernard Baruch, who, as Economic Adviser to the Peace Conference, imposed the crushing reparations burden on Germany, impossible for them to pay, and forcing them to seek political relief. A ruinous inflation wiped out the middle class and set the stage for a revolutionary program; whether it was to be Communism or some other faction was not a primary concern for the conspirators. Whoever it might be, they would be in firm control.

The way was now clear for the emergence of Adolf Hitler in Germany. His political party, the National Socialists, received the worldwide appellation of "Nazi" because it was the political party of the Ashkenazim, the German Jews (ashkenazim means Germany in Hebrew). Documents exist with the signature of Adolf Hitler just above that of Max Warburg , who, with the Oppenheimers, was the principal backer of the "Nazis." Hitler also had considerable occult support from the adepts of Ostara; a society which practiced the principles of Tibetan magic, as adapted to Aryan racial theories. The cult centered around Ostara, the Anglo-Saxon Goddess of Spring, to whom Oster month, or April, was dedicated. Hitler's birthday was April 20, which may explain why he was chosen to head this movement. During the Nazi period, it was a day of great celebration throughout Germany. On April 20, 1935, Hitler was presented with forty-one airplanes by the S.A., with the following address:

"My Fuhrer! The S.A. beg their leader, in celebration of his birthday, on the 20th of Easter Month [the pagan Ostermond-Ed.] 1935, to accept their contribution to the rearmament of the German people-the S.A. fighter squadron."

Tibetan magic claims to be untainted by its principal rival, Kabbalism; it also claims to be more powerful than any other known school of occultism, either Egyptian, Kabbalistic, or Hindu magic. Some of the Ostara adepts close to Hitler became practiced in the highest principles of occult Lamaism. It was the overconfidence produced by the early successes of the regime, which had followed the advice of these adepts, the expansion into Austria and Czechoslovakia, and the unexpectedly easy military successes in the first two years of World War II, which led them to their downfall. Whether Ostara actually is superior to Kabbalism and its other rivals may never be known, but whatever magical support Hitler and his circle may have been able to call upon, they were no match for the international organization of the Masonic Order of Canaanites. Hitler's greatest flaw was his lack of experience on a larger stage; it is doubtful if in his entire life he ever heard of the Canaanites. Both Hitler and Mussolini, early in their regimes, were quick to outlaw the Masons, failing to realize that Freemasonry and the Illuminati have always been underground movements. They had been proscribed numerous times in numerous countries; these bans only gave greater encouragement to their furtive conspiracy. Neither Hitler nor Mussolini realized the awesome power of the "determined men of Masonry" who exercised total control over the "democratic" powers.

Another considerable influence in the early days of the National Socialists was the Ariosophists, the Aryan branch of the Theosophists. Based in Vienna, the Ariosophists exercised dramatic influence on Hitler's writings during his formative years. It is doubtful if he ever knew that Theosophy was merely an extension of Kabbalism, or that he was involved with those whom he considered his sworn enemies.

Once World War II had been satisfactorily launched, it seemed that nothing could stop Hitler's triumphant progression across the battlefields of Europe. He failed to realize that Napoleon had also strode victoriously over those same fields, only to die miserably of arsenic poisoning on a remote island. No one in Germany could see that this was merely Act One of a carefully staged drama. Act Two would open with the entry of the United States into the war, a possibility never envisioned by Hitler, and Act Three would be Gotterdammerung, the melodramatic immolation of Germany and Brunnhilde.

Involving the United States in World War II was predicated on the successful operation of an end run play, which Hitler never considered. He had no intention of provoking the United States; when the British intelligence director, Sir William Stephenson, repeatedly murdered young German sailors on the streets of New York, the German government ignored the incidents. Despite the expenditure of millions of dollars on frenetic war propaganda, the American people remained insensitive to the "threat" of Nazism. Charles Lindbergh, Jr. led a nationwide "America First" campaign which seemed certain to keep us out of the war. The answer to the Roosevelt-Churchill dilemma was Pearl Harbor, one of the most artfully planned slaughters of American soldiers, sailors, and marines in our history. It seemed that everyone in a position of authority in London and Washington knew that the Japanese intended to attack Pearl Harbor, which was hardly surprising, because the Japanese secret codes had been broken months before. The nightmare of the plotters was that the Japanese commanders might inadvertently find that their codes had been broken and call off the attack on Pearl Harbor, since they would know that the defenders would be warned. The Washington conspirators, while breathlessly following the slow course of the Japanese fleet toward Pearl Harbor, avoided intimating to Kimmel and Short, the American commanders in Hawaii, that they were in any danger. Alerting them, of course, would warn the Japanese and cause them to turn back. The Japanese commanders later said that at the first sign of an alarm, they were prepared to turn back toward Tokyo without pressing their attack.

A meeting of the conspirators at the White House on the evening of Pearl Harbor found them haggard with suspense; only a few more hours, and they would know whether they had "won," that is, whether the Japanese would attack and destroy the American fleet and installations at Pearl Harbor. Never has any group waited for "bad news" with such intensity. President Franklin Delano Roosevelt, who lived throughout his life on handouts from his mother, the opium money amassed by her father, Warren Delano; Bernard Baruch, who had imposed the reparations debt upon Germany; General George Marshall, whom Senator McCarthy was later to call "a living lie"; these were the men who had staked everything on this gamble to involve the United States in World War II; if it failed, they had no backup plan. Hitler refused to pose any threat to the United States.

A book describing Stephenson's exploits in the United States, "A Man Called Intrepid" on p. 329 provides irrefutable proof that the conspirators knew what was to happen. Roosevelt used his son, Col. James Roosevelt, to convey his private communications to Stephenson to ensure secrecy. From information provided by James Roosevelt, Stephenson cabled Churchill in London, "Japanese negotiations off. Services expect action within two weeks."

This message was delivered in London November 27, ten days before Pearl Harbor.

Roosevelt's Chief of Staff, General George Marshall, a principal at the grim midnight meeting at the White House, later testified before Congress that he could not remember where he was at the time of the Pearl Harbor attack; yet an item in the Washington Post showed that he had addressed a veterans' organization a few hours before; he had then gone on to the White House. Marshall, a person of totally amorphous character, is presented to our youth as a great moral leader.

In the campaign to get the United States into World War II, Roosevelt relied almost completely on the assistance of the British Secret Intelligence Service. Its Special Operations Executive had been founded July 1940 under the direction of "C," one Sir Steward Menzies. Menzies was reputed to be the illegitimate son of King Edward VII; educated at Eton, he had always moved in the highest circles of the British aristocracy. He was awarded the DSO in World War 1. Lady Menzies of Menzies had been one of the founders of the British Fascist movement in 1923, with some of the largest landowners in England: the Earl of Glasgow, 2500 acres; Duke Abercorn, 2000 acres; Marquess of Ailsbury, 40,000 acres; Earl of Cardigan, 10,000 acres. A later group, the Anglo-German Fellowship, had been financed by F. C. Tiarks, partner of the Schroder Bank, and director of the Bank of England, which provided crucial financing for Hitler's regime. Also in the Fellowship were the Duke of Wellington, Admiral Sir Barry Domvile, and Lord Mount-Temple, chairman of the Navy League.

The cipher and signal branches of SOE were set up in Marks and Spencer's headquarters building; its chairman, Israel Sieff, had been a founder of the Fabian Political Economic Planning movement. With Menzies were the cofounders of SOE, Hugh Dalton, brought up at Windsor Castle (his father had been tutor to George V), Sir Frank Nelson, later Acting Director General of the United Nations, Sir Robin Brooke, later a director of the Bank of England, Hugh Gaitskell, later Prime Minister, and Lord Christopher Mayhew.

The SOE operators took General William Donovan in hand to create their subsidiary organization, the American Office of Strategic Services. The British, who were past masters at every type of espionage and covert action, found willing, if inept, students in the millionaires' sons who volunteered for the OSS. President Lyndon Johnson later remarked about their successors in the CIA, "Do you realize that those boys are all the sons of millionaires whose fathers were terrified to have them enter into the family brokerage business?" Apparently a good time was had by all in London during World War II, such stalwarts as Paul Mellon, his brother-in-law David Bruce, Henry Morgan of the J. P. Morgan family, and many other fraternity brothers from Yale, Harvard, and Princeton.

World War II did manage to meet its quota of one hundred million victims, many of whom were entire families of the people of Shem, such as the victims of the fiery holocausts at Dresden and Cologne. Because they were the victors, no trials were ever held of the perpetrators of these atrocities. The Masonic Canaanites had succeeded in bringing off another great triumph, massive human sacrifices before the altar of Baal. One of the first tasks demanded of American Army officers when they entered Germany was that they reestablish the Masonic Lodges, which had been closed by Hitler. In Italy, the victors quickly reopened the Grand Orient Lodges throughout the country. They were heavily financed with covert funds from the OSS, and later received large payments from CIA operatives in Italy.

CHAPTER 10

THE MENACE OF COMMUNISM

For thirty-five years, the present writer wrote on and spoke about "Communism" without knowing what it was. After consulting hundreds of reference works on Communism, I had found not one mention of the fact that Communism was but one branch of the world revolutionary forces of the Masonic Order of Canaanites. We have previously pointed out that the members of the First Communist International were Lionel de Rothschild, Karl Marx, and Heinrich Heine. Not only did Karl Marx maintain close ties with the Jesuits and Freemasonry throughout his career; he was also directly related to the British aristocracy through his marriage to Jenny von Westphalen, a descendant of the Countess of Balcarras and Argyll, two of the oldest titles in England. The Countess had been governess to William of Orange before he invaded England and chartered the Bank of England. It was the Masonic connection which obtained a steady income for Karl Marx, through commissions for writing for New York newspapers. Lenin also maintained close Masonic ties during his years in Switzerland, before he returned to Russia to lead the Bolshevik Revolution. In Switzerland, he had become the member of a secret Lodge under the name of "Ulianov Zederbaum." He received regular financial support, as well as occasional visits, from Sir Alfred Milner (founder of the Round Tables, and the Council on Foreign Relations), and Lord Palmerston, foreign minister of England. Both Milner and Palmerston had attained the 33rd, or revolutionary degree.

Meanwhile, the richest man in the world, the Czar of Russia, seemed helpless in the face of his country's slow slide into anarchy. Long before the advent of Rasputin, his court had been rife with occultists. The Tribune de Geneve headlined a dispatch on December 21, 1902, "RUSSIA: An Occultist at Court. The Daily Mail correspondent at Odessa telegraphed that paper the real facts concerning the occultist Phlippe's presence at the Tzar's court. Philippe has gained great influence over the Czar." The dispatch further stated that Philippe Nizier of Lyons had been presented to Nicholas by Grand Duke Nicolas Nicolaevitch. Earlier, in Lyons, Nizier had been sued for the unlawful practice of medicine. A French doctor, Gerard Encausse, had written voluminously on Kabbalah and magic. He had been introduced by Philippe to the Grand Duke. Encausse wrote his treatises on magic under the name of "Papus." The Swiss Gazette noted, December 20, 1902, "Few people know that there exists in Paris a kind of small University of Occultism, where students register, examinations are passed, and academic degrees conferred. For instance, one can obtain a diploma of Bachelor of Occult Science, or Doctor in Kabbalah. Papus is President and organizer."

Thus, the occult influence at the Court of Czar Nicholas is traced directly to a school of the occult in Paris. It is not too fanciful to conjecture that this school operates with the backing of the Grand Orient of Paris, since Freemasonry is always concerned with the occult. The Czar's later inability to act decisively in times of crisis, which led directly to the downfall of his government, may have been due to drugs or hypnotism. The world's most powerful autocrat was described by observers as "remarkably passive" and unable to take direct action when his regime was threatened with revolution. Indeed King Louis had reacted in much the same way at the onset of the French Revolution during the weeks before he was deposed and sent to the guillotine. It is difficult to believe that such absolute autocrats would meekly resign themselves to "the will of the people" and go unresisting to their deaths.

Apparently at the mercy of the occult influences at his court, Czar Nicholas was arrested, and a Provisional Government was set up. This government was headed by Kerensky, a 32d degree Mason, who had been chosen as head of the Provisional Government by Josef Sliozberg, the Grand Master of the International Order of B'Nai B'Rith in Russia. Kerensky had only one mission; to hold the fort until Lenin arrived on the sealed train from Switzerland. After the Bolshevik Revolution, Kerensky was permitted to peacefully emigrate to the United States, where he became a well-paid lecturer at leading universities. The Masonic Order of Canaanites always takes care of its own.

Princess Paley, wife of the Grand Duke Paul, stated that the English Ambassador at St. Petersburg, Sir George Buchanan, fomented and directed the Russian Revolution on direct instructions from Lloyd George, head of the Liberal Party in England.

The Bolsheviks were provided with ample funds for their takeover of Russia. On September 21,1917, Trotsky received a telegram from Stockholm: "The management of the Bank of Max Warburg & Co. informed him that a current account had been opened for him at Stockholm for the purposes of his undertaking." Trotsky had previously been presented with $10,000 in cash by the Rockefellers when he sailed from New York; other funds were forwarded to him from Berlin through the Disconto Gesellschaft, the Nya Bank, and the Siberian Bank, among other intermediaries, such as HelphandParvus, Ganetsky, Koslousky, and Krassin. After the Revolution, Krassin went back to work for Siemens, the giant German electric company; as Russian representative, he was supported by Hugo Stinnes, Felix Deutsch, manager of A.E.G., and by Walter Rathenau.

Although all of the Czar's enormous deposits in foreign banks was retained by those banks without payment to any member of his family, a small portion of his Russian holdings were set aside by the new Bolshevik government as a secret fund which was exercise final control in the Soviet Government during the ensuing decades. This trust was composed of Dzerzhinsky, founder of the Cheka, the British secret agent Sidney Reilly, and W. Averell Harriman. The trust was a continuation of the Parvus fund which had brought Lenin to power, an operation which had been directed by the influential behind-the-scenes figure, the Venetian Count Volpi di Misurata, a black nobility figure who had put Mussolini in power, orchestrated the numerous Balkan Wars, and secretly directed the Russian Revolution.

Oddly enough, the Bolshevik Revolution was greeted with enthusiastic approval of many of the world's leading financiers. One of the most prominent of their number, Jacob Schiff, senior partner of Kuhn, Loeb Co., New York, telegraphed his greetings, as recounted in the New York Times, March 19, 1917: "A persistent foe of the tyrannical autocracy, the merciless persecutors of my co-religionists, may I congratulate through you the Russian people upon what they have now so wonderfully achieved and wish you and your colleagues in the new government every success." The Minister, Milioukoff, a longtime friend of Schiff, replied, "We are united in hatred and antipathy to ancient regimes now overthrown." Here again is a direct quote from the Will of Canaan "hate your masters."

One of the most misunderstood events in history is the Allied "invasion" of Russia after the Bolshevik Revolution. This "invasion" again was featured recently in the Soviet Press as urgent reason not to "trust" the United States. In fact, the Allied troops were sent to Russia to divert the successful Counter Revolution of the White forces, and at the same time, to give the Red Army propagandists, principally Trotsky, a rallying cry to the faltering Red campaign, that "Mother Russia" was being invaded by "foreign troops." This proved to be an irresistible call to the Russian peasants, who immediately rallied behind the Red Army and gave them total victory. In fact, several divisions, mostly British and American, were sent to Siberia, where they remained for a year and a half, without participating in any action. None of the troops had any idea of what they were doing there; they returned home as mystified as when they had departed. Had they been assigned to "invade" Russia, of course, they would have landed on the European coast and marched straight toward Moscow, which could have been easily taken by these well-armed and trained divisions.

They had actually been sent to Siberia to betray the White Russians. This maneuver was exposed in the New York Times, February 15, 1920, "when Vladivostok was liberated from the Kolchak faction." "There is a pronounced pro-American feeling evident. Revolutionary leaders mounted the steps of buildings across the street, making speeches calling the Americans real friends, who, at a critical time, saved the present movement."

The "mystery" of the American military presence in Russia was never a mystery to its secret Masonic Canaanite backers. The three directors of the Federal Reserve Bank of New York who were financing the Bolshevik effort realized that under Trotsky the Red Army was losing the war. Its orgy of senseless terrorism and slaughter had turned the peasantry against the "liberators," and the White Army was gaining daily in support. To reverse the situation, the Federal Reserve Bank directors ordered the Allied troops into Russia. Quartered near the Kolchak forces, they gave the impression that they were there to support the White faction. The Russian people were given to understand that the Allied forces were sent to restore the old autocracy. The press of America and Britain now united the Russian peasantry behind the revolutionaries, and Kolchak's army was soon in full retreat. This was the explanation of the "pro-American feeling" in Vladivostok. The Allied presence in Siberia ensured the triumph of the Red Army and the imposition of a brutal dictatorship on the people of Russia.

There is ample documentation for the subsequent acts of terrorism which horrified the Russian people and permanently turned them against the Bolsheviks. The American Rohrbach Commission reported on some of the revolutionary atrocities: "The whole cement floor of the execution hall of the Cheka of Kiev was flooded with blood; it formed a level of several inches. It was a horrible mixture of blood, brains, and pieces of skull. All the walls were be smattered with blood. Pieces of brains and of scalps were sticking to them. A gutter of 25 centimeters wide by 25 centimeters deep and about 10 meters long was along its length full to the top with blood. Some bodies were disembowelled, others had limbs chopped off, some were literally hacked to pieces. Some had their eyes put out of their heads the face and neck and trunk were covered with deep wounds. Further on, we found a corpse with a wedge driven into its chest. Some had no tongues. In a corner, we discovered a quantity of dismembered arms and legs belonging to no bodies that we could locate."

Once the White Russian threat of retribution had gone, the Bolsheviks unleashed the full fury of their Canaanite bloodlust. They converted the entire nation of Russia into a gigantic concentration camp, in order to slowly torture and kill the remaining descendants of the people of Shem, who had ruled them for one thousand years. Solzhenitsyn later informed an incredulous world that the soviets had murdered sixty-six million people in Russia from 1918 to 1957. He cited Cheka Order No. 10, issued on January 8, 1921: "To intensify the repression of the bourgeoisie." This, of course, meant the people of Shem. Under this order, the concentration camps were established on a permanent basis. Typical of the bosses of these camps was Lazar Kogan, who calmly watched thousands of slave laborers die during his stint as overseer of the construction of the White Sea Canal. He greeted a new inmate with this incredible statement, "I believe that you personally are not guilty of anything. But, as an educated person, you have to understand that social prophylaxis was being widely applied." "Social prophylaxis" was a typical Canaanite euphemism for the massacre of the people of Shem. The prospective victims were no longer considered to be human, but only as corpses waiting to be tossed onto the scrap heap. They were known simply as "zeks," slang for the Russian term for prisoner, "zakluchenny."

After a half-century of unequalled barbarism, the "Russian experiment" was exposed in all its horror by Solzhenitsyn. He writes of the camps, "Many camp points were known for executions and mass graves; Orotukan, and Polyarny Spring, and Svistoplas, and Annuskha, and even the agricultural camp Dukcha, but the most famous of all on this account were the Zolotisty Goldfields ... At Zolotisty they used to summon a brigade from the mine face in broad daylight and shoot the members down one after another. (And this was not a substitute for night executions, they took place, too.) When the chief of Yuglag, Nikolai Andreyevich Aglanov, arrived, he liked, at line-up, to pick out some brigade or other which had been at fault for something or other and order it to be taken aside. And then he used to empty his pistol into the frightened, crowded mass of people, accompanying his shots with happy shouts. The corpses were left unburied."

Solzhenitsyn goes on for many pages to describe the horrors of which our liberals knew nothing, "But some transports of condemned zeks arrived too late, and they continued to arrive with five to ten people at a time. A detachment of killers would receive them at the Old Brickyard Station and lead them to the old bathhouse to a booth lined with three or four layers of blankets inside. There the condemned prisoners were ordered to undress in the snow and enter the bath naked. Inside, they were shot with pistols. In the course of one and a half months about two hundred persons were destroyed in this way. The corpses were burned in the tundra."

Solzhenitsyn continues, "A. B. V. has told how executions were carried out at Adak - a camp on the Pechora River. They would take the opposition members 'with their things' out of the camp compound on a prisoner transport at night. And outside the compound stood the small house of the Third Section. The condemned men were taken into a room one at a time, and there the camp guards sprang on them. Their mouths were stuffed with something soft and their arms were bound with cords behind their backs. Then they were led out into the courtyard, where harnessed carts were waiting. The bound prisoners were piled on the carts, from five to seven at a time, and driven off to the 'Gorka,' the camp cemetery. On arrival they were tipped into big pits that had already been prepared and buried alive. No, not out of brutality. It has been ascertained that when dragging and lifting them, it was much easier to cope with living people than with corpses. The work went on for many nights at Adak."

Solzhenitsyn is not the only person to describe life in the Soviet concentration camps. Consider the following description of life in a gulag: Sergei Grigoryants says that the prisoners are awakened at 5:30 a.m. and served a watery fish soup and brown bread for breakfast; at 10:30 the main meal, which is watery soup; the dinner is porridge. Grigoryants says that the prisoners are constantly tortured through lack of food and the cold in the cells. Soviet law requires that the temperature in the cells be at least 64.4 degrees Fahrenheit; this is solemnly tested by the camp inspectors. They bring an electric heater into the cell, turn it on until the temperature reaches 64.4 degrees, make the appropriate notation on their report, and then take the heater to the next cell. The temperature then returns to its usual forty degrees. A lamp is kept constantly burning all night in the cells, so that the prisoners never really rest. Grigoryants says that some 500,000 prisoners a year are released to return to Soviet society, and that their presence has a very alarming effect upon the entire country. Here again, how pertinent is this report? It was published as an interview with Grigoryants in the New York Times of February 22, 1987!

It would be logical to suppose that this Socialist society was built on the confiscated fortune of the late Czar Nicholas II, but this is not the case. In 1913, the Czar was undoubtedly the richest man in the world, with a personal fortune amounting to some thirty billion dollars in 1913 dollars. He personally owned 150,000,000 acres of land, and had some 30,000 servants, 500 automobiles in his personal fleet, 6,000 horses, 2 yachts, a personal gold reserve of one billion dollars in the Imperial Bank, with five hundred million dollars worth of jewels, including the $200,000 Great Mogul diamond, a Crown valued at $75 million and 32,000 diamonds. He controlled one-sixth of the surface of the entire globe. On the night of November 6, 1917, at 2:00 a.m., Red Guards drove a truck to the Imperial Bank and removed all of the Romanoff gold and jewels. Much of the gold was later shipped directly to Kuhn, Loeb Co. in New York. We may recall that the senior partner of Kuhn, Loeb Co., Jacob Schiff, had put up some $20 million of his own funds to finance the Revolution. Apparently it was a good investment. Victor Hammer fenced many of the Crown jewels to collectors in Europe and the United States.

The Dowager Empress Maria escaped with the considerable jewels in her personal collection. Both King George V and King Christian of Denmark repeatedly tried to get her to "entrust" her jewels to them for "safekeeping" or at least for "appraisal." She steadfastly refused, knowing that she probably would never see them again. When she died in 1928, special agents seized the jewels and immediately whisked them to Buckingham Palace. Her more important pieces later were seen in Queen Mary's personal collection.

After the Revolution of 1905, the Czar had prudently prepared for further outbreaks by transferring some $400 million in cash to the New York banks, Chase, National City, Guaranty Trust, J. P. Morgan Co., and Hanover Trust. In 1914, these same banks bought the controlling number of shares in the newly organized Federal Reserve Bank of New York, paying for the stock with the Czar's sequestered funds. Thus the Romanoff family actually owns the controlling interest in the Federal Reserve Banks today!

Other deposits of the Czar included $35-50 million in the Bank of England, $25 million in Barclay's, $30 million in Lloyd's Bank, $100 million in the Bank of France, $80 million in the Rothschild Bank in Paris, and $132 million in the Mendelssohn Bank in Berlin. Since 1917, a cloud has hung over the financial structure of the Western democracies, threatening their jerrybuilt financial structure, the fear that some court somewhere, might eventually rule that the Czar's funds must be turned over to the rightful heirs. This would affect not only the ownership of the Federal Reserve Bank stock, but, with payment of interest, would mean the end of our ten largest financial institutions. Does anyone wonder why the United States government, which is under the total direction of the Big Ten Banks, continually makes every effort to finance and feed the crumbling Soviet empire? Can anyone predict the financial calamity which would ensue if the Romanoffs were restored to the throne of Russia, and asked for their money back, or if they got a court ruling anywhere in the world to that effect?

This catastrophe loomed on the horizon at one point. The New York Times of July 20, 1929, reported on the progress of a lawsuit brought by the Czar's mother and thirty-two of the Romanoff heirs against Guaranty Trust and National City Bank. F. Dudley Kohler, an attorney representing James Egan, Public Administrator, issued the following Legal Notice which appeared in the Law Journal, "Notice is hereby given to all persons, corporations, banks, trustees having assets, deposits and securities of the late Nicholas II, that a statement and account of same is forthwith demanded, and in the event that no such statement of account is rendered, all such persons will be held responsible for the amounts, plus interest and the cost of discovery proceedings." Both the case and Kohler then disappeared from the pages of the New York Times. Apparently no account or statement was ever given. To have done so would have provided legal evidence of the debt, and would have made repayment inevitable. Charles Recht, counsel for the Soviet Union, retained Edward H. Fallows to represent the Soviet government, but no further legal proceedings are to be found.

Nevertheless, the Romanoff demand did have tremendous repercussions. The threat of a tremendous withdrawal from two of New York's most over-extended and precarious banks caused an underground pressure against call money, or cash, on Wall Street, which then precipitated the Crash of 1929. Even though the Masonic Canaanites controlled the courts in the United States, they could not be certain that the Romanoffs might not find a court in some other country which would grant them a judgment, or even an injunction against Guaranty Trust, a J.

P. Morgan controlled bank, and National City Bank, the Rothschild and Rockefeller bank in New York. This threat, coming at the very height of the stock market boom of the 1920s, cast a pall over the wheelings and dealings of the speculators, and caused immediate pressure on short term funds, resulting in the Great Depression.

To avoid such threats in the future, Roosevelt-Litvinoff agreements were concluded between the United States and Russia in 1933 and 1934. In these agreements, the United States unilaterally recognized all claims of the Soviet Government to funds of the Imperial Russian Government. Whether this could be made applicable to the funds of Czar Nicholas has never been tested in court.

The Roosevelt-Litvinoff Pact also put the diplomats of the world on notice that Roosevelt had now formalized the extended support formerly rendered to the Soviet Government by "private interests" such as the Federal Reserve Bank of New York and J. P. Morgan Co. since 1917. Not all of this was from private banks. It included a gift of $20 million from Woodrow Wilson's Special War Fund which had been voted him by Congress; the money was dispatched to Russia by way of Elihu Root. The Red Cross, Kuhn, Loeb. Co., and many other Wall Street firms had been active in financing the Soviet Government; henceforth, that burden would be borne directly by the American taxpayers, through subsidies provided to the Communists by the U.S. Government.

The dedicated financial support of the Communists by the world's leading bankers did not go unnoticed. Francois Coty, founder of the perfume firm, wrote, in "Tearing Away the Veils," published by Revue Internationale des Secret Societies, 1930, Paris, "The terms, Capitalism, Socialism, Communism, are so many themes distributed among well-paid demagogues to create confusion in the minds of the masses destined to become slaves. Universal Slavery is the immediate aim of the Bleichroder Group which they strive to attain through the medium of a new war." The Bleichroders were the German representatives of the House of Rothschild.

Wyndham Lewis, who during the First World War had co-edited Blast and Vortex with Ezra Pound, wrote in his book, "Count Your Dead; They Are Alive!", "A Rothschild or a Morgan makes his money in a very different way from a Nuffield or a Ford. The former deals in money as a commodity. His business is essentially allied to that of a moneylender. He makes nothing ... He toils not, neither does he spin. But for all that, he is no lily, as a rule! The latter, on the other hand, of the Nuffield-Ford type, are creative in the sense that they do at least make something ... Without Loan Capital there would be no Communism. The straight Bolshevik --say a Pollitt or a Strachey-- though perfectly ideological-- does not understand Capitalism ... Even Henry Ford is only a gigantic kulak [Ezra Pound called him 'the epitome of the American hired hand.' Ed.], and of all things the Marxist hates most on earth he hates the kulak most. With Loan Capital; on the other hand, he has many affinities. Indeed, if Loan Capital were allowed to proceed on its way without interference, it would automatically result in Communism ... I felt that the Soviets were altogether too thick with the Capitalists. I remarked that these Lords of Capital who do not seem to hate Communism quite as much as we would expect do not belong to us. We get nothing out of these people, but they get a great deal out of us. The richer they become-and they are a very few - the poorer we become."

Wyndham Lewis' observations may have been inspired by the activities of the Left Book club, which was directed by Victor Gollancz during the 1930s, featuring Harry Pollitt, head of the Communist Party of Great Britain, John

Strachey of the Daily Worker, and Claud Cockburn, alias Frank Pitcairn, editor of The Week, who was special correspondent for the Daily Worker at the Spanish Civil War battlefields. Gollancz headed many front groups, such as Friends of the Soviet Union, Young Communists League, and Committee for the Victims of Fascism. No intellectual has ever started a Committee for the Victims of Communism.

After the Bolshevik Revolution, there were abortive Communist uprisings in Germany and Hungary. The German revolution was quickly eradicated, but Bela Kun, in Hungary, actually established a short-lived Communist Reign of Terror. His mass murders and lunatic orgies (he had formerly been a mental patient) left the nation bankrupt and devastated. When a legal government was restored, the Hungarian government published the archives of the Masonic Lodges, proving that the "Communist Revolution" had entirely originated as the work of the Freemasons. The Hungarian government then closed down all Masonic Lodges throughout the country. The Hungarian government later sought a loan from the United States to rebuild their shattered economy. Their officials were promptly informed that the "United States government" made only one stipulation before granting the loan-that all the Masonic Lodges be restored and reopened. This proves that even in the 1920s, the Masonic Canaanites had already assumed full control over the government of the United States.

Another great slaughter of the people of Shem during the twentieth century occurred during the Spanish Revolution (1936-1939). The massacres were significant because they were a war of the Canaanites against Christians, and because they took place on the Iberian Peninsula (from Heber, of the people of Shem).

The slaughter of Christians in Spain began with the transfer of Soviet Russia's former peace delegate at Geneva, Rosenberg, also known as Moses Israelssohn, with his staff of one hundred and forty trained killers to the office of the Ambassador to Spain in August of 1936. This cadre of highly trained specialists in torture and murder inaugurated one of the most brutal campaigns in the history of Europe. Their atrocities were largely ignored by the world because the corps of journalists covering the Civil War were totally dedicated to the success of Communism; they only reported news which was unfavorable to the "fascists," as the Canaanites had contemptuously termed their opponents since the Romans had destroyed their world capital at Carthage.

The Rosenberg murder teams were euphemistically called "World Revolutionary Movement Purification Squads." Their work of purification consisted mainly of massacring priests, nuns, choirboys, and women, these being groups which were least likely to offer any armed resistance. Arthur Bryant, in his well-documented "Communist Atrocities in Spain," tells of one murder squad which went to the Dominican Convent in Barcelona and respectfully informed the Mother Superior that "because of possible mob violence," the nuns should accompany the squad to a place of safety. They were then taken to the suburbs and murdered. The Communist leader justified his action as follows, "We needed the building. We didn't want to muss it up before we occupied it." E. M. Godden, in his book, "Conflict in Spain," says, p. 72, "During the last week of July, 1936, the bodies of nuns were exhumed from their graves and propped up outside the walls of their convents. Obscene and offensive placards were attached to their bodies." In Madrid, it was estimated that one-tenth of the population of Spain was murdered by the Communist "purification" squads by 1939. De Fonteriz in "Red Terror in Madrid," describes how Cheka murder teams organized by Dimitrov and Rosenberg carried out a program of torture and killing so obscene that it cannot be reprinted here.

Early in World War II, Soviet murder teams captured 15,000 Polish officers, the most educated and responsible element in the population; they were never seen again. They were taken to three KGB-operated camps, Starbiesk, Kozielsk, and Ostashkov, where they were systematically murdered and dumped into unmarked graves. When the German army captured this area, known as Katyn Forest, they were led to the graves. At the Nuremberg Trials, the Soviets claimed that the Germans had committed these massacres; however, a Congressional Committee reported on July 2, 1952, that the Soviet NKVD had committed the massacres, which had been planned personally by Stalin as early as the fall of 1939.

The domination of the people of Shem by the Masonic Canaanites always results in an aura of total hopelessness; all justice, all honor, and all hope for the future now disappears. The eminent journalist, Don Cook, states in his book "Floodtide in Europe," that all journalists who go to Communist countries are struck by the "smell of Communism." "Worst of all to me was the peculiar and unmistakable smell of Russia and the Communist world which pervaded Leipzig." He continued, "Everyone who has ever set foot in the Soviet Union knows that smell - a stale, heavy, unwashed smell." He calls it "the smell of old lavatories, carbolic soap, unwashed bodies." The Soviets have never bothered to produce such necessities as telephone books, soap, and toilet tissue in their "Socialist economy."

Because it is an almost total waste of the energies and talents of its captive people, the Soviet Union can exist only by massive infusions of capital from the Western democracies. Few Americans realize how much of the money extorted from their wages by the Internal Revenue Service is transferred directly to the Federal Reserve Banks, and from there to Switzerland, where it is transferred to five Soviet banks. A defector from the Soviet Union reported in the New York Journal American, March 2, 1964, that of a remittance of $1,200,000 sent by the United States government to the CIA office in Vienna, the fund was distributed as follows: one-third to the Soviet Secret Police; one-third to the Communist Party of Italy; and one-third sent back to the United States to finance the Communist Party of the USA. Since World War II, when the OSS was handing out gold to the Communists in Italy, the process has become more formalized. James Angleton, head of covert action in the CIA and former CIA chief in Italy, set up organizations in which funds were channeled to Masonic groups in Italy, the foremost being P-2, which included most of the leading Italian government figures and businessmen; P-2 was penetrated by Andropov after he took over the KGB. Lord Sackville of England had introduced Freemasonry to Italy in 1733; it became the vehicle through which the British Secret Service "unified" Italy through Garibaldi and Mazzini to produce "the new Italy." The Italian Under Secretary of State, alarmed at the control which the Freemasons exercised over the Italian government in 1913, called for a law forbidding Masons from holding any sensitive office, "compromised by any hidden and therefore uncontrollable tie, and by any motive of suspicion or lack of trust by the public." The measure was never passed, and the unfortunate Under Secretary disappeared from his office. However, a decade later, Mussolini did outlaw the Masonic Lodges in Italy, causing the Canaanites to scream worldwide imprecations against "the brutal dictator" and "fascism."

Today, the "Red Billionaire," Jean-Baptiste Doumeng of France, carries on the vital work of feeding the helpless Soviet Union with the finest produce of the European "free democracies." He is a partner with Guy de Rothschild in distributing vegetables, the firm Sragri. Doumeng also directs the firms Inter-Agra and SOCOPA, which recently furnished one million tons of soft wheat to the Soviet Union at far below market price. Doumeng regularly ships meat and butter to the Communists at prices one-fourth of those which are charged European consumers. The Soviet Union frequently reships these commodoties back for resale at twice the price paid for them, thus gleaning hard currency from the European economies. None of this would be possible except for the international power of the Masonic Order of Canaanites.

CHAPTER 11

THE PROMISE

Despite the tremendous bloodlettings of the people of Shem during the twentieth century, in 1983, Robert Lacey, in his book, "The Aristocrats," noted that the nations which he called "white" but which are predominantly Shemite nations, continued to lead the world in per capita income. He lists

(1) the Arab Emirates; (2) Kuwait; (3) Lichtenstein; (4) Switzerland; (5) Monaco; (6) Luxembourg; (7) Denmark; (8) Germany; (9) Sweden; (10) Jersey; (11) Belgium; (12) Quatar; (13) United States.

We note that no Asian or African country made the list; also, that the United States, probably the most thoroughly dominated country in the world, groaning under the heel of the Canaanite parasites, occupies the Masonic number of thirteen on the list. The United States also ranks well down the list in such primary concerns as infant mortality, quality of medical care, education, and other important indicators. The principal cause of the United States' precipitous drop in world rankings is the continuous looting and raping of the nation by the Masonic Canaanite conspirators. For instance, of a defense budget of $248 billion in our peacetime economy, some $140 billion is paid directly to the NATO nations of Europe, our "allies" in the struggle against world Communism. The United States dispenses some additional $200 billion annually in "aid" to other countries such as the State of Israel, of which some $50 billion is channeled to the

Soviet Union and her satellites through food subsidies and monetary manipulations. The Soviet central bank, Gosplan, routinely sends officials to Switzerland to meet with the representatives of the Federal Reserve System at the Bank for International Settlements, where they plan new raids on the Treasury of the United States. A network of European banks regularly transfers funds to the Soviet Union which are routed to them from a number of United States government agencies.

Our entire government planning is aimed at maintaining enormous giveaways, which in turn creates the "necessity" for ever-increasing taxation of American citizens. Our most productive element, the people of Shem, regularly pay from 80% - 90% of their gross income to federal, state, and local tax agencies, often through "hidden" taxes on everything they buy and consume. Certainly no people on earth has ever been assessed such onerous tax burdens as the people of Shem have paid since 1913.

Much of the United States budget is debited to items such as maintaining 340,000 troops in West Germany. Melvyn Kraus of the Hoover Institution, in his recent book, "How NATO Weakens the West," states, "The Germans see the U.S. troops as a continuing army of occupation that makes them into an inferior partner in the Atlantic Alliance. Ike wrote in 1951 that in ten years all American troops should be returned to the United States." Yet, thirty-six years after that admonition, the U.S. contingent remains at full strength. Whether these troops are stationed there to "protect the West against an attack by the Soviets," as is usually claimed (military leaders report that our troops could only delay a Soviet attack by three hours before being annihilated), or whether they are stationed there to protect the Soviet supply lines, which bring them a steady flow of meat, butter, and wheat from European nations, as well as the financial aid transmitted through "neutral" Switzerland, is never discussed by the "free press."

It is noteworthy that these policies originate in the Babylonian buildings of the U.S. Congress. It is also noteworthy that these multimillion dollar structures are riddled from top to bottom with hordes of rats and cockroaches. The Washington Post reported on March 17, 1987, that the Congressional offices were purchasing special roach traps for $99 each, so that the staffers could eat their lunches without fighting off swarms of enormous flying brown cockroaches. These physical manifestations of total decay in our governmental structure give clear warning of what lies ahead; total moral chaos.

Political observers have always been aware of the ongoing nightmare of the Soviet leaders-a sudden shortage of bread in Moscow or other large Soviet cities. Given their corrupt system of distribution, this is not an idle fancy. The scenario continues with food riots, the police joining in with the rioters, and the downfall of the Soviet government within a matter of hours. In a society where only a privileged few enjoy the necessities of life, fewer than the French people had when they participated in the French Revolution, this government can never count on the support of its people.

To alleviate this nightmare of the Soviet officials, every official of the United States government tries to forestall this calamity. Few Americans realize that the principal thrust of our political program is not to "defend" this country against Communism, but to defend the Soviet government against its own people. Similarly, the principal aim of every United States government program is not to improve the economy or to guarantee the freedom of the American people, but to defend the swarm of Masonic Canaanite parasites against the growing anger of the American people. An ever-increasing tyranny is inflicted upon the people of Shem; increasing taxes; increasing regulations; increasing demands on the citizens by federal, state, and local officials; and all of this tremendous effort has but one goal; the prevention of food riots in Moscow. Only the international power of the Masonic Canaanites could so enslave the people of one nation as to make them the unwilling accomplices in the continued enslavement of another nation.

The function of the media is to obscure what is going on; it can never be entirely concealed. Therefore, the "free press" continually leads the public off on false scents -- Watergate, Irangate, San Salvador, South Africa. Any Congressmen who spends one moment on any of these "problems" should be arrested and taken out of his office to face charges of high treason. These are not the concerns of the American people or of any of its lawfully elected representatives, who have taken an oath to defend the Constitution of the United States. The occasional revelation of a free lunch is hailed as an instance of corruption but the important bribes, from $10,000 up, are never reported in the press. For instance, on May 9, 1934, the B'Nai B'Rith Masonic organization, which was holding its national meeting in Washington, presented a check for one million dollars to President Roosevelt as a personal gift. In 1987, the story of the year is the Iranian arms sales controversy. Here again, B'Nai B'Rith plays a central role. On December 3, 1986, the Washington Post noted that Prime Minister Yitzhak Shamir of Israel had cleared the $42 million arms sale with Seymour Reich, president of B'Nai B'Rith International, the "scandal" which threatens the Reagan presidency.

Reagan is power less to defend himself by disclosing the B'Nai B'Rith operation. All of those involved are in violation of 18 USC 794, "Gathering or delivering defense information to aid a foreign government. .. shall be punished by death or imprisonment for any term of years or for life."

The Reagan presidency itself represents the high water mark for the black nobility Canaanite control of our government. The Jesuits had boasted that a secret sign was to be given to the world when the ecumenical movement had successfully overcome its worldwide opposition. This sign would be the swearing in of a U.S. President while facing the symbolic occult obelisk. On January 20, 1981, for the first time in history, the swearing in ceremonies were moved to the west front of the Capitol. Reagan was sworn in while facing the Washington Monument, the mystical symbol of the Canaanites and the Babylonians.

Battered by the inflation and extremist policies of the Carter Administration, a weary American populace hailed the Reagan election as a genuine turnaround for their government. The Reagan staff was selected from such "rightwing" organizations as the Hoover Institution, Heritage Foundation, and American Enterprise Institute. The directors of these groups turned out to be the same financiers and wheeler-dealers who controlled the "leftwing" foundations, Rockefeller, Ford, and Brookings.

The Heritage Foundation was run by Sir Peter Vickers Hall, England's leading Fabian Socialist, who placed the Englishman, Stuart Butler, in charge of Heritage's policy-making apparat. Hall, of the munitions family, is also prominent in the Club of Rome.

When Reagan gave a dinner at the White House for Prince Charles, the guest list included Gloria Vanderbilt, Brooke Astor (who controls the John Jacob Astor fortune), Betsy Bloomingdale, Jerome Zipkin, William Buckley (of Skull and Bones and the National Review), and Rupert

EUSTACE MULLINS

Hambro, chairman of the London bankers Hambros; his cousin Charles had been chief of SOE during World War II.

These chosen "leaders" manipulate every aspect of American society, not the least of which is their control of music and the fine arts. Lincoln Kirstein was quoted in the New Yorker, December 15, 1986, on the manipulation of the American art scene, "John D. Rockefeller's notion of Lincoln Center was that it was a piece of real estate which he controlled. He had no interest in the performing arts really, or in any other kind of art. On the other hand, he had enormous interest in control" The Rockefellers singlehandedly created the Museum of Modern Art, which foisted "modern" art on the American public, making millions in the process. Reproductions of soup cans and beer cans were sold for many thousands of dollars, while the more traditional museums, also controlled by Rockefeller appointees, scooped up the more valuable symbols of our culture. They also promoted the Impressionist painters into the multimillion dollar class, the highest prices being paid for Picasso and Manet. Most critics agree that Picasso produced no important work after 1915, yet he painted thousands of pictures during the next sixty years. Kirstein comments of Manet, op. cit. "Manet is clumsy, unfinished, a pathetic transposition of three painters, Goya, Velasquez, and Titian. [A few days later, a Manet sold in New York for eleven million dollars! Ed.] One of the worst influences in cultural history is the Museum of Modern Art. It is a corrupt combination of dealer taste, marketing, and journalism ... it shows the general effect of personalization and idiosyncrasy."

The authority on symbolism in modern art is Margaret Stucki. She points out that Josef Albers, who came to the United States as a penniless refugee, achieved remarkable success due to nationwide promotion of his painting, a series called "Homage to the Square," the square being the flat side of the cube, which, as General Albert Pike pointed out, was the basic symbol of Freemasonry. Albers was set up as chairman of an art school at Black Mountain, North Carolina; this college was named after Mt. Blocken in Europe, where the Witches Sabbath was reputed to take place; it is a flat topped mountain which is represented in the Great Seal as a pyramid with the top chopped off. The present writer studied art at the Institute of Contemporary Arts; a fellow student, Noland, whose works now command huge sums began to paint Masonic symbols, the chevron, the target, and other "abstract" symbols. So-called non-representational art is not non-representational at all; it is the secret reproduction of occult symbols. Salvador Dali spent years studying occult symbolism at the previously mentioned Papus Institute in Paris. He always carried a forked cane which he had reproduced from ancient drawings of a wizard's staff; he was touted in the United States by Caresse Crosby, of the Black Sun Press (the black sun is an occult symbol representing the far side of the sun).

"Abstract" art was promoted by the Rockefellers because it is the modern depiction of the cults of the ancient world, principally the demon worship of Baal. These mystical symbols are understood by only a few cognoscenti, the Gnostics, or knowing ones, who perpetuate the secret organizations and dabble in their mystical powers. These same symbols are to be seen in the background of many Renaissance paintings, when Baal-worship was sanitized as "NeoPlatonism." Aby Warburg, of the Warburg Institute, spent his life studying these occult symbols of the Renaissance, except for a fortuitous nervous breakdown lasting four years, which kept him out of army service during the First World War. Warburg traced the development by which the classical representation of deities in art were transformed into occult symbols by the artists of the Renaissance, in which they now appeared in a demonic mien. Warburg was able to trace this symbolism through the emblems reproduced on heraldry and the costumes used in these paintings. This occult symbolism now is the mainstay of the modern "abstract" school of painting.

Abstract art also represents the Canaanite forces at work to deliberately debase the high standard of living reached by the people of Shem in the Classical World. The occult symbols which were infiltrated into Renaissance art were an important step in this program, but their real success did not come until the twentieth century, when rags dipped into paint and flung onto canvas, or pieces of scrap from junk heaps, became the new version of "high art." This was but one aspect of the ongoing campaign against the people of Shem, which was enshrined in the principles of "liberalism." Harold Laski defined liberalism as the political counterpart of capitalism. Liberalism is also the political program of Freemasonry, which has always been anti-capitalist. It is especially opposed to the development of modern technology, which dealt the deathblow to the profitable slave trade of the Canaanites, as machines replaced the use of slave labor.

The United States is now in the forefront of the Masonic Canaanite conspiracy to dismantle the modern industry which has been developed by the people of Shem. As a result, we now have the Rust Belt, miles of deserted factory buildings from the East Coast to the West Coast; thousands of independent farmers driven off their farms by loan capital, ruined because they were independent producers, or kulaks, and a threat to the Masonic Canaanite control of capital.

The linchpin in the Canaanite program to destroy American industry was the assault on our auto productions, which provided one of every seven jobs in the United States. This was accomplished by enlisting our defeated "fascist" enemies, Germany and Italy, in a plot to flood the United

States with foreign cars. Anyone suggesting such a possibility in 1948 would have been considered insane. The entire program was implemented by one man, General William Draper, of Dillon Read. His firm had previously handled the financing of Germany's rearmament program in order to make World War II possible; he was appointed the czar of postwar Germany's economic program, where he organized. Volkswagen and other producers to mount a serious challenge to American production. After setting up this program, in 1947 he was moved to Tokyo as Under Secretary of the Army, where he single-handedly created the "Japanese miracle." While General MacArthur postured as the "new Emperor" of Japan, it was Draper who ruled the country from behind the scenes. He commissioned Joseph Dodge to control the development of the Japanese auto industry; Dodge later became the president of Detroit's largest bank. The DRAPER PLAN resulted in a massive two-pronged attack against American auto production. The result was bankruptcy for thousands of small producers throughout the United States, who turned out parts for Detroit's mass production. To this day, Draper's name is unknown in Detroit, despite the fact that he brought the city to its knees. It was a typical operation of the Masonic Canaanites.

Every agency of the federal government has now been enlisted in the campaign to destroy American industry and production. The principal weapon is the Internal Revenue Service, which seeks out and destroys anyone who is engaged in the productive use of capital. The IRS moves in and confiscates all assets, so the business can never again go into production. This is a deliberate policy; those groups which are cooperating in the campaign to destroy the United States are automatically granted "Tax Exemption' by the IRS, whether through reducing our production capacity, encouraging homosexuality to reduce reproduction, or to defend the United States against its internal or external enemies who are headquartered in Washington. The special fury of the IRS is unleashed against any American who is considered a "patriot" or even a "conservative." Churches and schools which teach Christianity are padlocked by federal agents and their proprietors thrown into prison. Those churches which preach the doctrine of the Masonic Canaanites are immune from such onslaughts. These "patriotic" churches and schools represent a serious threat to the "final solution" which the Canaanites have planned for the people of Shem. "Plan Naamah," named after the demonic being who first introduced human sacrifice and cannibalism to the world, is a documented plan for the systematic extermination of all the people of Shem in the United States.

Plan Naamah is simply the American version of the massacres perpetrated during the French, Russian, and Spanish Revolutions. The plan is a simple one; newspapers, radio, and television will announce an imminent attack (the recent TV series Amerika was an important step in conditioning the American people to nonresistance in such an event; the "Russians" took over the country without a struggle). Everyone will be instructed to assemble in schools and auditoriums in every town and city in the United States. Only the fair-skinned people of Shem will actually obey this command; others, of Canaanite extraction, will be told that they should return to their homes. Once they have been herded into these buildings, the people of Shem are to be killed, but only according to regulated procedures, that is, with hatchets, clubs, and knives.

The use of guns will be prohibited, probably because there were no guns in the time of Naamah. Their use would violate "religious" principles. Also, the use of more primitive weapons assures a much greater flow of blood, which is always a basic objective of ritual slaughter. Should any Canaanite be inadvertently present, he or she will be protected by using the secret password, "Tubal Cain," the brother of Naamah, and the password of the Freemasons.

Plan Naamah will remain in effect until the people of Shem have been entirely eliminated throughout the United States. The teams of specially trained killers will be provided by the hordes of "immigrants" who have been imported into the United States during recent years specifically for this program. The people of Shem will be selected for extermination primarily by their physical characteristics, fair skin, blue eyes, although this will not be the sole qualification; lists will have been drawn up of the people of Shem in every area; these lists will be the final means of "selection." This will be the final strike against the "blue bloods," a term which originated after the Moors had invaded and conquered Spain (the Iberian Peninsula, home of Heber, the people of Shem). The Spanish coined the term "sangre azul," or blue blood, to mark those old families which refused to be contaminated with Moorish or other Canaanite admixtures. Those with very fair skin could be seen to have veins which showed blue against this background, while those of swarthier appearance showed no "blue blood."

Until Plan Naamah can be finally implemented, various other plagues are to be visited on the American people by the Masonic Canaanites, such as the current plague of AIDS. On January 30, 1987, the press carried headlines by the national director of public health, Otis Bowen, that AIDS might kill millions. On the next page was an interview with Bishop John Spong, Episcopal Bishop of Newark, urging ministers to bless and recognize homosexual relationships as "committed partners"; he announced that he would bring the matter up for discussion at the Congress of Bishops in Chicago. A few days later, a Unitarian minister, Rev. Carl Thitchener, passed out condoms on Sunday to his congregation; it was later revealed that he had been convicted of assault, and was also charged with parading naked before a group of Brownie Scouts. These ministers represent a widespread group which actively promote promiscuity and homosexuality, which is actively encouraged by the courts. Chief Justice Sol Wachtler of the New York State Court of Appeals (a classmate of the present writer at Washington Lee University in the 1950s) recently ruled that an adult bookstore could not be closed down because sexual acts were routinely being committed in the story by its patrons. "Freedom of expression in books, movies, and the arts, generally, is one of those areas in which there is great diversity among the states ... New York has a long tradition of fostering freedom of speech."

The hero of the Canaanites is Freud, who actively promoted the use of cocaine for his patients; it is now the drug of choice in the entire entertainment industry, and is usually distributed at their parties. In his book "Civilization and its Discontents," Freud describes the prohibition against incest as "perhaps the most maiming wound ever inflicted throughout the ages on the erotic life of man." Incest, of course, is the oldest taboo among civilized peoples.

Debased though these teachings may be, they are basic to the program of the Canaanites. Even more dangerous is the infiltration of the Christian churches by groups such as the Fundamentalists, the Dispensationalists, and the Premillenarians. We have pointed out that few Fundamentalists realize that they are directly descended from the New England Abolitionsts and their ties to the Transcendentalists and the Unitarians, who basically rely on the Cabala and other occult influences for their ministry. This will come as a shock to those who have accepted the teachings of these groups, but the historical record is clear. It descends in an unbroken line from the demon worship of Baal to the present day. The Premillenarians teach that Christ will suddenly return, as taught by Origen. Another offshoot, the Postpremillenarians, teach that Christ will return and reign for one thousand years. During this period, the Jews will be converted.

The Dispensationalists believe that the time is approaching when man will be tested for his obedience to some specific revelation of the Will of God. There are seven dispensations: (1) the innocence of Eden; (2) conscience, the expulsion to avoid evil; (3) human guilt, including capital punishment by government; (4) promise, and blessing to the seed of Abraham; (5) law-the disciplinary system; (6) church belief in the Gospel of Jesus Christ; and (7) Jesus' Kingdom, the Millenium, with God's promise to Israel fulfilled; Satan's final rebellion when he is cast into the fire; Christ delivers the Kingdom to His Father.

The promises of these groups, which deluge millions of television viewers each day through radio and television, the multimillion dollar "TV ministries" are based upon misinterpretations. The dispensationalists claim that their doctrine is based upon Christ's parable of the fig tree, which actually refers only to nature and the physical seasons. It does not apply to Israel or to any other nation. In spring, when the fruit of the Palestine fig made its appearance before the leaves, it was a certain sign of the approach of summer. Jesus used this parable in connection with His Great Prophecy, which he delivered during Passion Week, in which He foretold the destruction of Jerusalem and the Temple, the end of the age, and General Judgment. Dispensationalists are now asking on television that we watch for "the leafing fig tree" as a sign from Heaven that we should support the Canaanite invaders of Israel.

The Canaanite propagandists operate a billion dollar industry in the United States which masquerades as "religion." If it were true religion, it would not automatically obtain tax exemption from the IRS, as each of these groups does. They are granted tax exemption by the government because they are broadcasting a message which the government wants the American people to receive. What is this message? It is the false doctrine that it is not the people of Shem to whom God made His Promise, but to the spawn of Canaan, those who live under the Curse of Canaan. Typical of the Canaanite propagandists is Jim Bakker, head of PTL (Praise the Lord). In 1980, Bakker published a book, "Survival to Live," in which he rejoiced in the execution of Haman and the massacre of the women and children of the people of Shem by the blood-crazed Canaanites. Bakker denounces Haman as one who had treatened the Canaanites, as told in the Book of Esther; Bakker terms the Canaanites "the anointed ones of God"! The television propagandists claim that these "anointed ones," the Canaanites, are the true people of Israel, and that God promised them the Land of Israel. Not only is this blatant falsehood; it is also highly profitable. Bakker joined Christian Broadcast Network in 1965; having learned the propaganda line, he branched out on his own. He now has a $129 million-a-year industry and operates a theme park called Heritage U.S.A. which had six million visitors in 1986; there are two 500 room hotels and 2,000 employees.

Bakker and his wife suddenly fled to their Palm Springs, California, mansion when it was revealed that he had been paying $115,000 blackmail to a former paramour, while his wife Tammy admitted to a seventeen-year "dependency" on various medications and drugs, for which she was now undergoing treatment. They have a half million subscribers who pay at least $15 a month to PTL, as well as a host of other enterprises. Bakker then resigned, calling in Jerry Falwell to take over PTL, and hinting darkly of a "rival evangelist" who was trying to engineer a "hostile takeover." Yes, it is big business, subject to all the intrigues of any profitable multimillion dollar operation. Tammy had raised some eyebrows when she made a pathetic national appeal for prayer to bring her dead poodle back to life! She and her husband had embarked on a whirlwind of spending for such things as gold bathroom faucets, huge rings, and other stigmata of the true martyrdom.

Bakker and his fellow operators ask no questions about how all this bounty flows to them. They preach against "secular humanism" and Communism without any inkling that their evangelical movement traces directly back to the very forces which they denounce. From 1830 to 1870, Jeremy Bentham's utilitarian socialism dominated English legislation, while a simultaneous program, Evangelicalism, was being promoted by the same forces to take over Christianity. Dr. Dale is quoted by A. V. Dicey in "Law and Opinion in England," Macmillan, 1924, "The Evangelicals must encourage what is called an undenominational church-it regarded with indifference all forms of Church polity-it demanded common religious teaching and common beliefs; it cared nothing for the Church as an august society of saints." In short, Evangelicalism, the forerunner of our present crop of Canaanite propagandists, was first of all, ecumenical; second, it cast aside the spiritual heritage of the Church in favor of a robust dedication to fund raising and political propagandizing for goals rarely openly revealed. The Evangelical Alliance was formed in London in 1846. A branch was soon formed in the United States which was first known as the Federal Council of Church of Christ, and is now known as the National Council of Churches of Christ, a leftwing propaganda group. Yet it shares the same origin as that of the television evangelists, who claim to be "anti-Communist"!

What is this origin?

The evangelical movement was sponsored by the same British Intelligence leader, Lord Shelburne, who had directed the French Revolution. Shelburne imported a French radical into England, Etienne-Louis Demont of Paris, who was the desciple of Count Saint Simon, the founder of "social science." Dumont's principal English disciple was Jeremy Bentham, now known as the "father of utilitarianism." Shelburne had become the power behind Britain's political scene by lending William Pitt, the Prime Minister, large sums of money. After Pitt's death, the British Treasury was obliged to payoff these debts, amounting to forty thousand pounds. Because of his international intrigues, Shelburne was the most feared and hated man in England. Edmund Burke called him "a Cat aline or Borgia in morals"; he was known publicly by a contemptuous nickname, "Malagrida"; the press caricatured him as a Guy Fawkes preparing to blow up his own comrades! Henry Fox called Shelburne "a perfidious and infamous liar." King George III called him "the Jesuit of Berkeley Square." This master of espionage used his power to enthrone three men as the intellectual dictators of English life, Jeremy Bentham, John Stuart Mill, and David Ricardo. Mill was named after Sir John Stuart, a close associate of Shelburne, who obtained for both Mill and his father James Mill high-paying posts with the notorious East India Company. Bentham was the son of a wealthy London lawyer, and lived off his large inheritance. Ricardo was a dealer in "consols" with-HIs friend Nathan Meyer Rothschild. All three were heavily influenced by Dumont and Saint Simon's teachings. They worked to create in the nineteenth century the climate in which collectivism was to flourish in the twentieth century. Dicey points out that "the fundamental principle of collectivism is faith in the intervention by the State in every matter, to be extended indefinitely." He also pointed out that collectivism meant the end of freedom of contract. Dicey pointed out in his Lecture IX, "The debt of collectivism to Bentham-the machinery was thus provided for the practical extension of the activity of the State." He pointed out that Bentham's policies effected the transfer of power from the landed aristocracy to the new middle class of merchants and bankers. Bentham taught a system of "Hedonic calculus" in which moral judgments were to be determined only by physical pain and pleasure; he also promoted a "psychological hedonism" based on the pleasure principle, which denied natural law. Bentham wrote, "Every person is the best judge of his own happiness," presumably indicating individualism, but his system of State control means that a bureaucrat decides everyone's "happiness." Mill wrote in his work "On Liberty," "Every Man to count for one and no man to count for more than one." This happy situation was to be reached by granting all power to a utilitarian state. This group also promoted the Anti-Slavery movement in the United States which culminated in the Civil War. Immediately after Bentham's death, the Reform Act was passed, in 1832. Dicey says this installed collectivism in Europe. Bentham's body was embalmed, and is now on display, dressed in his usual clothes, surmounted with a wax head, at University College, London.

The reader may doubt that a case has been made here that the same forces of British Intelligence, the Bank of England, and the East India Company, which foisted totalitarian utilitarianism, also known as Communism, on the world, also created our modern "television evangelicals." However, the line of descent is clearly drawn, from the demon worshippers of Baal to their emergence in a more intellectual mien as Pythagoreans, Platonists, Neoplatonists, the Enlightenment, and the French, Bolshevik, and Spanish Revolutions. Throughout, the line is demarcated by the teachings of Cabala, the denial of natural law, the denial of spiritual development of mankind, and the goal of enthroning the Masonic Canaanites as unchallenged masters of the world.

The real message of Christ is not understood by these propaganda groups. The Bible tells us precisely what God intended and what Jesus Christ would provide. First,

Resurrection: God said, "I will ransom them from the power of the grave: I will redeem them from death" (Hosea 13: 1'1).

Then there is the Vision of Isaiah 26:19: "Thy dead men shall live: together with my dead body shall they arise! Awake and sing, ye that dwell in the dust: for thy dew is the dew of light, and the earth shall cast out the dead." Jesus promised, "Verily, verily I say unto you: if a man keepeth my saying, he shall never see death" (John 8:1).

Second, the Promise. The television propagandists deliberately conceal the identity of those to whom God made His Promise. Jeremiah 31:31: "Behold, the days are coming, saith the Lord, when I will make a new covenant with the House of Israel, and the House of Judah ... I will put my law within them, and I will write it upon their hearts."

This promise was not made to the Canaanites, whom God despised, and to whom even Jesus denied His Compassion while He was on this earth. We find the true heirs of the Promise positively identified in Galatians 3:14, "that in Christ Jesus the blessing of Abraham might come upon the Gentiles, that we might receive the promise of the Spirit through faith: To give a human example, brethren; no one annuls a man's will, or adds to it, once it has been ratified. Now the promises were made to Abraham and his offspring. It does not say 'to offsprings,' referring to many, but referring to one, 'And to your offsping,' which is Christ. ... For if the inheritance is by the law, it is no longer by promise; but God gave it to Abraham by a promise ... And if ye be Christ's, then you are Abraham's offspring, heirs according to promise."

The "Promise," then, is quite clear, "If ye be Christ's." Obviously this excludes the Canaanites who have invaded and illegally seized Israel. Thus far, I have written much about evil, which plagues man's existence. Now we can write about good, that is, God's Promise to the people of Shem, the people who have carried His Word throughout the world. In every nation, the people of Shem have been persecuted and massacred by the Canaaniates, the true anti-Semites. Often the people of Shem have been helpless before these attacks because they did not know how to identify their enemies, the true enemies of God. With Satan's help, the Canaanites attacked and seized the Land of Israel. The Bible says, "if ye be Christ's" then you are the true heirs of Israel. The Canaanite invaders now occupying Israel are not "Christ's"; they are the revilers and mockers of Christ. Thus God's anger is not only against the Canaanites, but also against God's people, the people of Shem, who have allowed this blasphemy of God. Hundreds of American youths were recently killed in Lebanon because they had been sent there by the Washington Canaanites, not to fulfill God's promise to the people of Shem, but to aid the Canaanites in their Satanic atrocities. Now God waits for the people of Shem to rally to their mission; to launch a new crusade to regain the Holy Land from the Masonic Canaanites. The sordid conspirators and their multimillion dollar propagandists must be challenged. To whom did God make the Promise? To Abraham's seed, those of Christ. Not one of the million dollar publicists for the Canaanites will mention this in their highly-paid television ministries. They must be exposed as mockers of Christ. They must be challenged with the truth.

We have been persecuted because we have fallen into the trap of the world, the dualism which offers us the choice of following God's Will, or of passively joining the Canaanites in accepting Satan as the leader, which means participating in the shedding of blood and the obscene rituals of human sacrifice. Today, America is obdient to the Will of Canaan, engaging lechery, robbery, and international Masonic conspiracy. America, who God intended to lead the world into the path of righteousness, now is called "the Great White Satan" because the fair-skinned people of Shem have been deceived into carrying out Satan's work on this earth. The choice is one which must be determined and made, and the decision is not far off; will the people of Shem accept God's Promise to Abraham, or will we continue to allow ourselves to be deceived by the Satanic Masonic Order of Canaanites? There is nothing in between-and if we persist in doing the Satanic work of the Canaanites-America will become NOTHING.

Printed in June 2021
by Rotomail Italia S.p.A., Vignate (MI) - Italy